WINTER IS COMING

IS

COMING

WINTER
IS
COMING

WHY VLADIMIR PUTIN *and*
THE ENEMIES *of the*
FREE WORLD MUST
BE STOPPED

GARRY KASPAROV

with MIG GREENGARD

PublicAffairs
New York

Published in the United States by PublicAffairs™,
a Member of the Perseus Books Group

Library of Congress Control Number: 2015948564

ISBN 978-1-61039-620-2 (HC)
ISBN 978-1-61039-621-9 (EB)
ISBN 978-1-61039-645-5 (international paperback)

Editorial production by *Marra*thon Production Services. www.marrathon.net

Book design by Jane Raese
Text set in 11.5-point Berthold Baskerville

FIRST EDITION
10 9 8 7 6 5 4 3 2 1

To the memory of Boris Nemtsov and
to every person in the world battling for freedom
and democracy as he did every day.

—GARRY KASPAROV

To Zoë, who makes it all possible,
and to Cleo and Rafa, who make it all worth it.

—MIG GREENGARD

CONTENTS

INTRODUCTION

On August 19, 1991, CNN was providing nonstop live coverage of an attempted coup against Soviet president Mikhail Gorbachev. Allied with the KGB, hardliners from inside the disintegrating Communist regime had sequestered Gorbachev at his dacha in Crimea and declared a state of emergency. The global press was full of experts and politicians worried that the coup would mark the sudden end of perestroika, or even the start of a civil war, as tanks rolled into the middle of Moscow.

I appeared as a guest on *Larry King* that evening, along with former US ambassador to the United Nations Jeane Kirkpatrick, a professor from California, and a former KGB operative. I was alone in declaring that the coup had no chance of success, and that it would be over in forty-eight hours, not the months Kirkpatrick and many others were predicting. The coup's leaders had no popular support, I insisted, and their attempt to put a halt to reforms they feared might lead to the breakup of the Union of Soviet Socialist Republics was doomed. The ruling bureaucracy was also split, with many feeling they had better opportunities for advancement after a Soviet breakup. I was vindicated with great efficiency, as Russian president Boris Yeltsin famously climbed aboard a tank, the people of Moscow rallied for freedom and democracy, and the cabal of coup leaders realized the people were against them. They surrendered two days later.

The coup attempt not only failed, but it accelerated the demise of the Soviet Union by presenting the people of the USSR a clear choice. Dissolution and an independent future was a little frightening, yes, but it could not be worse than the totalitarian present.

Like dominoes, republic after Soviet republic declared independence in the following months. Back in Moscow, two days after the failure of the coup, a jubilant crowd tore down the statue of "Iron" Felix Dzerzhinsky, the fearsome founder of the Soviet secret police, in front of the KGB headquarters.

It is difficult for me now to read the comments members of that crowd made to the press without becoming emotional. "This begins our process of purification," said a coal miners' union leader. An Orthodox priest said, "We will destroy the enormous, dangerous, totalitarian machine of the KGB." The crowd chanted "Down with the KGB!" and "*Svo-bo-da!*" the Russian word for freedom. Police took off their berets to join the march as messages like "KGB butchers must go to trial!" were scrawled on the base of the hated statue. A doctor said this protest was different from those of the previous months: "We feel as though we have been born again."

And so it shocks the imagination that eight years later, on December 31, 1999, a former lieutenant colonel of the KGB became the president of Russia. The country's nascent democratic reforms were halted and steadily rolled back. The government launched crackdowns on the media and across civil society. Russian foreign policy became bullying and belligerent. There had been no process of purification, no trials for the butchers, and no destruction of the KGB machine. The statue of Dzerzhinsky had been torn down, but the totalitarian repression it represented had not. It had been born again—in the person of Vladimir Putin.

Jump forward to the beginning of 2015 and Putin is still in the Kremlin. Russian forces have attacked Ukraine and annexed Crimea, six years after invading another neighbor, the Republic of Georgia. Just days after hosting the Winter Olympics in Sochi in February 2014, Putin fomented a war in Eastern Ukraine and became the first person to annex sovereign foreign territory by force since Saddam Hussein in Kuwait. The same world leaders who were taking smiling photos with Putin a year ago are now bringing sanctions against Russia and members of its ruling elite.

Russia threatens to turn off the pipelines that supply Europe with a third of its oil and gas. A metaphorical mafia state with Putin as the *capo di tutti capi* (boss of all bosses) has moved from being an ideologically agnostic kleptocracy to using blatantly fascist propaganda and tactics. The long-banished specter of nuclear annihilation has returned.

There are two stories behind the current crisis. The first is how Russia moved so quickly from celebrating the end of Communism to electing a KGB officer and then to invading its neighbors. The second is how the free world helped this to happen, through a combination of apathy, ignorance, and misplaced goodwill. It is critical to figure out what went awry, because even though Putin is now a clear and present danger, Europe and America are still getting it wrong. The democracies of the world must unite and relearn the lessons of how the Cold War was won before we slide completely into another one.

Putin's Russia is clearly the biggest and most dangerous threat facing the world today, but it is not the only one. Terrorist groups like al-Qaeda and the Islamic State are (despite the latter's name) stateless and without the vast resources and weapons of mass destruction Putin has at his fingertips. The attacks of 9/11 and others like it, however, taught us that you don't have to have a national flag or even an army to inflict terrible damage on the most powerful country in the world. What's more, state sponsors of terror are benefiting as democratic terrorist targets fail to organize an aggressive defense. The murderous regimes of Iran, North Korea, and Syria have enjoyed considerable time at the bargaining table with the world's great powers while making no significant concessions.

It's not new to talk about the challenges of the multipolar world that arose with the end of the Cold War. What is lacking is a coherent strategy to deal with these challenges. When the Cold War ended, the winners were left without a sense of purpose and without a common foe to unite against. The enemies of the free world have no such doubts. They still define themselves by their opposition to the principles and policies of liberal democracy and human rights, of which they see the United States as the primary symbolic and material representative. And yet we continue to engage them, to negotiate, and even to provide these enemies with the weapons and wealth they use to attack us. To paraphrase Winston Churchill's definition of appeasement, we are feeding the crocodiles, hoping they will eat us last.

Any political chill between Washington, DC, and Moscow or Beijing is quickly criticized by both sides as a potential "return to the Cold War." The use of this cliché today is ironic, given that the way the Cold War was fought and won has been forgotten instead of emulated. Instead of standing on principles of good and evil, of right and wrong, and on the universal values of human rights and human life, we have engagement, resets, and moral equivalence. That is, appeasement by many other names. The world needs a new alliance based on a global Magna Carta, a declaration of fundamental rights that all members must recognize. Nations that value individual liberty now control the greater part of the world's resources as well as its military power. If they band together and refuse to coddle the rogue regimes and sponsors of terror, their integrity and their influence will be irresistible.

The goal should not be to build new walls to isolate the millions of people living under authoritarian rule, but to provide them with hope and the prospect of a brighter future. Most of us who lived behind the Iron Curtain were very aware that there were people in the free world who cared and who were fighting for us, not against us. And knowing this mattered. Today, the so-called leaders of the free world talk about promoting democracy while treating the leaders of the world's most repressive regimes as equals. The policies of engagement with dictators have failed on every level, and it is past time to recognize this failure.

As Ronald Reagan said in his famous 1964 speech "A Time for Choosing," this is not a choice between peace and war, only between fight or surrender. We must choose. We must not surrender. We must fight with the vast resources of the free world, beginning with moral values and economic incentives and with military action only as a last resort. America must lead, with its vast resources and its ability to mobilize its fractious and fractured allies. But it is obsolete today to speak of American values, or even of Western values. Japan and South Korea must act, Australia and Brazil, India and South Africa, and every country that values democracy and liberty and benefits from global stability. We know it can be done because it has been done before. We must find the courage to do it again.

———

Five years after Putin took office and began to rebuild the Russian police state he so admired, I experienced a rebirth of my own. In 2005, I retired from twenty years on top of the professional chess world to join the fledgling Russian pro-democracy movement. I had become world champion in 1985 at the age of twenty-two and had achieved everything I could want to achieve at the chessboard. I have always wanted to make a difference in the world and felt that my time in professional chess was over. I wanted my children to be able to grow up in a free Russia. And I remembered the sign my mother once put up on my wall, a saying of the Soviet dissidents: "If not you, who else?" I hoped to use my energy and my fame to push back against the rising tide of repression coming from the Kremlin.

Like many Russians, I was troubled by the little-known Putin's KGB background and his sudden rise to power by overseeing the brutal 1999 war to pacify the Russian region of Chechnya. But along with my countrymen, at the start I was grudgingly willing to give Putin a chance. Yeltsin had badly tarnished his democratic credentials during his 1996 reelection by using the powers of the presidency to influence the outcome, and I confess that I was one of those who thought at the time that sacrificing some of the integrity of the democratic process was the lesser evil if it was required to keep the hated Communists from regaining power.

Such trade-offs are nearly always a mistake, and it was in this case, as it paved the way for a more ruthless individual to exploit the weakened system.

The 1998 default had left the Russian economy in a very shaky state, although it is worth pointing out in hindsight that gross domestic product (GDP) growth had already rebounded well by 2000. But at the time, crime, inflation, and a general sense of national weakness and uncertainty made the technocratic and plainspoken Putin an appealingly safe option. There was a feeling the country could slip into chaos without a stronger hand on the helm. Physical and social insecurity have always been easy targets in fragile democracies, and most dictators rise to power with initial public support. Throughout history, endless cycles of autocrats and military juntas have been empowered by the people's call for order and "*la mano dura*" (hard hand) to rein in the excesses of a wobbly civilian regime. Somehow people always forget that it's much easier to install a dictator than to remove one.

Of course I did not expect my new career in what can only generously be called Russian "politics" to be an easy one. The opposition was not trying to win elections; we were fighting just to have them. That's why I always said I was an activist, not a politician, even when I won an opposition primary for the 2008 presidential election. Everyone knew I would never be allowed to appear on an official ballot; the point was to expose that fact and to try to strengthen the atrophied muscles of the Russian democratic process. My initial goal was to unite all of the anti-Putin forces in the country, especially those that ordinarily would never imagine even being seen together. The liberal reformer camp I belonged to had nothing in common with the National Bolsheviks, for example, except for being marginalized, persecuted, and betrayed by Putin's plan to hold on to power for life. And yet our fragile coalition marched in the streets of Moscow and St. Petersburg, the first serious political protests since Putin had taken office. We wanted to show the people of Russia that resistance was possible, and to spread the message that giving up liberty in exchange for stability was a false choice.

Unfortunately, Putin, like other modern autocrats, had, and still has, an advantage the Soviet leadership could never have dreamed of: deep economic and political engagement with the free world. Decades of trade have created tremendous wealth that dictatorships like Russia and China have used to build sophisticated authoritarian infrastructures inside the country and to apply pressure in foreign policy. The naïve idea was that the free world would use economic and social ties to gradually liberalize authoritarian states. In practice, the authoritarian states have abused this access and economic interdependency to spread their corruption and fuel repression at home.

To take one easy example: Europe gets a third of its energy from Russia in total, though some individual countries get considerably more. Meanwhile, Europe draws 80 percent of Russia's energy exports, so who has the greater leverage in this relationship? And yet during the Ukraine crisis we have heard it repeated constantly that Europe cannot act against Russia because of energy dependency! Eight months after Putin annexed Crimea and three and a half months after evidence mounted that Russian forces had shot down a commercial airliner over Ukraine, Europe was still "considering" looking at ways to substitute Russian gas. Instead of using the European Union's overwhelming economic influence to deter Putin's aggression, they feign helplessness. An EU boycott, or even a hefty tax, on Russian energy imports would threaten to completely destroy the Russian economy, which is now entirely dependent on the energy sector to stay afloat. But Europe lacks the political will to make significant sacrifices in the short run to meet the far greater long-term threat that an unchallenged Putin represents to global security and, by extension, their globalization-dependent economies.

Engagement also provides modern authoritarian regimes with more subtle tools for escaping censure. They have their initial public offerings (IPOs) and luxury real estate in New York City and London, providing fees and tax revenue that greedy Western politicians and corporations are loathe to give up in the name of human rights. Unfree states exploit the openness of the free world by hiring lobbyists, spreading propaganda in the media, and contributing heavily to politicians, political parties, and non-governmental organizations (NGOs). There is very little backlash when these activities are exposed. Citizens in the free world occasionally show outrage when a sweatshop is exposed in the media, but in the end they care little for the social environment of the countries that produce their oil, clothing, and iPhones.

As Russian oligarchs spread their wealth and Putin's political influence around the globe, Western companies returned the favor by investing in Russia. Energy giants like Shell and British Petroleum (BP) couldn't wait to get a shot at Russia's immense energy reserves and the long-dormant Russian marketplace was an irresistible target, no matter how many concessions were needed to make deals. Human rights in Russia were the least of Western corporations' concerns. Even after Western firms were repeatedly betrayed, cheated, and threatened by their Russian partners and kicked out of partnerships or the country, they came back looking for more like beaten dogs to an abusive master.

The most remarkable example was BP CEO Robert Dudley fleeing Russia in 2008, when he was the CEO of a joint venture with a group of Russian billionaires. Harassed continually and afraid of arrest (and that he was being poisoned, according to one account), Dudley fled and went into hiding. And yet a few years later he was back in Russia for a photo op with Putin himself announcing an oil exploration deal with state-controlled oil company Rosneft! And while foreign investment has made up some of Russia's GDP growth—most was due to the huge rise in oil prices—little of it improved the lives of average Russians. Most of these new riches turned right around and ended up in Western banks and real estate in the name of Putin's oligarch elite.

So while our ever-evolving opposition movement made some progress in drawing attention to the undemocratic reality of

Putin's Russia, we were in a losing position from the start. The Kremlin's domination of the mass media and ruthless persecution of all opposition in civil society made it impossible to build any lasting momentum. Our mission was also sabotaged by democratic leaders embracing Putin on the world stage, providing him with the leadership credentials he so badly needed in the absence of valid elections in Russia. It is difficult to promote democratic reform when every television channel and every newspaper shows image after image of the leaders of the world's most powerful democracies accepting a dictator as part of their family. It sends the message that either he isn't really a dictator at all or that democracy and individual freedom are nothing more than the bargaining chips Putin and his ilk always say they are. In the end, it took the invasion of Ukraine to finally get the G7 (I always refused to call it the G8) to expel Putin's Russia from the elite club of industrial democracies.

By 2008, when Putin loaned the presidency to his shadow, Dmitry Medvedev, it should have been clear to all that Russian democracy was dead. The only other names on the ballot were the loyal opposition in their appointed roles: Gennady Zyuganov of the Communists and Vladimir Zhirinovsky, who has been playing the part of far right extremist since 1991. Both served, and still serve, as harmless window dressing to provide the merest appearance of democracy. And yet one democratic leader after another lined up to play along with the charade. George W. Bush phoned his new counterpart to offer congratulations. French president Nicolas Sarkozy warmly invited Medvedev to Paris. Similar encomiums were offered by the leaders of Germany, the United Kingdom, and too many others to list. This, despite the fact that the election had been boycotted by the main European election monitoring body, the Organization for Security and Cooperation in Europe (OSCE), to protest against restrictions imposed on observers.

Two months after Barack Obama was sworn in, he and Secretary of State Hillary Clinton launched a new foreign policy initiative to "reset" the United States' relationship with Russia.

And not in the realist way you might expect after Russia had invaded tiny Georgia just months earlier to establish independent enclaves that are still occupied by Russian troops today. No, this was an American charm offensive. (One complete with misspelled props—the infamous "Reset Button" Clinton presented to her Russian counterpart Sergei Lavrov actually said "overcharge" in Russian, not "reset.") The Obama administration wanted to believe the youthful and cheery Medvedev was a reformer, a potential liberalizer who would change Putin's course. You can call this naïveté from the early days of "hope and change" if you like, but incredibly, this policy of engagement continued long after it became clear Putin was still very much in charge and that his plan to turn Russia back into a police state was unchanged.

Putin's "Operation Medvedev" was a total victory. He gained four more years to further eliminate all domestic opposition while avoiding any consequences on the international front. When Putin predictably returned to the president's office in 2012 he barely bothered to make the election presentable. Like most dictators, Putin has good animal instincts when it comes to evaluating his rivals, and he knew he would face no real opposition from other world leaders. And, also like all dictators, Putin grew bolder with every successful step. Dictators do not ask why before they take more power; they only ask why not. When Putin looked carefully at the way leaders like Merkel, Cameron, and Obama treated him, he never found any reason not to do exactly as he pleased.

One needn't be a student of history to recognize this pattern, nor to see how it led to war in Ukraine. The complacency that set in among the nations of the free world after the Iron Curtain came down could not be easily shaken off to deal with someone like Vladimir Putin. He exploits engagement to his advantage while conceding nothing. For years, as the human rights situation in Russia steadily deteriorated, Western politicians and experts such as Condoleezza Rice and Henry Kissinger defended Western feebleness in confronting Putin by saying Russians were better off than in the days of the Soviet Union.

First off, a sarcastic congratulations to them for damning us with faint praise! But instead of making comparisons to the 1950s or the 1970s, what about to the 1990s? It is not difficult to improve on life under the totalitarian Communism of Stalin or Brezhnev, but what about life under Yeltsin? What about the destruction of every newborn democratic institution in Russia while the Rices and Kissingers of the world looked on? If the human rights of the Soviet people and the political prisoners in the vast gulags mattered, and they mattered very much, to so many leaders and citizens of the free world, why do dissidents in the twenty-first century not deserve similar concern and respect? Effective policies are based on principles. Ronald Reagan would talk with his Soviet counterparts but, as Václav Havel once told me, Reagan would also toss the list of political prisoners on the table first!

In my first years as an activist I often said that Putin was a Russian problem for Russians to solve, but that he would soon be a regional problem and then a global problem if his ambitions were ignored. This regrettable transformation has come to pass and lives are being lost because of it. It is cold comfort to be told, "You were right!" It is even less comforting when so little is being done to halt Putin's aggression even now. What is the point of saying you should have listened and acted when you still aren't listening or acting?

The mantra of engagement, and of refusing to address the crimes of dictatorships—especially if they are important business partners—has become so entrenched in the last twenty years that even the invasion of a sovereign nation in Europe cannot break its hold. The United States and the European Union have levied sanctions against Russian officials and industries, if mostly too little and too late. And yet they still refuse to admit the need for condemning and isolating Russia like the dangerous rogue state Putin has turned it into. This generation of Western leaders refuses to admit that evil still exists in this world and that it must be fought on absolute terms, not negotiated with. It's clear at the moment that the democracies of the twenty-first century are not ready for this fight. It is still an open question whether or not they can and will make themselves ready.

———

It is very dangerous to believe that the fall of a symbol is the same as the end of what that symbol represented, but the temptation to do so is nearly irresistible. People have a strong affinity for symbols and narratives of all kinds, especially when they look like the happy ending of a long and dark fairy tale. The Berlin Wall was a literal and figurative division of the world into good and evil, light and darkness. When ecstatic Germans poured across the fortified border and took hammers to the hated Wall, it was easy to believe that evil itself had been defeated.

Celebration was warranted, of course. Hundreds of millions of people were waking from a totalitarian nightmare that had lasted for decades. The "Evil Empire" had fallen. A span of over sixty-seven hundred kilometers—a quarter of the globe, reaching from the Chukotka Peninsula in the Russian Far East to Berlin—escaped from Communist repression and economic blight to the bright hope of democracy and free markets nearly overnight. It was a glorious, unforgettable moment.

There were also more practical reasons to celebrate. The existential threat of nuclear war was lifted. Three generations had grown up with duck-and-cover drills and dinner table talk of "mutually assured destruction." Countless billions of dollars had been invested in military measures and countermeasures that were now going to become redundant. The resulting "peace dividend" was going to lead to a new era of prosperity, or so the widely accepted storyline went.

I have written about what I call "the gravity of past success" in chess. Each victory pulls the victor down slightly and makes it harder to put in maximum effort to improve further. Meanwhile, the loser knows that he made a mistake, that something went wrong, and he will work hard to improve for next time. The happy winner often assumes he won simply because he is great. Typically, however, the winner is just the player who made the next-to-last mistake. It takes tremendous discipline to overcome this tendency and to learn lessons from a victory.

The natural response, the human response, in the aftermath of winning the Cold War was to embrace the former enemy. Clinton and Yeltsin hugged and laughed. The European Union and NATO welcomed the former Soviet Bloc nations with open arms and invested billions of dollars to aid the newcomers. When it came to economic and political reform, the sticks of isolation and containment were dropped in favor of a purely carrot-based Western policy. The EU and other institutions offered the newly free countries incentives to join as full partners if minimum conditions of political transparency and economic reforms were met. This principle of engagement was a great success in Eastern Europe, despite the bumpy road for many.

But this expansive method was also applied in places where the forces of oppression had not been rooted out. Countries where Soviet-style repression had merely been renamed were invited into the club with few demands, and little reciprocity. The prevailing attitude in the West was "It's okay, they will come around eventually. Democracy has won, the bad guys are on the wrong side of history. We just have to keep engaging with them and wait." But the proverbial forces of history do not win wars on their own. And experience has shown that you can often do just fine being on the wrong side of history if you are on the right side of a pipeline.

In hindsight it is amazing how quickly the lessons of the Cold War victory were forgotten and abandoned. At the moment of greatest ascendancy of the forces of freedom and democracy in history, the West stopped pressing the advantage. With overwhelming military, economic, and moral power on its side, the West changed strategies entirely.

In today's era of globalization and false equivalence it can be hard for many of us to recall that most Cold War leaders had seen true evil up close during World War II. They had no illusions about what dictators were capable of if given the chance. They had witnessed existential threats with their own eyes and seen the horrors of the concentration camps. They also knew that nuclear weapons could be used in war; for generations that followed, that thought was almost literally inconceivable. It is a shame that today Adolf Hitler and Joseph Stalin have become caricatures, as if they are mythological beasts representing an ancient evil vanquished long ago.

But evil does not die, just as history does not end. Like a weed, evil can be cut back but never entirely uprooted. It waits for its chance to spread through the cracks in our vigilance. It can take root in the fertile soil of our complacency, or even the rocky rubble of the fallen Berlin Wall.

Communism did not disappear when the Wall came down. Nearly 1.5 billion human beings still live in Communist dictatorships today, and another billion and a half live in unfree states of different stripes, including, of course, much of the former Soviet Union. The desire of men to exploit and to rule over others by diktat, and by force, did not disappear when the Wall fell. What did disappear—or, at least, what faded dramatically—was the willingness of the free world to take a firm stand in support of the oppressed.

This shift is understandable, as it represented the public's desire to end decades of tension and standoffs. Bill Clinton, who took office in 1992, was the first baby boomer president, and he epitomized the mindset that it was time to move beyond the harsh Manichean worldview of the Cold War. Meanwhile, the dragon's teeth were growing. Belorussian dictator Lukashenko began his lifetime tenure in 1994. His Central Asian dictator colleagues, Nazarbayev of Kazakhstan and Karimov of Uzbekistan, have been in power for over a quarter century. It is no coincidence that two of the countries from the former Soviet Union with the greatest potential to break free of Russia's dire gravitational pull, Georgia and Ukraine, have both been attacked by Russia and partially occupied.

It is true these thugs and autocrats do not represent a threat to the global order anywhere near that posed by the Soviet Union, despite Putin's attempts to cobble together a "USSR-lite" via trade agreements, intimidation, and puppet leaders. Beyond its military capability, the USSR was a threat because it aggressively propounded a toxic ideology, Communism, which was capable of spreading far beyond its borders. Until recently, Putin has felt capable of looting Russia and consolidating power without re-sorting to anything resembling ideology. "Let's steal together" has been his ruling elite's only motto, using government power to move money into the pockets of those wielding that power. But as the economic situation in Russia has deteriorated, Putin has been obliged to turn to the later chapters in the dictator's handbook to find new ways to justify his role as the supreme leader.

Since 2013, the Kremlin and its various mouthpieces have ac-companied the latest crackdowns on gays and the media with overtly fascist rhetoric about "un-Russian" behavior, treason, and betrayal of the nation. Some of these speeches, including a few of Putin's own, so closely resemble those of Nazi leaders in the 1930s that they seem only to change the word "fatherland" to "motherland." But as Hitler knew, you eventually run out of in-ternal enemies and have to look abroad. The demonization of the United States in state-run media had been going on for a decade, but it wasn't enough.

When Putin's puppet president in Ukraine, Viktor Yanukovych, fled the country after the "Euromaidan" protests demanding greater European integration, Putin seized his chance. Citing the need to protect Russians in Ukraine, he first occupied and annexed Crimea and then began inciting violence via Russian-supported "rebels" in Eastern Ukraine. Soon after, despite the Kremlin's increasingly absurd claims to the contrary, Russian troops and heavy arms turned the conflict into an actual invasion.

A war on any grounds is terrible, but Putin's dangerous turn to ethnically based imperialism cannot be ignored. Those who say the Ukraine conflict is far away and unlikely to lead to global instability miss the clear warning Putin has given us. There is no reason to believe his announced vision of a "Greater Russia" will end with Eastern Ukraine and many reasons to believe it will not. Dictators only stop when they are stopped, and appeasing Putin with Ukraine will only stoke his appetite for more conquests.

Ukraine is just one battle the free world would like to ignore in a larger war it refuses to acknowledge even exists. But pretending you don't have enemies does not make it true. The Berlin Wall and the Soviet Union are gone, but the enemies of freedom who built them are not. History does not end; it runs in cycles. The failure to defend Ukraine today is the failure of the Allies to defend Czechoslovakia in 1938. The world must act now so that Poland in 2015 will not be called on to play the role of Poland in 1939.

The Cold War was won not just by military or economic superiority, but on values I, a former Soviet citizen, unironically call traditional American values, ones that the Western Bloc adopted as well. We cannot resolve the problems of globalization with the same legal and economic tools that created it. We need new, morality-based frameworks to confront the dictatorships in Russia and China now that they have so thoroughly become a part of our globalized world. We need new alliances to combat the stateless terror networks that use our technology against us. These frameworks and alliances must be based on moral principles, the only weapon the enemies of democracy cannot match. This is even more obvious when those enemies possess nuclear weapons, making a military confrontation unimaginably dangerous.

The hazy battle lines of these modern conflicts can only be addressed by bright moral lines. The free world's enemies can be identified by their targets. They know that if liberal democracy and free market policies succeed, then they are out of business—and so they fight for their very survival. To meet these attacks we must turn our principles into policies. We must identify and understand what we are fighting for, and fighting against. We must be willing to defend our values as if our lives depended on them, because they do.

We must resist the distractions, excuses, and straw man arguments presented by dictators and thugs on one side and echoed by appeasers and cowards on the other. They talk ceaselessly of what might happen if the free world stands up to Putin or the consequences of taking direct military action against ISIS. But what they do not want to address is what will happen if insufficient action is taken, if the status quo of appeasement and engagement is allowed to continue. Avoiding a new Cold War sounds like an admirable goal, but what if we are already in one? And what of the actual war and invasion and annexation of European soil that has already happened in Ukraine? Denial is not an acceptable policy. Fretting only about what might happen when the current situation is already catastrophic is a pathetic attempt to defer tough decisions. Ignoring your cancer and arguing with the doctors who diagnosed it will not save you, no matter how much you fear treatment.

There is no way to be sure exactly what will happen if the nations of the free world, led by the United States and NATO, confront Putin in Ukraine (or, for that matter, decide to wipe ISIS off the map). What we can be sure of is that action will eventually be necessary and that it will require more resources, more sacrifices, and more lives lost for every day that goes by. Putin, like every dictator ever known before him, grows in confidence and support when he is unchallenged. Every step he can trumpet as a success to the Russian people makes it harder to remove him and more likely he will feel bold enough to take even more aggressive steps.

It is true that if America, Europe, and the rest of the world's democracies finally realize the era of engagement is over and strike at Putin and the other thugs by cutting them off and providing overpowering support to their targets, conflicts may worsen before they can be extinguished. This view—the willingness to accept short-term sacrifice for the long-term good—requires the sort of leadership the free world has very little of today. It requires thinking beyond the next poll, the next quarterly report, and the next election. The policies of the Cold War held remarkably firm for decades, across administrations, and eventually ended in a great victory for the side of freedom. Since then, one president after another, one prime minister after another, passed the buck of human rights in Russia until Putin had enough momentum to launch a real war on European soil.

A popular straw man argument is to suggest that intervention against aggression might lead to World War III or even a nuclear holocaust. To the contrary, the only way the current crisis will continue to escalate is if Putin is not confronted with an overwhelming threat to his hold on power, which is the only thing he cares about. If Putin is allowed to go from victory to victory, wiping out any opposition at home while gaining territory and influence abroad, the risk of an all-out war increases dramatically. Adolf Hitler did not attack Poland in 1939 because the Allies stood up for Czechoslovakia; they didn't. Hitler did not move into the Sudetenland because the world protested vigorously at his Austrian Anschluss, but because the response was so feeble. It was only after all of his early triumphs were accomplished so effortlessly, against so little opposition from the Western democracies, that he had the confidence to go too far.

Of course Putin is no Hitler; that unspeakable evil will never be matched—although those who lived through the horrors of Stalin, Mao Zedong, and Pol Pot may disagree. It is important, though, to remember that in 1936—and even in 1937 and 1938— Hitler was no Hitler either! The adulation of the foreign athletes and dignitaries at the Berlin Olympic Games, the unopposed ease of the Nazi army's first steps over the post-WWI German borders, the eager capitulation of Chamberlain: these are the things that allowed Hitler to become the monster.

In terms of global influence, Russia's industrial and military power today is no match for that wielded by Nazi Germany. But Putin has one thing Hitler never had: nuclear weapons. And he is not shy about reminding us of that fact. I forced myself to listen to Putin's October 2014 Q&A session in Sochi twice because I couldn't believe he was so casually praising Soviet leader Nikita Khrushchev's terrifying nuclear gamesmanship. But we should all listen carefully to what Putin says, because he has a track record of following through with his threats when left unchecked.

If, however, the leaders of the free world come to their senses in time and present a strong united front against Putin—one with economic sanctions, substitution for Russian energy, diplomatic isolation, and economic and military support for his targets—it will provide a foundation for a new alliance of the world's democracies. Dictatorships will be given the choice of reforming and joining the community or being steadily marginalized and left behind. The European Union employs this model internally; each prospective member state must meet explicit standards of economic development and human rights. Yet the same EU is happy to do business with brutal dictatorships like Putin's Russia that it could never accept as members. Ending Putin's war and ending this hypocritical policy of engagement can happen at the same time.

The first order of business in this book will be to establish why this undeclared war is real and why it matters. Lacking obvious symbols to focus on and without an evil empire to fight, it will be difficult to rally the world's democracies to take action, and yet they must. Then we will examine how two decades of Western retrenchment and retreat have encouraged autocrats like Putin and terrorist groups like ISIS to flourish around the world.

Democracies get the leaders they deserve, as the saying goes, and so we must look at the shift in values and priorities that has made appeasement and defeatist realpolitik the currency of choice in foreign policy today. Removing the moral component from foreign affairs has been a catastrophe from which it will take a very long time to recover. The last section of this book is dedicated to a comprehensive plan to implement that recovery, beginning with questions every candidate for leadership in the world's democracies should have to answer.

Throughout the book I will share my personal observations and experiences as an activist in Russia and in my work today as the chairman of the New York–based Human Rights Foundation. Of course my political battles actually started back in the 1980s, with my rebellion against the Soviet sports authorities as a chess champion and my interviews to Western publications about the iniquities of the Communist system that often got me into hot water. But the most important story in this book is not my own. It is the story of how Vladimir Putin, with the indifference, and in some cases the support, of the free world that had brought down the Soviet Union, put an end to the democratic experiment in Russia.

PROLOGUE

The rise and fall of Russian democracy would make for a painfully short book. It took just eight years for Russia to go from jubilant crowds celebrating the collapse of the Soviet Union in 1992 to the ascendance of former KGB agent Vladimir Putin to the presidency. Then it took Putin another eight years to corrupt or dismantle nearly every democratic element in the country—balance in the branches of government, fair elections, independent judiciary, a free media, and a civil society that could work with the government instead of living in fear of it. Uncooperative oligarchs were jailed or exiled and the press quickly learned what could and could not be said. Putin also consolidated the Russian economy, clamping down on free market reforms and emphasizing the creation of "national champions" in the energy and banking sectors.

A potential turning point came in 2008, when Putin's constitutional limit of two four-year terms was ending. Few expected him to retire gracefully, or at all, but exactly how he would keep control while keeping up appearances was a hot topic of debate. Putin had channeled power not just to his party or to his office, but to himself personally. His leaving would have been like ripping the spine out of the KGB mafia state he and his allies had spent eight years building. He could amend the Russian constitution to run again, but at the time Putin was still sensitive about keeping up democratic appearances. For one, it would have been awkward for his fellow G8 leaders to welcome him after any primitive power grab, and staying in the good graces of the leaders of the United States, Japan, and Western Europe was very useful to

Putin at home. How could he be called anti-democratic, let alone a despot, if he was embraced so heartily by the likes of George W. Bush, Silvio Berlusconi, and Nicolas Sarkozy?

Putin's dilemma gave those of us in the Russian opposition movement a brief glimmer of hope that the 2008 election could turn into an opportunity to change the course of the country. We knew the election itself would be rigged from start to finish, but we hoped exposing this corruption could lead to more people joining our cause. Russians were aware they were losing their freedoms under Putin, and they could still be sensitive about having their noses rubbed in it, as the massive 2011 protests later showed.

Putin's decision was a tactical masterstroke. Instead of keeping the presidency himself, he endorsed his first deputy prime minister, the young Dmitry Medvedev, who was generally seen as far more liberal and pro-Western than his boss. The election was as predictable and rigged as could be expected, with Medvedev scoring a small fraction less than Putin had in 2004. (The joke at the time was that it would have been unacceptably ill-mannered for Medvedev to earn a higher percentage than Putin—or for him to be taller than Putin.) Medvedev immediately named Putin his prime minister and the two men switched offices in a graceful pas de deux on the grave of Russian democracy. Four years later, Medvedev duly handed the presidency back to his master, having changed the constitution so Putin could now sit for two six-year terms. In the 2012 election even less effort was made to hide the fact that Russia had truly become a dictatorship once again.

There were a few bumps in the road, however. Just three months before the presidential election on March 4, the largest political protests of the post-Soviet era had erupted spontaneously after the parliamentary elections were so blatantly rigged that it was too much for many to stomach. Over the next months, hundreds of thousands of Russians took to the streets, many chanting "Putin Must Go!" and "Russia Without Putin!"

I frequently participated along with other opposition leaders like Alexei Navalny and Boris Nemtsov, but it was the surprising appearance of tens of thousands of typically apolitical and apathetic Muscovites in Bolotnaya Square on December 10 that gave us hope that something might be changing. Since 2005, I had been at the front of many marches where we had been outnumbered by the riot police by at least ten to one. On December 24, in Sakharov Prospekt, the odds were reversed at last. Standing before a sea of opposition flags uniting against corruption and Putin, who could not dream of a new future?

But the momentum could not be maintained. Draconian new laws against the freedom of assembly were quickly passed, allowing for huge fines and criminalizing nonviolent protest. Many opposition leaders and members were harassed, arrested, and interrogated over their roles in organizing the protests. The Kremlin committed massive resources against the protests; the last mass demonstration on May 6, 2013, was brutally dispersed and led to the so-called Bolotnaya Square case that records show has involved more than thirteen thousand witness interviews and that led to dozens of protesters being sentenced to years in prison.

At the same time, the Kremlin-controlled media began to intensify its portrayal of the protesters and opposition leaders as dangerous extremists and quite possibly traitors to the motherland. Not only would the revolution not be televised, the would-be revolutionaries had no access to television. There were still a few significant protests after Putin's so-called election was announced, but it became clear to me in 2012 that democracy was truly dead in Russia. I could no longer envision a peaceful transition away from Putin. If he fell it would be messy and likely violent. After I was called several times to come in for one of the prosecutor's special interviews—you go in as a witness and come out as a suspect, if you come out at all—I decided not to return to Russia in 2013.

Here I would like to rewind and look again from outside of Russia. Oil price boom, propaganda, repression, and a compliant population notwithstanding, Putin could not have achieved what he did without considerable outside help. After all, it is not so easy to create a dictatorship in this day and age. Among other factors, global communication makes it difficult to prevent a country's people from envying the rights and riches of their neighbors. This is one reason Putin has always done everything possible to support authoritarian regimes in Russia's neighbors.

The global trend toward democracy in the second half of the twenty-first century is one of the greatest achievements of humankind. Before World War II, a vast majority of the world's democratic governments were found in Europe and the Americas. Samuel Huntington documented this "third wave" of democratization in his 1991 book of the same name, while Francis Fukuyama's was memorably titled *The End of History* in 1992. Liberal democracy and capitalism were the big winners of the last great ideological competition we would ever know. Totalitarianism and Communism were the big losers. The good guys won the Cold War, McDonald's opened in Moscow, and it was time for a much deserved celebration.

But in Russia, the story was different. The end of the Cold War presented an opportunity, not just for economic advancement but for a welcoming embrace among the world's democratic powers. Even as the Soviet Union crumbled, Russia, by far the largest and most powerful member, kept many of the USSR's privileges and positions, as well as keeping the world's largest nuclear arsenal while Ukraine, Belarus, and Kazakhstan were successfully pressured into giving theirs up. Russia took the Soviet spot on the United Nations Security Council and, despite perpetual unfounded complaints about suffering humiliation at the hands of the victorious West, there was nothing in the way of reparations demanded by the winning side. In fact, the United States and several other countries provided badly needed loan guarantees and other aid to Russia, directly and via the International Monetary Fund (IMF). Russia was even paid for bringing its troops back from Germany. This was not just charity. Collapse and chaos in the nuclear-armed giant would not have been in anyone's best interests.

Nor were there any trials or truth and reconciliation commissions, internationally or domestically, about the former USSR. After decades of genocides, mass relocation and imprisonment, and totalitarian repression, it was decided to let bygones be bygones and move into the bright new future without recrimination. Of course many of the new leaders and officials had a personal interest in not digging too deeply into the cruel past. I'm not proud of having once been a member of the Communist Party myself, even if joining had been a calculated move so that a lack of party affiliation did not hurt my developing chess career. (I left the party in January 1990.)

The dominant position soon became one of "avoiding witch hunts," even if that meant leaving people with blood on their hands in positions of power. More critically, it left the roots of the powerful Russian security apparatus intact, if renamed and with a considerably lower profile for the time being. Yeltsin didn't want trials and the Russian KGB archives remained off limits. Former officials were given tacit promises of financial security and immunity from prosecution in exchange for facilitating the transfer of power. This same formula was employed by Yeltsin when he hand-picked Vladimir Putin to become his successor in 1999.

Western nations unanimously collaborated with this dubious cover-up. It is remarkable how quickly even many of the most hawkish Cold Warriors were willing to forgive and forget as soon as the USSR ceased to exist. "Witch hunt" implies persecution with false pretenses and/or a lack of evidence. But what if there are plenty of actual witches around, and plenty of evidence of witchcraft? Don't forget that Lenin's mausoleum in the middle of Red Square was never removed.

I think the sense of jubilation overwhelmed people on both sides of the Iron Curtain. We could learn about the rest of the world, travel, read newspapers that were actually interesting. We could talk about politics that actually mattered, and even vote! Few Russians had the appetite for gloomy trials detailing the horrors we knew all too well had occurred in the Soviet Union. This turned out to be a terrible mistake that Russia, and the rest of the world, is still paying for today.

———

There is no single moment where Russia lost its way and Vladimir Putin, or someone like him, became inevitable. There was no specific turning point in the West's dealings with Russia marking the shift from confrontation over human rights to engagement. It was a slow and steady process. Time and again, the United States and Europe turned a blind eye to the crimes and misdemeanors of Gorbachev, Yeltsin, and Putin in the hope that everything would work out on its own. US presidents in particular always placed far too much faith in individuals in Russia, instead of supporting the structural and institutional reforms that could have guaranteed the survival of democracy.

The West's acceptance of authoritarianism in the former USSR actually began before the "former" had been firmly appended. In 1988, Ronald Reagan's devout belief in the moral superiority of individual freedom and the free market was replaced by the cautious pragmatism of George H. W. Bush. By early 1991, Gorbachev was losing control of his timid reform program as the winds of change blew in hard from Eastern Europe. Bush did his best to support Gorbachev's efforts to hold the USSR together, delivering his infamous "Chicken Kyiv" speech on August 1, 1991, where he enraged many Ukrainians by warning them against pushing too hard for independence from the USSR.

Gorbachev's desperate attempts to preserve socialism and the Soviet Union eventually failed utterly, turning him into an accidental hero in the West. I won't even give him the minimal credit some offer for not sending in the proverbial tanks to crush the anti-Communist uprisings that were taking place all across the Soviet Bloc, especially since Gorbachev did send in military to Latvia and Lithuania, where he believed he could get away with

6

it. He was hardly a risk taker where his own neck was concerned and didn't want to end up like Romanian Communist dictator Nicolae Ceaușescu, whose rapid overthrow and execution in December 1989 was still fresh in everyone's mind.

When I spoke in the European Parliament in September 1991, I compared Gorbachev to Louis XVI, who also recalled parliament and declined to use force against the revolutionaries in the hopes they would spare his life. In that regard Gorbachev had better luck than Louis, despite having a roughly similar approval rating with his own people. There are also similarities with the last Russian tsar, Nicholas II, who likewise attempted to stave off revolution and maintain his autocracy via shallow reforms. He convoked a parliament, issued a constitution, and still ended in misery. (I cannot resist pointing out that Gorbachev, Nicholas II, and Louis XVI also all had intelligent, influential, and unpopular wives: Raisa, Alexandra, and Marie Antoinette. Raisa was certainly aware of the violent fate met by the others, and I imagine she encouraged her husband to avoid the use of force in order to increase their chances of escaping with their skins, and her furs, intact.)

Boris Yeltsin, in contrast, was a true populist at heart despite being a career party official. He backed up his faith in the people with action and with ambitious political reforms. Internationally speaking he had a weak hand and he knew it, compensating by alternating between bluster and charm with foreign leaders. Yeltsin managed to preserve a regional sphere of interest despite the terrible weakness of Russia on the world stage during the 1990s. That he succeeded in doing this is to his credit—and to the immense discredit of Bill Clinton and the other G7 leaders who allowed it to happen.

The 1990s were a series of huge missed opportunities for the global forces of democracy. The economic, military, and moral might were all on one side more so than at any time in history. Instead of pressing this advantage by, for example, reforming the United Nations with a robust new human rights framework, the

7

advantage was squandered. The United States and its European allies had the capability and the leverage to exert tremendous pressure for positive reforms—capability they exercised effectively to win the Cold War. Instead, as soon as the Berlin Wall fell they switched to relying almost exclusively on incentives and engagement, which were quite effective in Eastern Europe but failed against determined autocrats like Vladimir Putin.

Every time Putin cracked down in Russia, or even when he interfered with neighboring nations, the West had the opportunity to push back. Instead, at every turn Putin was rewarded with even closer ties to the world's leading democracies and, more importantly, with greater access to their lucrative markets. It is impossible, of course, to say with certainty that Putin's course toward dictatorship would have been altered or prevented by a strong stand by the free world. But I believe it to be so.

Putin is not an ideologue. He and his cronies accumulated tremendous wealth, and the threat of not being able to enjoy it freely in the West would have been a very serious threat. Unlike their Soviet predecessors, Putin and his allies are not content with a late-model ZIL limousine and a nice dacha on the Black Sea. They want to rule like Josef Stalin but live like Roman Abramovich, the close Putin buddy who spent his riches buying a famous English soccer team and yachts the size of soccer fields. Putin's oligarchs travel the world and keep their wealth abroad, and this gives Western governments real clout if they have the courage to use it.

That was even more the case early in Putin's first term, when he was still testing what he could get away with. Like any born autocrat, Putin respects only power. He takes a step, looks around, sniffs the air, and then, if there are no negative consequences, he takes another step. With each advance, he gains more confidence and becomes harder to stop. Muted expressions of concern from diplomats and foreign ministers are the greenest of lights to someone like Putin. Such chatter is in fact designed to be meaningless in his interpretation. After all, if the United States were truly concerned it would do something instead of just talking about it while doing nothing.

The appeasers' motives range from ill-advised optimism about Putin's true nature to cynical political careerism that sees a belligerent and energy-rich Russia as too difficult a problem to deal with. It was easier for many Western leaders to pretend there wasn't a problem in Russia than to admit it would be difficult or impossible to solve it. Then there's a separate category for those leaders like Silvio Berlusconi and Gerhardt Schröder, men for whom cooperating with Putin was literally business as usual.

Despite the attempt to rebrand the method as "engagement," the smell of appeasement is impossible to mask. The fundamental lesson of Chamberlain and Daladier going to see Hitler in Munich in 1938 is valid today: giving a dictator what he wants never stops him from wanting more; it convinces him you aren't strong enough to stop him from taking what he wants. Otherwise, goes the dictator's thought process, you would stand up to him from the start.

The warning signs about Putin's nature and intent were plentiful. His rise to power was aided by his brutal response to the 1999 apartment bombings, terrorist acts that many still suspect to have been a Reichstag-style provocation. (But unlike the Reichstag, there was actual blood spilled.) Carpet-bombing and torture of civilians across Chechnya were presented as part of the global war on terror, which was a complete fabrication. Later, Putin's contempt for the value of human life was confirmed in two hostage situations, the first in 2002 when federal troops using a still-unspecified gas killed many dozens of hostages in the Nord-Ost theater standoff in Moscow. The second came in 2004, when security forces using military weapons demolished a school full of child hostages in Beslan, resulting in the deaths of hundreds.

The Kremlin's rapid subjugation of the Russian press was, along with a rise in oil prices of over 700 percent by 2008, the biggest reason behind the perceived success of the regime of Vladimir Putin. Very early on in his first term as president, Putin learned that control of the Fourth Estate was essential to controlling the other three. The lesson stemmed from the public outcry over the botched rescue of the crew of the *Kursk* nuclear submarine, which sank after an explosion during a training exercise in the Barents Sea in August 2000. Instead of taking names in the military or cleaning out our Augean bureaucracy, Putin went after the free press.

Media outlets were taken over by forces friendly to Putin and his closest associates. The owner of NTV, Vladimir Gusinsky, spent three days in jail in June 2000 and was forced to give up his company. In fact, in what would become a typical "negotiating method" of the day, he was forced to sign over his company before being allowed to leave jail. He fled to Israel while his channel was appropriated and absorbed into the Kremlin's portfolio in April 2001, and today, ironically, NTV is probably the dirtiest of the official propaganda stations against some very tough competition in that field. This "soft censorship" was accompanied by the more conventional kind, with its lists of non grata names and verboten topics. Media power was centralized in the same fashion as political power, and with the same purpose: looting the country without causing a popular revolt.

The corruption of the Yeltsin era is burned into Russia's collective memory only because we learned about it in the press at the time. In the 1990s, the competing oligarchs waged war against one another in their media outlets. It was not a fight fought fairly or decently, but a preponderance of facts came to light and thousands of honest journalists worked to bring the truth to the Russian public. Under Putin, the only light came from the endless stream of glowing articles about him and his administration.

In the typical pattern, the Western response to these bold steps toward despotism was limited to press releases expressing concern while business went on as usual. Putin was welcomed as a full member of the G7, which is supposed to represent great industrial democracies. For those who excuse the invitation due to Russia's size and influence, note that China is not a member. Russia's inclusion was a reward for democratic reforms and it should have been rescinded as soon as Putin rolled back those reforms. It says a great deal that Russia's membership was not revoked until Putin invaded Ukraine and annexed Crimea in March 2014.

Putin's strong opportunistic instincts led him to make perhaps the most important phone call of his life on September 11, 2001. He was the first foreign leader to call President George W. Bush and offer full support after the terror attacks. By so doing he earned the sympathetic Bush's trust and the benefit of the doubt for seven long years. (This must have changed when Russia invaded Georgia in 2008, but that itself was a reflection of how much Putin had grown in ambition and confidence during Bush's term.) Putin succeeded in portraying Russia as a US ally—in Afghanistan in particular—while actively working against US and European interests elsewhere.

Bush 43's ability to stand up to Putin's many transgressions was further constrained by a chance comment several months earlier when the two men first met, in Slovenia on June 16, 2001. It was after that meeting that Bush uttered this famous evaluation: "I looked the man in the eye. I found him to be very straightforward and trustworthy and we had a very good dialogue. I was able to get a sense of his soul." After that comment, Bush couldn't take Putin to task without admitting a serious misjudgment of his character; and admitting mistakes was never Bush's strongest suit. To be fair, Bush and the United States had a new set of top priorities after 9/11. But it is still a little surprising in hindsight that an administration with experienced Cold Warriors like Cheney, Rumsfeld, and Soviet/Russia expert Condoleezza Rice completely failed to put any pressure on Putin.

As the saying goes, however, as bad as things get they can always get worse. Barack Obama came into office with hardly any foreign policy experience and saddled with overwhelming domestic challenges. He also had a clear mandate from an American people burned out on long unpopular engagements in Afghanistan and Iraq: fix America and leave the rest of the world alone. There was little chance that Obama, the idealistic newcomer, would challenge Putin in any meaningful way despite adding the Orange Revolution–savvy Mike McFaul to his foreign policy team.

What happened was still much worse than I expected. The Obama administration trotted out its reset plan, complete with Hillary Clinton's inaccurate button. Imagine the message this warm overture sent to Vladimir Putin. (Technically, the recipient of the message was Dmitry Medvedev, but let's not trifle with such absurd pretenses.) If Putin occasionally seems incredulous at the relatively robust international response to his 2014 invasion of Ukraine, perhaps it's because he is simply waiting for his next reset button.

In her 2014 memoir, Hillary Clinton goes to great lengths to defend the Reset and to explain that she was never taken in by Putin. Ironically, this post-facto position follows the same pattern as the memoirs of her political adversaries: George W. Bush, Condoleezza Rice, Dick Cheney, and Donald Rumsfeld. With near unanimity, often with very similar phrasing, they all say they knew Putin was a bad guy, but they had no choice but to do business with him. (Bush 43 is the most forthcoming about the possibility he had misjudged Putin, as I'll discuss later.)

As someone who has been yelling from every rooftop and op-ed page about Putin's nature and ambitions for over a decade, the sight of so many powerful US politicians agreeing with me as soon as they are out of office is infuriating. Their books give no space at all to what they might have done differently to influence Putin's behavior while they had the power to do so. The idea that the United States might have threatened to isolate Putin, to cut him and his billionaire cronies off, to use the stick after he had eaten all their carrots, never comes up.

When the US government finally did take limited steps to respond to the Putin regime's many abuses, it came only after Putin had achieved total power in Russia and a sense of complete impunity. And the move didn't even come from inside the administration. The Magnitsky Act legislation that levied asset and travel sanctions on some Russian officials for human rights abuses was championed by American-British investor Bill Browder. One of his Russian investment group's lawyers, Sergei Magnitsky, was arrested in 2008 by the same corrupt law enforcement officials whose massive fraud he had exposed. A year later he died in pre-trial detention after being beaten and failing to receive adequate medical attention.

The Magnitsky legislation was Browder's retaliation in a way, and at first the Russian officials on the list were only a few who were directly related to Magnitsky's persecution and death. It's notable that the Obama administration fought against it from the start, and it was only signed into law as part of a House bill that also normalized trade with Russia, which had previously been restricted in some ways by the famous 1974 Jackson-Vanik amendment.

The Obama administration followed Europe's embarrassingly cautious lead in applying sanctions against Russia and to Putin's allies in the wake of Russia's 2014 invasion of Ukraine. Despite the overwhelming and bipartisan congressional support for doing more—arming and training Ukraine's military in particular—Obama continued to echo Merkel, Hollande, and other European leaders talking about "finding a peaceful solution" when there was already a war in progress. They insisted on referring to Putin as someone who would negotiate in good faith, even after he triumphantly admitted in March 2015 that he had been lying about the presence of the Russian military in taking Crimea a year earlier.

I do not believe that Merkel and Obama are so oblivious, especially Merkel, who was born in the Communist German Democratic Republic. So the only explanation is that they still find the Putin problem so politically thorny that it's easier to pretend there isn't one. And it may even be true, for them personally, for a while. Perhaps they only wish to postpone total catastrophe until they are safely out of office and can leave Putin to their successors. In any case, it is a moral capitulation that has produced very real costs.

1

THE END OF THE
COLD WAR
AND THE FALL
OF THE USSR

In the middle of the summer in 1989, I gave a long interview to a magazine that practically personified Western decadence in the Soviet imagination: *Playboy.* But it wasn't just the publisher of my interview that raised eyebrows in the Soviet Union. Despite the increasing atmosphere of *glasnost*, openness, between America and the USSR, and the slow loosening of political repression under Mikhail Gorbachev's perestroika, my outspoken criticism of Soviet society and my praise for America and Americans in particular were something of a scandal. The fall of the Berlin Wall on November 9 was still five months away and largely unimagined. A month after that, Gorbachev and President George H. W. Bush would declare that the USSR and the United States were no longer enemies. But even in this rapidly changing environment my comments sounded close to treason to some in the Kremlin.

PLAYBOY: You sound like an American. Americans always want to be winners.

KASPAROV: This is a very human quality. It proves that Americans are very close to true human nature.

For Soviet authorities steeped in the myth of the moral superiority of Communism and the Soviet man, comments like these were quite serious. In today's world it may seem quaint, or else catastrophically oppressive, but socialist ideology and perceptions of morality were very much part of the Cold War arsenal. When the Soviet sports authorities attacked me for wanting to retain my chess winnings, they condemned not only my disobedience, but my lack of socialist solidarity. For me to say that my neighbors in Baku should see my keeping the Mercedes I won in Germany as normal, healthy thinking was radical and subversive.

Of course my interview wasn't as much of a public scandal as Russian actress Natalya Negoda appearing nude in the same magazine earlier in the year after playing a call girl in a movie that shocked the prudish Soviet society. Her photos and my interview in a publication that was still banned in the USSR, and the confused responses they provoked, were indicative of the perestroika period. Our country's tentative steps toward greater openness were tantalizing, but we knew we could be punished and the reforms rolled back at any time. There were no clear rules any longer, and more and more people were finding the audacity to test just where the lines were at a given moment.

In 1987, Gorbachev said he wanted to build Alexander Dubček's "socialism with a human face," to which I responded that Frankenstein's monster also had a human face. Communism goes against human nature and can only be sustained by totalitarian repression. Without outside assistance, or massive amounts of natural resources like oil, repression leads to economic stagnation. Then there is the moral and spiritual stagnation of a society were individual success and excellence are all but forbidden.

Of course there were specific events that helped expose the fatal flaws in the Communist system and force Gorbachev into his desperate attempts to reform and save the country. One was the

April 1986 disaster at the Chernobyl nuclear plant in Ukraine, and how the crisis was handled revealed official levels of incompetence, corruption, and mendacity beyond those of any banana republic. (Anatoly Karpov and I donated the prize fund from our 1986 world championship match to the Chernobyl victim relief fund.) Then there was the Soviet war in Afghanistan, which was going into its tenth year by 1989, and had been as ineffective, unpopular, and expensive as the American and NATO sequel would be.

Thanks largely to increasing Soviet exposure to news, ideas, and opinions, especially those from the outside world, the Soviet establishment found itself in a dilemma. If the authorities reacted as usual and cracked down over small transgressions, they would lose credibility as reformers and prove the critics' point that Soviet society was backward and stagnant. But they also knew that if they permitted a small amount of criticism it would encourage others to speak out. The authorities' responses were increasingly confused and inconsistent. Different manifestations of this catch-22 are what finally brought down the Soviet Union, despite Gorbachev's best attempts to hold it together.

Well before the Wall came down, it was clear to many of us on the "wrong" side of the Iron Curtain that major changes were inevitable. We had no idea what shape they would take, or where they would begin, but it was quite a novel experience for most Soviets to talk seriously and openly about anything to do with political transformation or a new direction for the country. And we weren't sure if the democratic reforms were real or simply a "one party democracy" distraction to help Gorbachev shore up power against the Soviet old guard and to buy time for his failing economy. People in the street talked about the ethnic violence that was already accompanying many of the republics' independence movements. We wondered whether or not millions of people would starve before economic reforms finally took place.

On March 26, 1989, the USSR held its first real election since its formation in 1922. The newly created Congress of People's

Deputies of the Soviet Union was intended to put a democratic face on the Supreme Soviet, the body that still held the real power. But the Communist Party only won 85 percent of the seats (instead of the usual 99.9 percent), and among the independent insurgents was Boris Yeltsin, who won the Moscow district overwhelmingly over Gorbachev's candidate.

Ironically, the USSR's limited experiments with democracy had their greatest early impact outside of the Soviet Union, in Poland. The sight of an actual election in the USSR, however sloppy and superficial, provided the Poles with the impetus for their own much more comprehensive experiment. Instead of adopting Gorbachev's dreamed of socialist reform, Poland overthrew its Communist masters completely and the rest of the Warsaw Pact nations quickly followed Poland's example.

The current despots of many former Soviet states lived through and understand the dangers of the free speech "cracks in the wall" dilemma and have worked very hard to avoid it in their own nations. Putin and other ex-Soviet autocracies view what happened in Gorbachev's regime as a negative case study. This is why they react so harshly against political criticism on a tiny blog or a single protester holding a sign.

Modern dictatorships have learned from the mistakes of their predecessors. They know that explosive energy will build unless there is a release valve. So they've created space for a strange kind of controlled dissent. The Echo of Moscow radio station and website are permitted to broadcast and publish material critical of Putin while smaller and less compliant outlets for dissent like my Kasparov.ru news service are banished from the Russian Internet. I was the chairman of Echo from 1991 to 1996, when it was independent. Now, while it still maintains an opposition character, it is owned by the media arm of state energy giant Gazprom and operates knowing it can be shuttered at any moment.

Similarly, protest rallies can be registered and may take place, but organizers and participants may still find themselves prosecuted. It's all part of the elaborate modern ballet of pseudo-democracy and pseudo-choice that also includes elections with predetermined outcomes and every television channel with a slightly different position on how very well Putin is handling everything.

The "color revolutions" associated with the pro-democracy movements in Georgia in 2003 (Rose) and Ukraine in 2004 (Orange) also provoke fear among the autocrats, who take preemptive countermeasures against youth movements, NGOs with foreign connections, and seemingly minor platforms for free speech like indie radio stations. But it is the Soviet experience that truly scarred Putin and the rest and that continues to shape their worldview and their behavior. And it is only my own experience as a Soviet and Russian citizen that allows me to understand Putin's moves and motivations.

It is very difficult to describe life in a Communist state to those who never lived in one. The human spirit is a resilient creature and tends to adjust to circumstances as best it can so as not to lose all hope. There is also a solidarity in deprivation, which is why stories of the affluent West had such subversive power in the USSR. It is much harder to maintain stoicism in the face of adversity when you find out your neighbors are doing much better than you are. That is human nature, the underpinning of free-market consumer capitalism, and why Communism was, and remains, such a perverse and alien thing.

In the summer of 1989, at the time of the *Playboy* interview, my own audacity was a product of youth, success, travel, and a life spent a healthy distance from Moscow. I turned twenty-six that year and had been the world chess champion since 1985. I was a national sports hero in the chess-crazed USSR and was still living in my hometown of Baku, Azerbaijan, one of the trans-Caucasian republics along with Armenia and Georgia that make up the furthest-flung points of the far-flung Soviet empire. (As I like to joke when speaking in the United States, I was born in the Deep South, right next to Georgia.) Jutting out into the Caspian Sea twelve hundred miles from Moscow, Baku felt like the distant colonial outpost it was.

From there, from my training camp on the sea speaking to the interviewer, I had the confidence to say:

Everyone has the same kind of normal human aspirations. There may be two political spheres in the world today, but normal life-style exists in only one of them—and that is not here in the Soviet Union. Life here is what I could call a distortion of normal life. It's like living in a house of mirrors. Well, the only way out is to smash those mirrors. For years, I had the feeling that something was wrong around us here in the Soviet Union; when I traveled in the West, the feeling only got stronger. I am looking for the same thing that everyone else is: a normal life, where a person can live well and express himself well. It's very important for me to try to bring the normal life to my people. The daylight.

I am proud of those words today, since they show I have been consistent in my fight. Twenty-six years later I am still devoted to bringing "the normal life" to those living in the house of mirrors of dictatorship. The tragedy is that this fight is still necessary in Russia, decades after the collapse of the Soviet Union.

There were plenty of myths and misunderstandings about the dissolution of the USSR at the time, but this was to be expected. The same Western experts, politicians, and pundits who failed to foresee the fall of the Berlin Wall until Germans were streaming across the border were also blind to how quickly the forces Gorbachev unleashed with his reforms would spin out of his control.

My fame and outspoken nature frequently afforded me the opportunity to discuss politics with people far above my "rating" in the field. I was always surprised by how much they overestimated the stability of Communism in Europe and of the USSR itself. It was as if they had forgotten that a wall built by human hands could be torn down by those same hands.

A few cases stand out in my mind. In October 1989, I attended a party where I discussed the future of Europe with Henry Kissinger and Jonathan Bush, the then-president's brother. They laughed and only humored me a little when I said there wouldn't be any Communist regimes left in Europe by the end of the year. They could tell I was just a typical young know-it-all, basing my wild opinions on optimism and the smell of change in the air instead of years of scholarship and analysis. And maybe they were right, but so was I.

Early in 1990, after a promising meeting with the editorial board of the *Wall Street Journal* that led to lasting cooperation, editor Bob Bartley got me an invitation to speak at the RAND Corporation in Los Angeles. There, the head of RAND said I should meet his friend Brent Scowcroft, Bush's national security advisor and a veteran hand, having held the same post under President Ford in the seventies. At that White House meeting I also met Condoleezza Rice, a Russia expert who was then the director of the Soviet desk at the National Security Council.

They asked me about Boris Yeltsin, who had become Gorbachev's main critic and rival in Russia. They called Yeltsin a loose cannon and a drunkard, and I could only reply by asking if they wanted to hear about his character or his political future. It shocked me that these experts seemed completely unfamiliar with the political terrain in Russia, where Yeltsin was clearly rising and Gorbachev was flailing and falling. It was clear they only spoke to their good friend Gorbachev and other people inside the Kremlin—after all, that's where the power and the nuclear weapons were.

I did a better job holding my tongue in this more formal encounter, but I was amazed at how calm and oblivious they seemed to be about what I was sure was a tidal wave of change coming in Eastern Europe and the USSR. They were far more interested in the mechanics of Gorbachev's reform proposals than the fact that everybody in the streets from Berlin to Vladivostok now felt willing and able to complain openly about their political leaders. I told Scowcroft that Yeltsin was sure to be elected to lead the Russian Supreme Soviet in May, and that he would use this mandate to continue to challenge Gorbachev. I don't think he believed me, and I understood he and the White House were more concerned about keeping a good relationship with Gorbachev than anything else.

The focus on the Kremlin and Gorbachev's concerns meant overlooking the broadly destabilizing impact of Yeltsin's battle of "Russia versus the USSR," as Scowcroft admits in the 1998 book he wrote with President Bush. "In retrospect, when Yeltsin started to reject the authority of the Union and the Party and to reassert Russian political and economic control over the republic's own affairs, he was attacking the very basis of the Soviet state, shaking its political structure to the roots." Exactly so, and he was successful. Not bad for a loose cannon!

In April 1990, in a car ride across the French countryside, I told an interviewer, Fred Waitzkin, who would go on to become a biographer, "Communism is dead. Next year, in 1991, the Soviet Union will not exist. Definitely. Mark my words. Next year, there will be no more evil empire. We will have private property in my country. Many of the republics will have their independence." When he recounts this conversation in his book *Mortal Games*, Waitzkin adds that to him my predictions seemed "gratuitous, even frivolous" because they were so out of touch with the conventional wisdom of the day.

I suppose it was around this time that I began to develop an immunity to the rolled eyes and raised eyebrows of interviewers, experts, and politicians, an immunity that continues to serve me well today. My track record certainly isn't 100 percent, but I would rather speak my mind than censor myself because of what others may think of me, especially about important topics. I had no qualms about shouting about the eminent death of

Communism and the need for the West to press harder for democratic reform in the USSR every chance I got.

I was particularly enraged about how Gorbachev was treated like a champion of freedom in Western Europe and America when, as I said to Waitzkin that night in France, "Gorbachev has succeeded in convincing the West that his is the fight of a decent man for a better future. This is a lie. He is the last leader of the Communist state, trying to save everything he can."

This was indeed the case, and remains so today, despite a Nobel Peace Prize and over two decades of Gorbachev's revisionist spin. But I also had personal reasons for my hostility toward the man who became the first and last president of the Soviet Union.

Tensions have always been high between Azerbaijan and Armenia, but the wide scale of interethnic violence was unprecedented in Soviet times. As the regional independence movements gained momentum, protests and violent rhetoric also increased. Soviet hegemony kept conflict between the two territories at a standstill, but when Moscow turned a blind eye the region erupted both politically and in violence. A pogrom against Armenians in Sumgait in February was followed by two years of feuding and Armenian emigration. As would happen in Baku, the official Kremlin response was muted and then, when violence started, very late to arrive with force. As one writer darkly joked at the time, British forces got to the Falklands faster than police and troops arrived in Sumgait.

In 1988, the Armenian population of my home city of Baku was around a quarter million. By January 1990, the only remaining Armenians in Baku were mostly mixed families, including my own. Violence erupted in the city and for seven long days and nights, groups calling for the expulsion of all Armenians from Baku terrorized the city and its surroundings. Over a hundred people were killed and close to a thousand were injured. I was fortunate enough to be able to charter a plane and help family and friends and as many others as possible to escape under the cover of night.

It was an entirely preventable tragedy. Eleven thousand Soviet interior troops were stationed in the city, but they were not ordered to intervene. It wasn't until nearly a week after the attackers had run out of targets that General Alexander Lebed brought the Soviet troops in and martial law was established. By that point, almost all of Baku's remaining fifty thousand Armenians had fled. It is impossible to imagine that the attacks could have been so efficiently targeted in a city the size of Baku without comprehensive inside information and coordination.

I believe Gorbachev wanted the outbreaks of violence to consolidate direct control over these hot spots in the Soviet empire. He let the violence run its course, then he sent in the troops to crack down on everyone and to install leaders loyal to Moscow by force. The Baku pogrom led to my only meeting with Gorbachev, in the Kremlin a few days after Lebed's army entered Baku on January 20. I wanted to talk about the 120 people who had been murdered and the tens of thousands who had been displaced. What was he going to do about the unfolding military confrontation between Azeris and Armenians? But Gorbachev ignored this line of discussion and kept asking me who should become the new first secretary of the Communist Party in Azerbaijan.

I continued to do what I could to help draw attention to what was happening in the USSR. I announced I would sell the winner's trophy of my 1990 world championship match with Karpov if I won and would use the money to create a fund for Armenian refugees from Baku, which I did. It came out to around ten million rubles, $300,000 at the time. My mother and I basically ran this fund out of our home in Moscow, putting me in personal contact with countless refugees. Their painful stories hardened my antipathy for Gorbachev.

An earlier incident around that 1990 match, my fifth match in a row against Karpov and split between Lyon and New York, revolved around which flag was going to appear next to my name during the games, the Soviet hammer and sickle or the revived prerevolutionary Russian tricolor. This may sound incredibly trivial, I admit. But to me, and to a Soviet culture obsessed with symbols, politics, and chess, it was a big deal. The Soviet Union would still exist for well over a year and the match organizers in New York were very worried about politicizing the event or upsetting the Soviet authorities. After all, this wasn't a *Rocky* movie with an American underdog; it was two Russians. (As Americans in particular tended to call all Soviets, however inaccurate it often was. American world champion Bobby Fischer once boasted he was going to "beat all the Russians" at a tournament, when in fact his opponents were Estonian, Latvian, and Armenian!)

Of course politicizing the match was what I wanted and I stuck to my demand and got my wish, for a while. After four games, both flags were removed from the table due to protests from the Soviet delegation. I switched to wearing a prominent Russian-flag pin for the rest of the match. As much as I loved chess and as much as chess had done for me, I had always known that there were more important things in life. I was lucky that my "disloyalty" to the chess goddess Caissa rarely cost me as dearly at the chessboard as it might have. Despite the trauma of Baku and the distractions of Russian politics taking up so much of the time I should have been preparing for Karpov, I managed to edge out another world championship victory. And I did it representing to the white, blue, and red flag of democracy and rebellion.

Even the Western critics who admit Gorbachev never desired the end of Communism or the USSR give him credit for "not sending in the tanks" as the Iron Curtain unraveled and the Soviet republics spun off from Moscow like water off a top. I will deny Gorbachev even this small point of honor, however. First off, he did use military force in several places, especially the Baltics. Yes, he could have ordered Soviet troops to shut down elections, arrest opposition leaders, and fire on protestors. But would they have listened? Even had some of them obeyed Moscow's orders and massacred thousands, it would have sealed Gorbachev's own violent end—and he was nothing if not a survivor.

It also would have been foolish for Gorbachev to take risky military action in Hungary or Czechoslovakia when he had to worry about stability in the USSR. When your own house is on fire you don't send the firefighters to your neighbor's house. Food shortages and political independence movements were flaring up all over. Gorbachev didn't send in the tanks to try to keep the USSR together by force because he knew it was too late and he knew it would mean his own neck. And by mid-1991, when things were completely unravelling, he had seen the backlash after Soviet forces killed dozens and injured hundreds at a Vilnius TV and radio station in January 1991, after the Lithuanians refused to back down from their declaration of independence (issued in March 1990, the first of the Soviet republics). Yeltsin, by then the president of the Russian Federation, immediately denounced the violence and called for the withdrawal of all Soviet troops from the Baltics. Foreign leaders also condemned the crackdown and Gorbachev knew he could lose Western sympathy and the billions in aid he needed to have any hope of keeping hold of power.

The Soviet Union was already without members when it formally dissolved on December 25, 1991. (A date that has no particular resonance in Russia, where Christmas is celebrated on the Orthodox date of January 7, if at all.) Russian president Boris Yeltsin had succeeded in steadily ripping power away from Gorbachev and transferring command and control to the Russian Republic. The three Baltic nations, Armenia, and Georgia had long since declared independence and had been admitted to the United Nations. The failed coup of August 19–21 opened the floodgates for the rest.

Gorbachev's hope to form a new union was falling apart when news came that hardliners in his government had declared a state emergency to prevent the August 20 signing of the New Union Treaty that would have officially transformed the USSR into a federation of independent republics. During the coup, Gorbachev was supposedly held incommunicado at his dacha in Crimea, but it is my belief that the coup was of his own devising, or at least that he was a willing participant. Instead of seeing his authority continue to dwindle, Gorbachev might have hoped he would be able to return to a strengthened position after "negotiating" with the hardliners after they had done the dirty work of cracking down on political opponents like Yeltsin. As I recounted at the start, there was no popular or military support for the coup and it fell apart in seventy-two hours. After that debacle, even the Central Asian republics that had been eager to join the new union quickly followed Ukraine and Belarus out the door and declared their independence. Mother Russia herself declared on December 12.

The good news for Gorbachev was that the West spent a long time in denial over what should have been considered fantastic news. After my disappointing experiences discussing my homeland with American experts, it came as no surprise that President Bush often sounded more alarmed than overjoyed by the prospect of the Soviet Union falling to pieces. The empire was evil, yes, but it was the evil he and everyone in his administration knew very well. Bush also felt he could rely on Gorbachev, although he was a man backed by the KGB and who had never been elected to anything, over the unknown quantity of the populist and popularly elected Boris Yeltsin.

There was more than rhetoric involved in these bizarre attempts to prop up an old foe. Billions of dollars in Western aid and loan guarantees were provided to keep the USSR on life support. Germany alone extended an $8 billion aid package that was part of the agreement on German unification. Germany's financial commitments to Russia would balloon to $45 billion by 1992 and they included money for sending Russian troops home and even building housing for them in Russia.

The United States also stepped in with assistance well before any outcome was clear on democratic reforms in Moscow. On December 12, 1990, President Bush announced a package worth over $1.3 billion in credit and credit guarantees and waived the 1974 Jackson-Vanik amendment that put strict controls on doing business with the USSR. Four months later, Bush authorized another $1.5 billion in agricultural loan guarantees. The United States also sent medical aid directly to the Baltic States after the Soviet crackdowns there, and to Ukraine for the victims of the Chernobyl nuclear catastrophe.

American and other G7 multilateral aid and credit to Russia and other Soviet states only increased over the next few years, with Russia by far the largest beneficiary. In March 1993, feeling the need to support Boris Yeltsin's government, which was under parliamentary pressure, the G7 put together a $43 billion assistance plan. Japan bowed to the pressure of its fellow G7 members and did not tie its nearly $2 billion in aid to the disputed Kuril Islands. The IMF and the World Bank also opened their wallets, with the World Bank making its largest project loan ever of $610 million to help rebuild Russia's oil industry. Russia failed to collect all of the offered aid due to failing to achieve some required economic reform requirements. Thankfully, it was too little and far too late to keep the USSR together.

Separately, during the 1990s billions of dollars came in to secure the Soviet nuclear weapons and related programs in Russia, Ukraine, Belarus, and Kazakhstan. This can hardly be called anything but a wise investment, since the last things anyone wanted to see was a lack of oversight of nuclear weapons and materials or a diaspora of Soviet nuclear scientists in need of employment.

All these numbers are tedious, but it is important to counter the popular Russian victimhood myth spread by Putin's propaganda and by his anti-American, anti-NATO sympathizers around the world. The story goes that Russia was humiliated by the West when the USSR collapsed, leading to resentment and mistrust. They say the Cold War victors "lost Russia" first by not providing enough assistance and then by expanding NATO too aggressively. Both accusations are demonstrably false. As I will discuss in more detail later, if anything the West has been far too willing to forgive and forget the past crimes and dangerous potential of its old enemy.

In reality, many Western leaders became trapped by the idea that Russia was "too big to lose" and had to be supported at all costs even when it was clear they were throwing good money after bad down a hole of post-Soviet corruption and mismanagement. The danger of hardliners kicking out Gorbachev or the Communists coming back and beating Yeltsin was considered too great. The brief August 1991 coup by hardliners against Gorbachev, whether it was real or of Gorbachev's own desperate orchestration, resulted in an immediate bump in American aid. Similarly, when the Russian Duma challenged Yeltsin's reforms in 1993, the US Senate immediately responded by pushing through a $2.5 billion aid package that had been delayed.

In *Anatomy of Fascism,* Robert Paxton includes in his concise definition "the belief that one's group is a victim, a sentiment that justifies any action, without legal or moral limits, against its enemies, both internal and external." The myth of Russian humiliation at Western, especially American, hands fits the victimhood model perfectly. The false narrative that Russia is surrounded by enemies who are intent on holding it back fills Putin's need for fuel for his increasingly fascist propaganda. For similar reasons, Putin's regime is as obsessed with Soviet suffering and victory in World War II as the Soviet Union ever was. Along with the victimhood claim (in this case, legitimate), the WWII fixation fits the Kremlin's desire to call all of its enemies fascists, despite all evidence to the contrary. Their bizarre logic goes, "We defeated fascists in WWII, and so everyone who opposes us is fascist."

Ironically, the roots of Russia's descent back into totalitarianism can be traced to the West doing too much to respect the legacy of the USSR as a great power, not too little. Russia was allowed to inherit the Soviet Union's seat on the UN Security Council when that organization, which had been designed to preserve the Cold War status quo, should instead have been reformed to reflect the new primacy of the free world. There were no demands for lustration—investigating and prosecuting, or at least ejecting, Soviet officials for their crimes—while Gorbachev was practically canonized in the West.

Not exactly humiliation, unless you count the embarrassment of needing billions in cash and aid from a former rival, a rival that generations of Soviet propaganda had portrayed as heartless and destructive. The USSR lost the Cold War, and losing is painful. This sentiment, feeling like losers, was a consequence of failing to move on from the nation that vanished under our feet. The USSR lost the Cold War, but it was a victory not just for the United States and the West, but for Russians and all Soviet citizens and everyone living behind the Iron Curtain. We were free to live, to speak, and to think for ourselves. The real loss came when we failed to uproot the KGB system and failed to put misremembered glory days behind us quickly, as most of the European Soviet Bloc succeeded in doing. This left Russia and other former Soviet states vulnerable to the humiliation myth and to men like Putin eager to exploit it.

2

THE LOST DECADE

Many today seem to have forgotten that the fall of the Iron Curtain, the end of the Cold War, and the collapse of the Soviet Union were distinct events. Closely related events, of course, but by the time the USSR officially disappeared the Berlin Wall had been down for over two years. Anti-Communist revolutions and secessionist movements of various stripes spread across Central and Eastern Europe in 1989, beginning with the Solidarity movement in Poland in April. The wave swept through Hungary, East Germany, Czechoslovakia, Bulgaria, Romania, and Albania.

In my recollection, the Soviet media covered these incredible events with the schizophrenia typical of the glasnost period. In theory, the press was free at this point, but television in particular was still under centralized Kremlin control. Programs that discussed the Baltic uprisings in an insufficiently critical way, for example, could suddenly disappear from the airwaves. It was also in response to these political shifts that a more aggressive form of propaganda began to appear on Soviet television instead of just bland news and light entertainment. The print media had come a long way since the party-line *Pravda* days before 1985 and periodicals were bold enough to accurately report the fall of one European Communist regime after another. The transformation was remarkably peaceful, with the notable exception of the execution of vile Romanian dictator Nicolae Ceauşescu, who had ordered his troops to fire on anti-government protestors and where an estimated eleven hundred people were killed during the violence.

China's Tiananmen Square protests and massacre should also be mentioned in any discussion of "the Spirit of 1989," especially since Gorbachev visited Beijing in May, right in the middle of the protests, three weeks before the tanks were sent in to crush the demonstrators. Dictators seem to learn from history much better than democrats, by the way. The Putins of this world view Gorbachev as having been too weak to hold the USSR together and take from Tiananmen the value of brutal force.

Far more blood would soon come from a sadly predictable quarter, Yugoslavia, which, while Communist, had remained officially nonaligned for decades. When dictator-for-life Josip Tito died in 1980, the tight lid he had clamped down on the many ethnic and territorial divisions in the patchwork Balkan nation began to rattle. Federal control was already very weak by the time the European anti-Communist movement arrived and led to the country's first multiparty elections. But instead of settling things, the elections highlighted the irreconcilable differences among the country's terribly intertwined republics and its ethnic and religious groups. The ethnic Albanian majority in Kosovo was resentful of the Serbs while separatist parties in Slovenia and Croatia promised independence at the same time Serb leader Slobodan Milošević worked to strengthen the federal system that he largely controlled. It was a recipe for disaster that would soon become the first test of the post–Cold War security system.

With enough problems already stemming from the 1989 revolutions, NATO and the Western powers were happy to ignore the initial phases of the Yugoslav wars as internal problems. Europe had to figure out how to deal with 130 million impoverished new friends and their fledgling democratic governments. The Bush administration was focused on the USSR and, from August 1990 to February 1991, with the first Gulf War and its aftermath. The US-led coalition to kick Saddam Hussein out of Kuwait was notable for being the first time the two superpowers had been on the same side of a crisis since the end of World War II. The Soviet Union had been Saddam's main supporter, so the joint US-USSR statement condemning his invasion was another signal that the Cold War was fading. (Although it later turned out that Gorbachev had hedged his bets and left Foreign Minister Eduard Shevardnadze to push the statement through on his own.)

The moral clarity and stubbornness of Ronald Reagan had done its job in the end. In 1976, Reagan lost the Republican nomination to Gerald Ford, but succeeded in introducing the "morality in foreign policy" plank into the GOP platform. It is no exaggeration to say this modest achievement changed the world, as well as my own destiny. The Wall was torn down as Reagan had demanded and the evil empire fell. Lesser problems were left to lesser men.

While I am not an admirer of the first President Bush due to his extreme loyalty to Gorbachev, and I railed against his fecklessness at the time, his administration did a fair job of cleaning up the pieces in the immediate aftermath of the dissolution. He had a mature and competent foreign policy team whose lack of vision and courage before and during the USSR's collapse wasn't such a drawback when it came to managing the fallout. Bush, James Baker, Brent Scowcroft, Dick Cheney, and the rest grudgingly began to work with "loose cannon" Yeltsin on practical matters of nuclear security and economic reforms.

I would still take issue with how those economic reforms and aid packages were handled, although it was a hugely difficult task under any circumstances. The history of left-wing dictatorships transitioning to democracy with market economies is a short collection of horror stories. Communism is like an autoimmune disorder; it doesn't do the killing itself, but it weakens the system so much that the victim is left helpless and unable to fight off anything else. It destroys the human spirit on an individual level, perverting the values of a successful free society.

It is no coincidence that right-wing autocracies have a much better track record of emerging from political repression and achieving democratic and economic success. Chile, Portugal, Spain, South Korea, Taiwan—their regimes were about power for the sake of power, without a deeper ideology. When their regimes fell, with elections in most cases, the roots, the human values of individual freedom, were still healthy enough to flourish. Communist ideology attacks both root and branch and poisons the soil. Many countries in Eastern Europe are still struggling, despite the stabilizing influence and massive financial support provided by the European Union for decades. For some nations it was psychologically easier to uproot Communism because it was seen as a by-product of the hated Soviet occupation and they were eager to throw it all out.

Of course this is hardly an endorsement of any type of dictatorship. I believe Churchill's famous phrase: "democracy is the worst form of government except all those other forms that have been tried." But it partly explains why the former republics of the USSR have struggled so badly and why the regimes of Cuba and North Korea have proven so durable. It is the difference between people resenting that they are not free and people believing they do not deserve freedom.

The year 1992 saw the beginning of a modest debate over what the new world order should look like. It was no longer split between two rival superpowers. Was it a unipolar world where the United States, with most of Europe in tow, would set the agenda and enforce its will? Or was it a multipolar or nonpolar world, with no center of moral gravity? The US, with its massive military, enormous economy, and lack of any political opposition, was the de facto global hegemon, whether it wanted to embrace the role or not. The real question was how it would use this influence.

In 2015, after two exhausting and mismanaged wars, a humbling financial crisis, the rapid rise of China, and America's apparent impotence in various global hotspots, it's easy to forget just how dominant the United States was in the 1990s. In 1992, the US economy of $6.5 trillion was nearly double Japan's, triple Germany's, and thirteen times larger than China's. Russia barely made it into the top twenty, where it would stay until the price of oil shot up enough to push it into the top ten. The balance in military spending and capability was even more tilted toward the US and NATO in the 1990s, as it was revealed that the fabled Soviet military machine was as antiquated and feeble as the rest of its economy. China's relatively small military budget wouldn't take off until the 2000s.

Even more importantly, victory in the Cold War provided the United States and the rest of the free world with ideological supremacy. Democracy and capitalism had triumphed, totalitarianism and socialism had lost. Again, this all seems obvious and inevitable today, but the ideology of Communism was a serious challenge for many decades in nearly every country in the world. With the collapse of the USSR, the argument was over. Even twenty-five years later, most outbreaks of socialist rhetoric are limited to populist would-be autocrats keen to redistribute wealth to their cronies and with stagnant economies dependent on natural resources.

The Bush team had already begun rhetorical disarmament from Reagan's unapologetic American exceptionalism and moral leadership. America's reach and power flashed briefly in the first Gulf War, although even there Bush went to great lengths to make stopping Saddam Hussein's rampage sound like a pragmatic move by a broad coalition. Bush did speak boldly and eloquently on the importance of American leadership, however. He later wrote about the need for "a new domestic consensus for the American role in the world" to avoid isolationism and protectionism.

Bush continued:

The present international scene, turbulent though it is, is about as much of a blank slate as history ever provides, and the importance of American engagement has never been higher. If the United States does not lead, there will be no leadership. It is our great challenge to learn from this bloodiest century in history. If we fail to live up to our responsibilities, if we shirk the role which only we can assume, if we retreat from our obligation to the world into indifference, we will, one day, pay the highest price once again for our neglect and shortsightedness.

Bravo! This passage approaches the urgency and clarity of Reagan, if not the charisma. Unfortunately, Bush said these inspiring and prescient words in his 1998 book with Scowcroft and not while he was in office. This concluding section of *A World Transformed* likely reveals Bush's regrets about not pressing this role harder himself as president.

He had passed on the golden opportunity to remove Saddam from power and punish him for his attack on Kuwait. Along with condemning Iraqis to another decade of terror and oppression, it sent a message to other aspiring conquerors. In the summer of 1992, we heard Western politicians' calls to bring the Yugoslavian dictator Slobodan Milošević before an international court for his aggression in Croatia and Bosnia. How, when Saddam was still alive and in command?

Which brings us back to Yugoslavia. There, superficially, everything appeared to be clear. Direct American interests were not affected, so there was no reason to send troops. But Bush, whose blind support of the territorial integrity of Yugoslavia invigorated Belgrade's confidence that it could risk military action, forgot that each innocent victim of the war weakened democracy and lent new power to waning totalitarianism. If, in an era of global military domination by a democratic superpower, we could passively witness the revival of Nazi practices—concentration camps and ethnic cleansing—it meant that Bush's talk of a "new world order" was empty demagoguery aimed at a naïve domestic audience.

Bush played on the fear of a prolonged Vietnam-style involvement in Yugoslavia, ignoring a fundamental change in the world scene. By that point there was no Soviet threat to back up Yugoslavia, so Bush could rapidly have affected events with much less force than would have been needed in the past. As was only demonstrated years later, after many tens of thousands had died, NATO air strikes were enough to undermine the determination of the "Greater Serbian" forces. The destruction by air of Serbian heavy equipment required Belgrade to face a war conducted on equal terms with Bosnia and Croatia. But Bush showed that rote support for "UN policy" meant more to him than saving tens of thousands of lives, and more than presenting a strong stance against aggression.

Yugoslavia also revealed the need for a new policy for the new post–Cold War era, and that the Bush administration had failed to imagine such a policy. When Deputy Secretary of State Lawrence Eagleburger visited his old friend Milošević in Belgrade in February 1990, he was shocked to find there was no common ground to be found. There was so much good news coming from Europe at the time that the Balkan powder keg was pushed to the background even after Eagleburger returned from his trip warning that "it's much worse than anybody thought and it's going to be much bloodier than we thought."

Bush quickly lost the chance to make amends in a second term thanks to an American electorate that turned its back on foreign policy in the blink of an eye. He lost to a man with no foreign policy experience, a man whose slogan, "It's the economy, stupid," efficiently discarded foreign policy and the Cold War from the campaign. (Third-party candidate Ross Perot syphoning his votes away didn't help Bush either.) Bush was certainly no Winston Churchill, but the way he was turned out of office after the end of the Cold War echoes the way British voters quickly turned against Churchill after he led the nation to victory in World War II.

I was then, as I am now, an advocate for the use of every available tool to stop aggressors like Hussein and Milošević, including military intervention. In this I have been consistently on the side of those who have suffered from violence and against those who spilled blood first, regardless of their ethnicity or religion. My sympathies were therefore clearly on the side of the beleaguered Bosnians and Croatians, despite Russia's long-standing support for Serbian nationalism. From 1993 to 1995 I gave a series of charity events to draw attention to and to raise funds for Croatian and Bosnian refugees, including a simultaneous exhibition in the besieged Bosnian capital of Sarajevo in July 1994.

Throughout 1992, Serbian paramilitary forces murdered civilians and terrorized Muslim populations. Bush insisted on working through the United Nations, with predictably absurd and tragic outcomes. For example, the arms embargo imposed on the region mostly prevented the Bosnians from defending themselves against the Serbs, who were well armed already.

On the day after the US presidential election, November 4, 1992, I wrote an editorial for the *Wall Street Journal* that was essentially an open letter to the US president, old or new. I wrote that I had no doubt that a serious warning from George Bush to Milošević could have stopped the aggression and bloody ethnic war in Yugoslavia. The entire world had seen the pictures from Kuwait and Iraq showing the effects of the American military invasion, and they knew that the United States could accomplish great military feats if the will was there.

I also made a call for a return to strong moral leadership and ending the hypocrisy of putting stability ahead of democracy and freedom. "Coming global changes require a strong moral leadership, and only the U.S. is powerful and politically creditworthy enough to make the decisions and take the actions indispensable to a new world order. . . . Pure idealism, you say? Maybe, but I want to believe that yesterday America elected the leader of the world."

Alas, as we know, America elected Bill Clinton. Clinton's 1992 campaign had deftly exploited the ongoing recession and the end of the Cold War to paper over his lack of qualifications in the international arena. He made it clear he was of a new generation that wanted to break with the past and all of its heavy responsibilities around the world, and the American people seemed to agree. If any symbolism were required, Clinton's campaign theme song's lyrics included "Don't stop thinking about tomorrow" and "Yesterday's gone, yesterday's gone."

The horrors taking place in Yugoslavia were reaching the Western media by the time Clinton got into office. Photos of Bosnian Serb detention camps full of skeletal prisoners instantly reminded people of images from the liberation of the Dachau and Buchenwald concentration camps. Ethnic cleansing was once again taking place in the heart of Europe. Still plodding along with UN and European leaders, Clinton failed to convince France's François Mitterrand and the UK's John Major to lift the arms embargo. The new president declined to take unilateral military action without the permission of his NATO partners in Europe.

By the time NATO finally intervened militarily over two years later in the first combat action in its history, an estimated 140,000 people were dead and millions of people had been displaced. Genocide and coordinated rape campaigns were taking place while UN peacekeeping forces were on the ground. You may recall the artillery attacks of the marketplace in the historic center of Sarajevo in February 1994 and August 1995 that killed a total of over a hundred civilians with many more wounded. The images of the second savage attack finally galvanized NATO to launch the air strikes against Bosnian Serb forces. Along with the July offensive by combined Bosnian and Croatian forces that freed Knin and Bihać, the NATO strikes helped force Milošević to accept the Dayton Accords and bring the war to an end.

Meanwhile, Russia supported its "Serbian brothers" and helped delay outside action, as it would do again in 1999 over NATO intervention against Serb forces attacking Kosovar Albanians. In the case of Kosovo, Clinton acted much more rapidly to intervene with force, even making a powerful televised speech to the American people on March 24, 1999, on why NATO was launching a bombing campaign against Milošević's Serbia. Reading it now, I'm struck by how much of Clinton's address could, and should, apply to what is happening in Ukraine today.

It's worth looking up and reading in full, but I will excerpt a few key lines:

> We act to protect thousands of innocent people in Kosovo from a mounting military offensive. We act to prevent a wider war, to diffuse a powder keg at the heart of Europe that has exploded twice before in this century with catastrophic results. And we act to stand united with our allies for peace. By acting now, we are upholding our values, protecting our interests, and advancing the cause of peace.

Clinton went on to explain—he was always a great explainer—why Kosovo mattered, why this faraway place few Americans had heard of was vital to US interests, and why it was important to act quickly before things got worse. In Kosovo, as with Putin's ongoing invasion of Ukraine, no NATO country was under attack. But, Clinton continued:

> If we and our allies were to allow this war to continue with no response, President Milošević would read our hesitation as a license to kill. . . . Imagine what would happen if we and our allies instead decided just to look the other way, as these people were massacred on NATO's doorstep. That would discredit NATO, the cornerstone on which our security has rested for 50 years now. . . . If we've learned anything from the century drawing to a close, it is that if America is going to be prosperous and secure, we need a Europe that is prosperous, secure, undivided, and free.

Again, bravo! Substitute "Ukraine" for "Kosovo" and "Putin" for "Milošević" and President Obama could repeat it nearly word for word to my great satisfaction. And, again, this powerful statement on the importance of moral leadership and using American and NATO power to protect innocent lives came inexcusably late. The powerful closing paragraph of Bush 41's book I quoted earlier about America shirking its responsibilities and retreating into indifference was surely a message to Clinton, who was in the middle of his second term at the time it was published. And Clinton, after vacillating over Bosnia and overlooking the 1994 Rwandan genocide of more than 800,000 people, was, in the penultimate year of his eight years in office, finally ready to use America's unrivaled might to do the right thing without delay.

Seventy-nine days after the NATO air campaign began, Serb forces withdrew from Kosovo and nearly a million people were able to return to their homes. Remember Kosovo when you hear people say sending weapons to Ukraine would only "escalate the conflict" or "lead to World War III" in the popular straw man argument. Of course the scenarios and opponents are different—Russia is not Serbia and Putin is not Milošević. But the lesson is that much good can come from the decisive application of power, both in the moment and with a deterrent effect, and that waffling has real consequences and fuels future aggression.

The seasonal cycles of history shape and are shaped by human policies and plans. The hard-hearted Cold War strategies of isolation and containment gave way to engagement and an overabundance of caution. Retrenchment allowed threats to grow unchecked and genocides to occur on multiple continents while the overwhelming might of the free world looked on. One of those unchecked threats fulfilled its destructive potential on 9/11, pushing the pendulum back toward intervention and, inevitably, overreaction. The two exhausting wars that resulted helped bring to power a US president with a mandate for, what else, retrenchment and engagement. Obama has fulfilled his mandate to the extreme, as nearly all of his predecessors did before him. Europe has been resting on its laurels for so long that it is struggling just to stand when faced with xenophobia and terror on the inside and an aggressive Russia on the outside. Once again the seasons are changing and new threats have been allowed to flourish and to escape their borders.

3

THE INVISIBLE
WARS

Most European nations are largely populated by the ethnic groups that have been there for centuries. Despite decades of immigration that has increased with European Union expansion and the lowering of many borders, France is still full of Frenchmen and Germany of Germans. The borders of many Central and Eastern European countries were rearranged over and over by force throughout the twentieth century, and even though many groups were finally allowed to go their own ways to independence in the 1990s, there are still a few odd or controversial areas, though most are blessedly peaceful today.

For the most part, disputes are agreements to disagree between friendly neighbors or internal independence movements inside stable democratic nations where ethnic passions are argued in the press or taken nonviolently to the polls. Many Catalans in Spain and many Scots in the United Kingdom might disagree about just how satisfactory the arrangements are, of course, as would many Quebecois in Canada.

The United States is a very different thing. It's a continent-spanning nation built from scratch by millions of immigrants from every part of the world on top of the bones of its native population. (Argentina has a similar history.) The brutal treatment of the Native

American population is not a popular topic for discussion in the United States today, I have found, and it's not hard to see why. It is as disturbing and embarrassing as slavery to many Americans, which is why it was a popular topic for instruction in the USSR. It was very important for Communist ideology to show we were superior in every way, including morally. (And intellectually, which was why chess was so heavily promoted, fortunately for me.)

Soviet propaganda was also expert in "whataboutism," a term coined to describe how Soviet leaders would respond to criticism of Soviet massacres, forced deportations, and gulags with "What about how you Americans treated the Native Americans and the slaves?" or something similar. For the most part it was a transparent and shabby rhetorical trick of deflection and changing the topic. As Putin has revived so many Soviet methods and traditions, whataboutism is popular once again today thanks to Russia's cadres of trained Internet trolls. Scarcely a critical tweet of mine on Russia goes by without a few instant replies saying that the United States (or Israel) did something similar, or worse, or something entirely unrelated but also quite bad. This technique is always popular with the leaders and supporters of autocracies because they have no answers for their own crimes. For example, Arab states often talk as if Israel's conduct with the Palestinians somehow justifies their own repressive regimes.

The Soviets had many good reasons to want to change the topic. In fact, tens of millions of reasons that became clear as soon as the USSR began to crumble. The works of Aleksandr Solzhenitsyn had already documented the horrors happening inside the USSR under Lenin and Stalin. They were banned in the USSR, and their author exiled, not only because they impugned these men but because of Solzhenitsyn's conclusions. He made the strong case that the entire Soviet system could only function due to coercion and the threat of imprisonment, as well as the free labor provided by the gulags. But there was much more to what Stalin had done to pacify his patchwork empire, and it would come back to haunt Russia and the world.

The United States is called a melting pot or a salad bowl to describe how its diverse waves of immigrants have mixed together as proud Americans. In an amusing tradition that probably goes back to the first ship to reach Plymouth Rock after the *Mayflower*, each generation likes to complain that the latest group of immigrants is far worse than their own group was, that they won't work or won't assimilate or are in some other way inferior. And yet despite being a nation built on conquest and despite all the squabbling, America keeps churning along, turning new immigrant ingredients into apple pies. I admire this quality greatly as a recent arrival myself, now with a green card despite a dubious job history of "thirteenth world chess champion" and "pro-democracy activist."

The Soviet Union was a very different creation, and food metaphors fall short. I would say the USSR was a Frankenstein's monster with mismatched body parts inexpertly sewn on to a Russian head. Instead of assimilating into a shared identity, most of these disparate republics were subjugated into a common Soviet Communist culture (if that word can even be used) by the sheer force of totalitarian bureaucracy and media. For all the Bolshevik talk about the obvious superiority of Marxism-Leninism, state terror and military force were the primary tools used in building and maintaining the Soviet empire.

The total failure of the USSR to move beyond that legacy of invasion and repression in seventy long years was clearly reflected by the eagerness with which the various republics detached from the rotting head of the Kremlin as soon as they had a chance. Even Ukraine, the ancient home of the first Eastern Slav proto-Russian nation-state and with so much in common with Russia, quickly ran for the exit to completely crush Gorbachev's hope for a new union.

There was also a power-grab incentive factor in many cases. Regional bureaucrats and party bosses dreamed of being autocrats and realized they would have more power and a greater ability to line their pockets in independent states, even if their economies and regimes remained largely dependent on Moscow.

Still, even the Central Asian republics that had tentatively agreed to stick things out with Gorbachev's new USSR-lite eventually abandoned him.

The fifteen former Soviet republics quickly recognized by the United Nations as independent nations turned out to be the least of Russia's problems. No fewer than five others declared their independence around the same time as the fifteen but failed to achieve it. Most are known to westerners only due to the fact that they remain disputed regions that occasionally flare into violence. Abkhazia and South Ossetia were semiautonomous regions of Georgia within the USSR and both claimed statehood when the USSR began to fall apart. After off and on conflicts they both instead remained as part of Georgia and were later exploited by Putin to provoke the 2008 war with Georgia. Both are now essentially occupied Russian zones, though still recognized by the UN as parts of Georgia.

Transnistria and Gagauzia had roughly similar experiences with the USSR and the newly independent Moldova. (I hope residents and experts forgive my simplifications for the point of expediency.) Putin's Russia has similarly meddled in these autonomous zones, as always, stepping into any nearby power vacuum. Nagorno-Karabakh, a long-disputed area between Azerbaijan and Armenia, also declared itself an independent state in 1991. Its current status is officially Azerbaijani territory, but it is de facto independent and essentially functions as part of Armenia.

But we are not quite done, and I have saved the worst for last. I think only real specialists will recognize the name Ichkeria. It is seldom used anymore, and to my knowledge was rarely used even when its full name, Chechen Republic of Ichkeria, was still valid. That is, if it was ever valid, which of course is the question that led to two wars, thousands of terrorist attacks, and hundreds of thousands of deaths, most of them civilians, and almost all of them inside Russia.

Most people today have heard of Chechnya, and always for negative reasons. Its name is associated with the export of brutal mafiosos, militants, and terrorists. It was back in the news recently when it was revealed that the Boston Marathon bombers, the Tsarnaev brothers, were Chechen Americans. Home to over a million people, predominantly Muslim, tiny Chechnya fought two vicious wars for independence from Moscow. The first started at the end of 1994, when Yeltsin tired of Chechen leader Dzhokhar Dudayev's anti-Moscow consolidation of power in his unrecognized republic. In the long tradition of overconfident leaders of large nations attacking small local forces in the mountains, the Russian offensive turned into an embarrassing quagmire that turned into a full-scale war that lasted twenty months. An estimated one hundred thousand civilians were killed and close to twenty thousand Russian troops. Human rights violations by the Russian forces were epidemic, and the Chechens turned to hostage-taking outside of Chechnya.

The brutality of the war and the terrible destruction of the Chechen capital of Grozny helped enrage and radicalize a generation of Chechens, who already had no love lost for Russia. Chechnya and its neighbors, Ingushetia to the west and Dagestan to the east, had declared independence from Russia as a united mountain republic in 1917 only to be yoked into the Soviet Union by force four years later. Despite the honorable participation by the region's inhabitants against the Nazis in World War II, Stalin had nearly all of them, close to half a million people, rounded up and deported to Kazakhstan in 1944. They were allowed to return in 1957 as part of the de-Stalinization process, but a huge number had starved or been killed.

It's no coincidence that most of these disputed and conflicted regions are located in the Caucasus. (Not Moldova, which is on the west side of the Black Sea between Ukraine and Romania.) There are patches upon the patchwork quilt of the region and innumerable bloody rivalries both ancient and new. This contentious region reaches from my birthplace of Azerbaijan in the south on the Iranian border and the Caspian Sea over to Georgia on the Black Sea with Armenia in between and Turkey to the south. In the north, on the Russian side of the border, it includes Dagestan, Chechnya, and Ingushetia as well as Kabardino-Balkaria (home of Mount Elbrus, the highest mountain in Europe) and north to the Kalmyk Steppe. It is home to over fifty ethnic groups, dozens of languages, and nearly every kind of religion.

Letting Chechnya and its ultraviolent neighbors become independent was never going to appeal to Russian leaders. It wasn't just that they were convenient punching bags to rally the domestic base. Nor did they have much in the way of resources. The problem was, if they became independent nations they would instantly gain the rights and protections of independent nations, free to make allies, sign treaties, and complain to the United Nations—all with no way these broken states could control the flow of violence. Dealing with a failed Russian state was bad. Dealing with a failed neighboring country was much worse, a lesson the Soviets had learned in Afghanistan.

Not to defend Yeltsin on the matter, but another factor made a split nearly impossible: the lack of clear borders. The USSR was made up of republics and the borders between them were quite clear. When the USSR broke up there were very few conflicts between the new nations over geography. But inside of Russia the borders had never been drawn so clearly since they had no sacred meaning inside the vast republic. So when the Chechnya-Ingushetia region declared for independence in 1991 nobody was sure exactly what that would mean. The breakaway's leaders insisted their new nation might extend all the way to Stavropol, two hundred kilometers west of Grozny, and it was difficult to deny their claim or make an alternative one based on anything concrete. Where did Chechnya begin and end? And what of neighboring Dagestan? It was a Pandora's box. Chechnya was also unique because there were no external influences on its rebellion. All the rest had neighbors pushing for or against rebellion in one way or another. But Chechnya's revolt was entirely internal.

It is tempting to jump ahead to the second Chechen war that brought an unknown prime minister named Vladimir Putin to the presidency. This first war not only set the stage for the second, but it is also an important illustration of the light-handed way the West treated Russia during the 1990s. Thanks to the magic of e-books I can tell you that Bill Clinton's memoir, *My Life,* mentions Chechnya exactly four times in its thousand-plus pages. Even if you discount the first half of the book that takes place before he became president, this is astonishing. It is also an accurate representation of where Chechnya and other global hot spots ranked on Clinton's radar while he was in office, especially during his first term. (The 1994 Rwandan genocide earns a few more mentions, mostly in the form of his regret at not having done anything to intervene.)

It's not as if the first Chechen war was widely ignored at the time. Human rights groups and the Western media covered the atrocities as closely as they could. The Russian military's failure to pacify the region as quickly as promised became an embarrassing issue for Boris Yeltsin as the 1996 election approached, forcing him to talk about it at public appearances. Remember, this was back when Russia still had a free media. The word "Chechnya" itself would practically be banned from the Russian press soon after Putin took power. Yeltsin even spent some awkward moments standing next to Clinton at press conferences in 1995 and 1996 answering questions about Chechnya, mostly denying that violence was taking place despite the overwhelming reports of war crimes.

It's a remarkable feeling to read those news conference transcripts today. A Russian president, pressed to answer tough questions from the Russian press! You could be forgiven for forgetting that such a moment had ever existed in Russian history. At their conference in Moscow on May 10, 1995, one reporter got straight to the point after hearing Yeltsin's usual dismissive remarks.

REPORTER: "President Clinton, you've just heard President Yeltsin describe the situation in Chechnya in a way that may be at odds with news dispatches coming from the

part of the country describing a massacre. And I wondered if—what your reaction is to his description, whether
you accept it, if not why not, and what impact these reports of terrible things there may be having on the countries eager to join NATO, and what you would have to say
to him about that?"

Clinton's response referred to how the civilian casualties and
the prolonged fighting in Chechnya had "troubled the rest of the
world greatly and have had an impact in Europe on the attitudes
of many countries about what is going on here and about future
relationships." He said he had urged Yeltsin to make a cease-fire
and "bring this to a speedy resolution," concluding that "it's been
a difficult thing for them [Russia] as well."

So then, what could the American president or the Organization for Security and Cooperation in Europe (OSCE) do about
a bloody civil war in Russia where tens of thousands of civilians
were being displaced, tortured, and murdered? One clue comes
from earlier in the same press conference, when President Clinton was asked what he would do about Russia's continued support for Iran's nuclear program.

REPORTER: "Will you resist Republican threats to cut off foreign aid to Russia?"

What!? Yes, this was the situation in 1995! Today, exactly
twenty years later, the Iranian nuclear program Russia built is
back on the front pages for mostly the same reason: fear over
Iran making a nuclear bomb. It all started while American aid
was helping keep Russia afloat (and helping Yeltsin get reelected
in 1996). Surely making such aid conditional on dropping support for the Iranian nuclear program or on ending the massacre
in Chechnya should have been discussed. In fact, such condi-
tionality was discussed quite a bit in the US Congress, in both
houses, in 1995 and 1996.

49

The Russian nuclear agency, MinAtom (succeeded by RosAtom in 2007), brought in desperately needed hard currency and was run with an alarming degree of autonomy. Its chief, Viktor Mikhaylov, had made a secret deal with Iran to deliver a gas centrifuge that would enable them to produce weapons-grade uranium, and he had done so without even telling Yeltsin. The rogue agency also had the support of Foreign Minister Yevgeny Primakov, who promoted close political and economic ties with Iran.

Clinton recounts in his book that when he first met Yeltsin in the Kremlin on that trip, they "shook hands" on Yeltsin publicly announcing Russia wouldn't give any nuclear technology to Iran that could be used for military purposes. He duly did so at the press conference, but Yeltsin wouldn't officially prohibit such weapons-related transfers until August 1996, over a year later.

Many members of Congress were outraged and added conditions to restrict aid to Russia if it continued to support Iran's nuclear program and to wage war on civilians. But the Clinton administration managed to include a provision in the Russian aid bill to "allow the President to waive this restriction if he deemed it in the interest of US national security. The Administration argued that it was inappropriate to condition aid to Russia on a particular desired behavior in either Iran or Chechnya inasmuch as the aid program was intended to benefit reformist elements in Russia and ultimately facilitate a transformation that might ensure a more cooperative relationship in the future."

That paragraph lays out everything that is wrong with dropping the moral element from foreign policy. For the sake of a vague hope for "a more cooperative relationship in the future," the Clinton administration fought to keep the Iranian nuclear program and Chechnya massacre off the table. The money wasn't the issue; a few billion dollars wasn't going to make or break either country, although Yeltsin certainly needed all the help he could get as the 1996 election approached. (I campaigned for him myself.) Instead of tying foreign aid and foreign policy to the immoral slaughter of civilians in Chechnya, Clinton expressed concerns, made vague remarks about how it might drive other countries toward joining NATO (which it did), and called it an internal affair.

Clinton and Europe missed the chance to draw lines of acceptable behavior for Russia, at least anywhere beyond the Baltic States. In Central Asia and the various conflict zones in the Caucasus, the West tacitly supported a Russian sphere of influence. As the *New York Times* reported in October 1994, two months before Russian forces stormed into Chechnya, the West refused to provide peacekeepers to the newly formed states, allowing Russian ones to step in to manage the conflicts they themselves had provoked.

Reagan and his moral foreign policy had shown the way, but it was now completely abandoned. It was not based on what could be done unilaterally. No one could ever imagine that the United States or NATO would directly aid the Chechen separatists, for example. The important element was to show clearly and consistently that human rights mattered and that human lives mattered. Clinton was so invested in hoping "for a more cooperative relationship" that he could not simply state that massacring civilians and helping a state sponsor of terror build a nuclear program were unacceptable.

This record of immoral passivity also puts more nails in the coffin of the myth of Russian humiliation. Clinton treated Yeltsin in good faith throughout, provided Russia with intelligence on Iran, began to massively demilitarize Europe, and even helped disarm other ex-Soviet states with the effect of guaranteeing Russian preeminence. Nineteen ninety-four was the year the leaders of Russia, Ukraine, the US, and the UK all sat side by side at a long table in Hungary to sign what would be known as the Budapest Memorandum on Security Assurances.

This brief document is far from a comprehensive treaty or even a security guarantee, but its intent and purpose was clear. Ukraine was giving up the third-largest nuclear arsenal in the world under heavy pressure from Russia and the United States. In exchange, Ukrainian president Leonid Kuchma wanted a public pledge from Clinton, Yeltsin, and John Major that they would "respect the independence and sovereignty and the existing borders of Ukraine" and "refrain from the threat or use of force against the territorial integrity or political independence of Ukraine."

Obviously Russia violated the agreement when it invaded and then annexed Crimea in March 2014. As for the other signatories, there are no means of enforcement in the memo and the only promised response is to seek UN Security Council action "if Ukraine should become a victim of an act of aggression or an object of a threat of aggression in which nuclear weapons are used."

When I spoke to the first Ukrainian president, Leonid Kravchuk, in Kyiv in late 2014, he was adamant that the United States had betrayed Ukraine to Putin by reneging on the obligations Clinton assumed in Budapest. He said it had always been Clinton, even more than Yeltsin, who had pressured him and the presidents of Kazakhstan and Belarus to relinquish their nuclear arsenals. No doubt this was a worthy goal and a worthy achievement at the time. But what does it say when twenty years later Ukraine is practically helpless against the giant nuclear-backed war machine of Vladimir Putin and the United States tells Ukraine sorry, but it should have read the fine print in Budapest?

To answer my own question, it tells the world that American security promises are worthless (and British ones, for good measure). The only point of Budapest was to demonstrate to any potential aggressor—all eyes on the Russian bear next door, obviously—that the United States was putting Ukraine under its nuclear wing. If such displays are meaningless, and having one's own nuclear weapon is the only way to be safe from aggression, it will not take long for other countries to move full speed toward acquiring them. Japan and Taiwan count on America to deter China. South Korea counts on America to deter North Korea. And whether they admit to it or not, half of the nations in the

Middle East have rejected a push for nuclear weapons to match Israel's because of America's long shadow. It is difficult to see that restraint lasting very long if President Obama continues to meet Russian military aggression with weak sanctions, worthless negotiations, and expressions of deep concern.

Since he is still very much a public figure, Bill Clinton himself should be asked what he thinks of Obama's indifferent attitude about the document Clinton signed in Budapest. Especially since they are of the same party and Hillary Clinton served in Obama's cabinet as secretary of state. It probably never occurred to any of the reporters in Budapest to ask Clinton what his administration would do if Russia rolled tanks into Ukraine as they have now done, but I would very much like to hear his answer today.

There is an irresistible tendency to look only for big moments in history. While such moments do exist, long-term trends and patterns usually matter more than any one decision or event. When we talk about the collapse of Russia's democracy and the Western appeasement that facilitated its collapse, it is important to look at how each moment fit into an overall pattern.

Bush 41 supported Mikhail Gorbachev to a fault and to the bitter end. Bill Clinton's administration was similarly enamored of Boris Yeltsin and supported him at the expense of a coherent and consistent policy of pressuring for economic reform and democracy in Russia. As I'll discuss in the next chapter, Bush 43 made the same mistake with Putin by putting his trust in an individual instead of the democratic institutions, policies, and principles Russia so badly needed. The West would find someone they liked, or felt they could work with, and jump in with both feet. When the results inevitably failed to live up to the unrealistic hopes, it was awkward or impossible to back away.

At the same time, American authority and credibility on the global stage was being whittled away throughout the 1990s. The

United States looked all powerful at the end of the Cold War, like the Wizard of Oz before the curtain was pulled back. By 1999, when Clinton finally got it right in Kosovo, the curtain had been pulled back, torn down, and burned in effigy. The "Blackhawk Down" catastrophe in Somalia, the genocides in Yugoslavia and Rwanda, conceding to Russia on Chechnya and limiting NATO expansion: each was a blow to global stability and its supposed guarantors in the United States and the European Union.

Far from the imperial overreach and hegemonic tendencies that Russia and China kept warning about, the United States retreated instead. By 1998, Clinton's personal credibility was also diminishing rapidly. The Monica Lewinsky scandal exploded in the headlines in January. The media circus, trial, and impeachment became a huge distraction for the government and the American people. Later in the year, Clinton had his wag-the-dog moment when he ordered a cruise missile strike on what turned out to be a benign pharmaceutical factory in Sudan.

As convenient as it would be to put all the blame for the collapse of Russian democracy on Putin, the truth is more complicated. Russia's return to dictatorship was not a sudden fall. Many small, quick steps in the same direction resemble a smooth slide. Just as when analyzing a completed chess game, what we call the postmortem, talking as if everything was going just fine until this or that event is usually absurd and harmful to the process of honest analysis. Of course huge isolated blunders in otherwise good positions do occur, but they are even rarer in diplomacy than in world championship chess.

This is a point of disagreement I often have with my more diplomatically minded friends today. They look back over twenty years of Russia-US relations and it doesn't look so bad, so the complete catastrophe of 2014 is viewed as a sudden shock. But as I have been warning frequently for at least fifteen of those years, Putin's latest eruption of repression and violence has been steadily building all the time and was only intensified by years of Western compromises and pretending that everything was fine. There was no big shift by Obama that provoked Putin, or any dramatic changes in Putin's attitudes or Russia's fortunes that necessitated the invasion of Ukraine. It was always moving in this direction, and the only question was whether or not Western leaders would change their ways to prevent such an eruption from taking place. Unfortunately, as we now know, the answer was no.

If the road to hell is paved with good intentions, compromises on principles are the streetlights. As I admitted earlier, I supported Yeltsin's 1996 reelection despite his increasingly undemocratic attitude toward Russia's institutions and the independence of our elections. Yeltsin abused the power of the state to fight off the challenge of the Communist Party that still had the power to terrify the reformers. It also had taken control of the Russian Duma in the 1995 parliamentary elections, so it was no imagined threat. Yeltsin was deeply unpopular, polling under 10 percent at the start of the year with only six months until the June election.

The Yeltsin administration's trope of accusing every critic and opposition figure of trying to drag Russia back to the dark past became less and less effective as the economy struggled. The outside world didn't think much of Yeltsin's chances either. In February, Communist Party leader Zyuganov was treated like a rock star at the World Economic Forum in Davos, of all places, the belly of the capitalist beast. Of course Zyuganov was completely clueless about what to do and would have been an unmitigated catastrophe as president, but it certainly looked likely to happen. It wasn't simply a case of people in hard times voting with their pocketbooks. There was a real sense of confusion and betrayal in Russia, and the natural target was the president.

Here is where we come to one of the most difficult concepts to explain to outsiders about the Russian rejection of democracy. When Soviets pondered the collapse of our country and the future ahead, democracy was not a very well-defined or well-understood concept to most of us. Yes, we desired freedom, rights, and all the things that come with an open society, but for most people these are abstractions. What we really envied about the West was opportunity; specifically the opportunity to improve our lot economically. The free world had elections and it had money and we had neither, so these things obviously went together: a package deal.

So when we happily mobbed the polls in 1991 to vote for Yeltsin the first time it was as if many Russians expected the ballot boxes to operate like ATMs: put your ballot in and money will come out! This conceptual misunderstanding later made it easier for an authoritarian like Putin to roll back civil rights by claiming that democracy had failed, that it had all been a Western scam to exploit Russia, and so on. The economic situation didn't help much either. If there is anything worse than empty store shelves it is shelves full of expensive new products you cannot afford to buy.

We had sobered up quite a bit by the time special parliamentary elections were called in 1993 after the constitutional crisis that nearly toppled the entire government. Yeltsin attempted to dissolve the Supreme Soviet in September, something he did not have the authority to do according to the constitution. In retaliation, the parliament impeached Yeltsin, who of course refused to recognize their act of defiance. After weeks of dueling protests and street violence, Yeltsin called in the special police and the parliament building was sealed off. It was quite uncertain what would happen. Pitched battles were taking place in the streets outside the government building and nearly two hundred people would be killed and hundreds more wounded.

Along with the rest of the world, I was watching all of this unfold on CNN from afar. My 1993 world championship title defense against Nigel Short began in London on September 7 and lasted, as matches did in those days, for six weeks. As it had been in 1990, it was difficult to focus on chess when my country was again facing revolution. Fortunately, I jumped out to a big lead in the match and could play with less psychological pressure. I felt comfortable enough to give a few interviews on the situation in Moscow, where I said Yeltsin was fighting for the free future of Russia.

After days of violence and frantic negotiations on all sides, the allegiance of the Russian army to Yeltsin was the decisive factor. In an unbelievable scene, on October 4 a row of tanks fired on the White House (as we call the parliament building) and the top floors of it caught fire. Special forces stormed the building and clamped down on the street protesters. Back in control, Yeltsin wasted no time in pushing through constitutional reform, demoting the parliament and creating the very strong presidency that haunts us today. The Supreme Soviet was obsolete, of course, but in a country with such a fragile civil society it is important to have power spread as thinly as possible.

In 1996, Yeltsin had little popular support but he could count on many of the oligarchs whose fortunes he had enabled and the financial backing of the West. Despite a campaign spending limit of $3 million, still out of reach of most parties, the Yeltsin campaign spent somewhere in the range of one to two *billion* dollars according to later investigations. Even more important was a huge loan from the International Monetary Fund in February. The $10.2 billion allowed the Yeltsin government to pay long overdue wages and pensions.

If that had been all, dubious financing and pork-barrel politics on steroids, it might not have done damage lasting beyond Yeltsin's term in office. But there was also the media influence and outright electoral fraud, weapons that are very hard to put back in the closet after being used. It was all enough to earn Yeltsin a narrow lead over Zyuganov in the first round, 35 percent to 32 percent. Yeltsin had a serious heart attack between the June 16 election and the July 3 run-off against Zyuganov, a potentially dangerous situation that was successfully hidden from the public thanks to government and media complicity. Yeltsin won the runoff 54 percent to 40 percent, with even more evidence of widespread voter fraud later coming to light.

At the time, had I known everything that was going on, it still would have been very hard for me to wish for anything other than a Yeltsin return. In 1996, Gennady Zyuganov wasn't the performing pet Communist he is for Putin today. He was a Communist revanchist who had fought against liberal reforms every step of the way and he would have been a dangerous man with the power of the presidency. There was a real possibility that an election that brought him to power would be the last election we would have for a long time. And yet the lesson of 1996 is that institutions must matter more than the man. The Yeltsin campaign undermined nearly every aspect of a democratic society and it never recovered. His successor would quickly take up Yeltsin's campaign tools of repression and corruption and apply them to everyday governance. Putin was no Communist, but he was a Soviet revanchist through and through.

———

I feel I must also apply to myself the standards I regularly urge on the leaders of the free world who so often put expediency and personal affinity over nurturing institutions. The fear of the unknown, of losing a reliable ally, often drives democratic leaders to the utmost hypocrisy. It leads them to support "friendly" dictators against their people, as was seen recently by the tepid reception the Arab Spring movement received in the Obama administration and in much of Europe. I have long railed against this in regards to how Putin was embraced by the G7 despite his crackdowns on civil liberties, but this is far from a uniquely Russian problem.

My thoughts on this have been further shaped by my work as the chairman of the Human Rights Foundation and at the Oslo Freedom Forum organized by the HRF and its founder, Thor Halvorssen. We invite dissidents from all over the world to speak about their movements and their fights for liberty. One common denominator is how dangerous and demoralizing it can be for the so-called leaders of the free world to downplay or to ignore their plights, or, as often happens, to openly support the authors of their repression. Often, European and American visitors were surprised to find out that their governments were actively supporting some of the world's most repressive regimes.

I may be idealistic, but I am far from naïve. I understand that every democratically elected head of state will do what is necessary to protect the interests of his or her people. In foreign policy, sometimes that will mean shaking a hand with blood on it or trading with a country with atrocious labor practices. We can, however, demand transparency and accountability for these deals. We do not have to like it and we can let our politicians know that it must change.

The world's dictators are very aware of the power wielded by the free world today. This is why nearly all of them role-play at democracy with sham elections and perform other acts of theater to stay in the good graces of the world's largest economies and militaries. Unfortunately, the free world is too uninformed, callous, or apathetic to use this influence. They enjoy the benefits of engagement with dictatorships—oil from the Middle East, gas from Russia, everything else from China—while the dictators use the money to fund repression. But not all dictatorships are the same.

The pro-democracy sit-in protests in Hong Kong that started in September 2014 led to speculation about why such an Occupy-style movement has so far failed to materialize against the dictatorship of Vladimir Putin in Russia. It's an awkward comparison at best; the student Hongkongers who could barely recall the 1997 handover from the United Kingdom to China were accustomed to their special status of rights and democracy relative to the rest of China. The flame of Russian democracy flickered only briefly before Putin squelched it, and the memories of the chaos and corruption of the 1990s are not fond ones for most Russians.

A more concrete answer is that the Communist dictatorship in China needs its people, especially its young and educated people. Hong Kong is still a large and strategically critical piece of the Chinese economy. That economy also depends almost entirely on consumers in the free world, consumers who have far more information about the protests than nearly anyone in heavily censored China. A Tiananmen massacre in Hong Kong, transmitted around the world on millions of Chinese-made iPhones, could make "Made in China" into a bloody mark. Anti-China boycotts could hurt the Chinese economy enough to lead to wide-scale unrest.

Putin, on the other hand, has no use for the people of Russia, especially its young and educated people. He and his junta have turned the country into a petro-state, and exporting natural resources to an insatiable global market doesn't require entrepreneurs or programmers, let alone writers and professors. Boycotting oil and gas also requires coordinated political will, a substance Putin now knows is far rarer in the free world than the platinum and diamonds in Siberia.

Decades of economic and political engagement with the West and improved standards of living were supposed to liberalize these dictatorships and provide leverage against them. But leverage is only useful if applied, and it is also double edged. Europe buys four-fifths of Russia's energy exports, giving it tremendous economic leverage over Putin, who has made the Russian economy totally dependent on oil and gas. But instead of aggressively developing alternative supply routes in order to be able to use that leverage to stand up to Russia, Europe dithers and cries foul when Putin blackmails Eastern Europe with the gas supply as winter approaches.

China and Russia have similar social compacts with their dictatorial governments: economic stability in exchange for their citizens' human rights. They both have heavily censored state propaganda instead of news, sham elections, and minimal freedom of speech and assembly. The skyrocketing price of oil through the 2000s allowed Putin to fulfill, if minimally outside of Moscow and St. Petersburg, his promises of pensions and payrolls—and oil is also why stoking Middle East instability that keeps the price high is always a priority for him. China started from a much lower point and managed to raise a billion people out of poverty by turning an entire nation into the world's factory.

Globalization, economic integration with rich free economies, made both the Russian and Chinese scenarios possible.

The reality is that most consumers in the developed world would rather not know where their phones and gas come from as long as the prices are low. If you know, you must act, so it is better not to know. The occasional scandal over inhuman working conditions in Chinese factories (or women's rights in Saudi Arabia) allows some liberals to feel better when a Nike or Apple announces an investigation that is quickly forgotten by the time the next shoe or gadget comes out.

Now then, is the case of China really such a failure, you might wonder. Should we have condemned those billion souls to poverty and hunger for the sake of politics? This is empathy from the innocent but it is also the false choice the autocrats love to present to the world. It is the false choice between freedom and food, between repression and stability. There is no reason China could not have enjoyed similar or greater economic success with a more liberal regime. In fact, there's a great deal of evidence that democratic countries perform better. Do not fall for the false choice. Repression may begin as a means to an end, but it always ends up being an end unto itself.

The protests in Hong Kong were also a refutation of what I have mockingly referred to as the genetic theory of democracy. For years I have been told that Russians (or Arabs, or Chinese) simply aren't disposed to democracy. They require a "strong hand" or "love a tough leader." This is just one of many theories people born in the free world use to mask their privilege, their inaction, and their shame. How could this be true when Taiwan is composed of the same people but is a flourishing democracy? What about East and West Germany, North and South Korea?

There are countless reasons democracy fails to take root, or why some military coups succeed and others fail. None of these reasons are based on ethnicity or geography. Our governments are human constructs, as are our traditions and beliefs. As Milton Friedman said, "Society doesn't have values. People have values."

We must decide what we value and decide what is worth fighting for and then—the most important part—we must fight for it. If we fail to do this we will lose to those who believe in other things, in worse things. We will lose to those who don't believe in the value of human life or liberty, and who are willing to fight to impose their dark vision for humanity on others.

We may call the rights we cherish inalienable or universal, but this isn't the same as being entitled to democracy, or even to basic human rights. No, these things must be fought for. And if it takes brave students in Hong Kong to remind the world of this, then their protest was a success, however brief it may have been.

4

BORN IN BLOOD

There were two wars in Europe in 1999, both sequels to wars that had concluded just a few years earlier and both with considerable impact on the future of Russia. The second to begin was in Chechnya, and it played a key role in the rise to power of Vladimir Putin. The first I have already discussed: the Kosovo war in Yugoslavia where the ethnic Albanian majority in Kosovo was attempting to gain independence from the Serb-dominated central government still controlled by the unrepentant and unrestrained Slobodan Milošević. NATO bombing had finally forced him to agree to the Dayton Agreement in 1995, ending the war in Bosnia. But the Kosovo Albanians still struggled under repression and were out of patience waiting for their own independence.

The Kosovo Liberation Army (KLA) began attacking Serb security forces regularly in 1998 and they were met by the brutality and indiscriminate use of force that the Serbian forces had become well known for in Bosnia. By September, a quarter million Albanians had been displaced, many without shelter. The UN Security Council issued a resolution expressing that most famous phrase in the dictionary of diplomatic impotence: "grave concern." In October, a NATO peacekeeping mission arrived but achieved little of lasting effect as both sides violated a cease-fire almost immediately.

As in Bosnia, it took a massacre of civilians to spur the great powers to act. Forty-five Kosovo Albanian farmers were rounded up and killed in the village of Račak in January 1999. This led directly to Clinton's speech to the American people and nearly three months of NATO air strikes and cruise missile attacks against Yugoslav forces. (And, in one tragic incident, the bombing of the Chinese embassy in Belgrade, killing three. NATO blamed the accident on an outdated map.)

By April, leaders of NATO nations were discussing an invasion of ground forces, which would have changed a great many things. Russia was openly advocating for the Yugoslav side in the conflict and the sight of NATO troops, especially American troops, on the ground as part of an offensive would have been very inflammatory in Russia. Russian weapons and supplies were also finding their way to the Yugoslav side. It was revealed in later reports that the main reason Milošević held out as long as he did was the hope that Yeltsin would intervene militarily on his side.

Milošević's vicious calculations were based on the belief that conflict with the West would strengthen his position in Serbia and that desperate refugees would destabilize neighboring countries, including Albania, Macedonia, Montenegro, and probably even Bosnia. The Balkans would be set on fire again and Western public opinion would prevent NATO from sending in ground troops. Then the Serbian military would play a decisive role in resolving the chaos, and of course reap the spoils.

Events, fortunately, did not turn out as he had hoped. The prestige of the free world was saved by the united actions of the major democratic powers. An impressive air campaign and the efficient organization of refugee camps sent a clear signal to every quarter in the world that the West was capable of supporting its moral claims with advanced logistics that totalitarian regimes simply lack.

Kosovo also demonstrated that the United Nations in its current form was, and is, irrelevant when it comes to solving such crises. It doesn't take a Nostradamus to predict the fate the Kosovars would have met had it been left up to the United Nations, where Russia and China have a veto, to deal with Milošević.

This brings me back to the role of Russia in the events in the Balkans. It seemed obligatory in the Western capitals to give Boris Yeltsin and his special envoy Viktor Chernomyrdin credit for convincing Milošević to accept the terms dictated by NATO. (That the G7 had so quickly become the G8 made it clear some sort of payoff had gone on.)

In my view this public appraisal contained serious flaws. If Milošević had accepted the Rambouillet peace deal months earlier, he could have prevented the creation of over a million refugees, the deaths of thousands of innocent civilians, and the destruction of Serbia. President Milošević torpedoed this deal with the open support of Russia, which categorically objected to the presence of an international police force in Kosovo.

Later, after Serbian resistance was shattered by NATO airpower, Russia changed its view on foreign troops entering into Kosovo and decided to play the role of "impartial" broker. Imagine someone jumping onto the train just a few seconds before departure and then arguing with the conductor about the ticket price.

If one assumes that Russia did have serious influence over Belgrade's decisions, then Yeltsin's government should have been held partly responsible for Milošević's stubbornness in conducting his murderous policy of ethnic cleansing. If Russia's influence was being overestimated, what was the point of US Deputy Secretary of State Strobe Talbott's overanxious shuttle diplomacy?

European and American leaders once again proved eager to salve Russia's "great power" ego and anxiety, and for what? It was a classic form of enabling an abuser, even if in Yeltsin's day it was more petty crime than major felonies. Russia was in denial and acting in a self-destructive fashion that also had impact abroad. Had the Western powers been firm about Russia's true status and used that as leverage to encourage transparency and reform, we would all be much better off today.

Instead, with their Serbian ally in ruins and Yeltsin exposed as a mass murderer, the Yeltsin administration and the Russian media were desperate to create some angle that would salvage their dignity. While Russians in the country's far east and northern territories were gravely concerned about obtaining a regular supply of food and fuel that coming winter, the Russian government was actively working to equip ten thousand peacekeepers for Kosovo.

In my *Wall Street Journal* op-ed after Kosovo, I had rare words of praise for Western leaders for their decisive action. I ended with a reminder that Kosovo would not be the last such intervention needed unless they combined their power to create a more stable world order. The United Nations had been created in 1945 to cement a political order following the Allied victory. But quickly the organization became a body of compromises in which the superpowers could veto any resolution deemed against the interests of their clientele. With the collapse of the Soviet Union this system no longer served the purpose of international peace and stability.

UN-crafted compromises were no longer necessary, and often dangerous. Indeed, strict adherence to the UN's resolutions by President Bush in 1991 ultimately spared Saddam—and prolonged the Gulf crisis indefinitely. Milošević tried to play a similar game by involving Russia as a mediator (ironically Yevgeny Primakov was the broker of choice there, as with Iraq) and demanding UN authorization for any Alliance action.

All of this made it clear that the world needed an international decision-making mechanism not hobbled by the ideological baggage of the Cold War. The UN's goal of freezing the status quo between two nuclear superpowers was obsolete. Democracy was ascendant and it was time to formally recognize this and to press the advantage. The indictment of Slobodan Milošević by a war crimes court was an excellent first step toward such a new world order but, as we now know, precious few steps were taken afterward.

In his definitive book on the Yugoslav wars, American journalist David Halberstam wrote an insightful passage about what led

66

Milošević to ruin and, eventually, to die in jail in 2006 while on trial for war crimes in The Hague.

> Milošević had managed to retain the view of many a totalitarian figure before him. He believed that if democracies were slow to act, it was a sign of weakness; if they were affluent, then they were also decadent. In addition, because their politicians and their citizens feared paying the price of war, they could be bullied. He once told the German foreign minister, Joschka Fischer, "I can stand death—lots of it—but you can't."

He was proved wrong eventually, but only after hundreds of thousands of deaths and millions more wounded and traumatized. Sadly, we can add to Halberstam's first sentence, "and like many a totalitarian figure after him." Putin performed the same ruthless calculus in his dealings with the free world over his invasion of Georgia in 2008 and over Ukraine today. Terrorists of every kind use this reasoning. They believe that democracies—our slow, affluent, fearful democracies—cannot stand up to suicide bombers and bloody massacres. They also believe the values of the modern world are both its weakness and a threat to their survival, and they are correct on both counts. Our challenge is to overcome our weaknesses without losing the values the enemies of the free world fear so much.

The type of evil Milošević represented has always been difficult to understand. He was urbane, intelligent, and able to present himself to different people in ways that flattered them and made them trust him. The Bush 41 foreign policy team was reportedly baffled by how "their friend" Milošević transformed from a well-mannered banker and bureaucrat into a fire-breathing Serbian nationalist who championed ethnic cleansing campaigns against his own citizens. This prompts a key question for this book and for our current world order: Are monsters born or are they made?

I do not intend to open a "nature versus nurture" debate about the genetic makeup of psychopaths or the long-term impact of a difficult childhood on personality. I have spent far too much of my life asking and answering questions about the origins of my chess success, and the only conclusion I'm confident in is that I was lucky to find a game that suited my talents perfectly very early in life. I'm happy to leave those theories to the psychologists and geneticists.

I'm referring to potential evil versus actualized evil and society's role in preventing the former from becoming the latter. At what point do others have to accept some of the responsibility for the crimes of a murderer? Crimes they could have prevented? Not in the sense that a murderer is not responsible for his actions, of course. There is already far too much excuse making for criminals of every sort, as if the concept of personal responsibility can be suspended as long as a motive can be concocted. Putin's invasion of Ukraine is no more tolerable if you believe he felt threatened by NATO expansion than if you don't believe he felt threatened. Telling Ukrainians they provoked Putin by rejecting him and moving toward Europe is like telling a harassed woman she should wear longer skirts. Do not lose sight of who is the offender and who is the victim! If we fail to maintain that moral balance and our perceptions of what is right and what is wrong, we are too vulnerable to propaganda.

The caveat is on the practical side of the matter. It is foolish to let down our defenses against an attack simply because we will be in the moral right should that attack come. Condemn, prosecute, and punish the violators, absolutely, but do not make it easy for them. Orson Welles's modern fable of the scorpion and the frog is a memorable lesson. The frog carries the scorpion across a river on its back, convinced by the scorpion's logic that it will not sting him because if it does, they will both die. In the middle of the river the scorpion stings the frog, who says, dying, "Logic?

There is no logic in this!" The scorpion replies, "I know, I can't help it. It is my character."

The practical moral is not to trust a scorpion because logic and being in the right doesn't help you very much when you're dead. Another lesson is that not everyone acts in mutual best interest, or even in their own best interest, and that true nature can override logic and self-preservation. I think of this whenever I hear European diplomats talking about wanting to reach a "win-win" scenario with Putin over Ukraine.

This attitude is admirable in some ways, and it is the definition of diplomacy to at least say that is your goal. It would be wonderful if every crisis or conflict could be ended to mutual benefit, or at least to mutual satisfaction. But assuming that can happen with Putin or with ISIS ignores the true nature of the enemy. Putin's only goal is to stay in power and he has moved beyond needing cooperation with the free world to do that. He needs conflict and hatred now, and how do you negotiate with that without betraying your ideals and your people? Al-Qaeda and ISIS want to cut off and destroy the modern world of rights and freedom. How does a pluralistic liberal society negotiate with that worldview to mutual benefit? It cannot.

When the logic of assumed mutual benefit keeps failing, it is time to try something else. We are not condemned to expose our backs to the world's scorpions over and over in the hope that next time, for once, they won't sting us.

Few humans are truly scorpions—complete psychopaths. Since the end of the ages of monarchy and empire, rising through political ranks to the highest stations requires at least some subtlety and intuition. (North Korea is one of the few modern exceptions and the result is obvious.) The crux of the "born or made" argument is potential meeting opportunity. Slobodan Milošević probably would have been just another party boss had the revolutions of 1989 not given him the chance to seek greater power through inciting hatred. Milošević was allowed to flourish in that role long enough to become responsible for the first genocide on

European soil since the end of World War II. He should have been removed from power by force in 1995, but he was given another chance, which he naturally interpreted as weakness in his opponents, and he struck again a few years later.

As I said at the start of this chapter, there were two wars in Europe raging in 1999. Both were civil wars, both were fought largely along ethnic and religious lines, and both saw horrible war crimes and acts of terror against civilian populations. And in both Kosovo and Chechnya, the war was part of a fight for political power in a distant capital.

By the end of summer 1999, a new glow of Russia-facing optimism could be detected from Western policy and financial circles. The Clinton administration and international financial institutions had declared the government of Prime Minister Sergei Stepashin one they could "do business" with.

Not only did Russia appear to have averted the total economic implosion many feared during financial crisis, but the market had recovered to around its pre–August 1998 levels, and international creditors were returning. But the fourth firing of a government in less than eighteen months put the lie to such superficial indicators of health.

It also proved the fallacy of the West's policy toward Russia. By mistaking superficial indicators for genuine progress, and placing unwarranted faith in the stale cast of political elites, Western leaders pursued a policy that rewarded nonreform, helped entrench a corrupt and undemocratic system of government, and, however unintentionally, punished the Russian people.

The departure of Sergei Stepashin was hardly significant. Like its predecessors, the Stepashin government failed to tackle the structural problems that stopped growth and investment from taking off to the benefit of the country as a whole. Its only real claim to achievement was preventing a further decline in the value of the ruble.

Eight years of so-called reforms left a small group of elites fantastically wealthy, while a huge and potentially explosive segment of Russia's population remained impoverished. Communism collapsed in the Soviet Union when an overwhelming majority of its citizens awakened to how terrible the system was for their well-being. There was real danger of a new awakening if hardship continued.

The demand for change that brought millions of Soviets to the streets in 1989–1991 was based on the belief that a more attractive alternative existed in the West. Western assistance to Russia was also considered by many of my compatriots as an imperative. That assistance, however, did not produce the great leap into modernity that Russians hoped for. The primary blame rests, of course, on the shoulders of Russia's leaders: both the so-called reformers and those who openly maneuvered to create a new Russian elite with much the same power and privilege their Soviet predecessors enjoyed.

What the West failed to understand, however, is that the average Russian was more likely to point a finger at foreign financial institutions and governments for imposing what many Russians perceived as a corrupt and dysfunctional capitalist system. That it wasn't really much of a capitalist system at all yet wasn't understood. This resentment was compounded by how Yeltsin (and later Putin) and other top officials routinely deployed anti-Western rhetoric to pass off any blame from landing on their own shoulders. This all contributed to an anti-reform sentiment that made implementing a true market-based economic system all the more difficult.

The reformers and the Western nations involved in the reforms made a crucial mistake in responding to the criticism. Instead of confronting Yeltsin and the Russian public with the truth about the corruption and real reasons progress had stalled, they tried to pretend everything would be fine. Instead of transparency and the strong medicine Russia needed, we were fed placebos and told we were going to get well soon. It was a form of treatment we were quite familiar with from the days of the USSR. Once again the difference between the clarity of the Reagan administration and the timidity of his successors was on display. There was no need to compromise principles in the name of "doing business" with the Russian regime.

Instead of a comprehensive policy on how to act and speak to the Russian people, as existed during the Cold War, the West only dealt with our increasingly corrupt leadership long after it was clear they weren't representing the people. The 1990s were a window of opportunity where Russians could access a wide variety of uncensored news media. We would have listened and become part of the debate. Instead, Yeltsin and Putin's anti-Western rhetoric and litany of lies about why reforms weren't working went unchallenged.

Western governments should have made it clear that credits and investments by commercial institutions in Russia would no longer receive taxpayer-backed guarantees. The loud and clear message from the West should have been that Russia's rulers would not be told by Washington how they should spend public funds. Whatever Russia's elites did with public money—steal it, transfer the funds to foreign bank accounts—at the end of the party they would have been held accountable by their disillusioned people. Instead, every string that the International Monetary Fund, United States, and European Union tied to their aid money was used as an excuse by Russian officials to scapegoat the West. Cutting those strings publicly would have reinforced the broken lines of communication between ordinary Russians and the free world.

There were smaller but nevertheless important ways the West could have communicated its interest in the Russian people. I had to deal with it more than most, but any Russian who endured the treatment of Moscow's Western embassies in the process of obtaining an entry visa, or harassment at the hands of customs officials in Western airports, could have been forgiven for buying into the stories the Communists and nationalists spread about a worldwide anti-Russian conspiracy.

The collapse of the Soviet empire was brought about not by the West indulging Soviet leaders, but by a consistent and principled fight for liberal democratic values. Accommodating the demands of aging Soviet leaders never yielded positive results. The real contribution came from consistent efforts to reach Russians, such as the work of Radio Free Europe/Radio Liberty and Voice of America, which were considered by many Soviets to be the most reliable sources of information about our own country.

In August 1991, when Boris Yeltsin's administration took over, the majority of Russians were prepared for a partnership with the civilized world. This mood had all but disappeared by 1999, a casualty of the persistent nationalist campaigns of Russian political leaders. A good rapport was never going to be revived by ritualistic praising of whichever Russian leader was at the helm. The West had few avenues to influence the feudal fights of Russia's ruling elite in the late 1990s. But it had a fighting chance to win back the trust of ordinary Russians, with whom the country's future ultimately lay, and it missed that chance.

That sense of the tense and acrid atmosphere in Russia in August 1999 provides context for the traumatic events of September. Three years had gone by since the end of the first major war in Chechnya with Russian troops, but the chaos and violence in the region had never completely abated. By spring 1999, Chechnya was essentially in a state of internal warfare. Warlords controlled most of the region outside of the capital of Grozny and kidnapping for ransom had become a primary source of income. The 1998 kidnapping and murder of four foreign engineers, three British and one from New Zealand, made the news worldwide. The case would be a factor in removing any chance for international sympathy for the Chechen people during the horrors to come.

Russian politicians would occasionally bang the drums of war about the need to go "teach the Chechens a lesson," and it was

73

later revealed that an invasion plan had already been drawn up by Prime Minister Stepashin. But it wasn't until the end of August that it all spilled over. Chechen warlord Shamil Basayev led a small army, including foreign fighters, into neighboring Dagestan. Then, over twelve days in September, four bombings of apartment buildings took place in different Russian cities, killing nearly three hundred people. While there had been smaller attacks before, these bombings were professional, nearly identical, and unlike any committed by the Chechens before or after.

As you can imagine, the public was terrified and furious. The Federal Security Service (FSB, the primary successor of the KGB) blamed the Chechens and Yeltsin demanded action. The man he turned to was not Stepashin, but his new replacement, Vladimir Putin. The new prime minister had been the head of the KGB for just a year before his sudden promotion to prime minister took place right before the bombings began. Before that, in reverse chronological order, Putin had been a fairly anonymous member of Yeltsin's presidential staff, a deputy chief in the federal property management department, and a member of the mayor's staff in St. Petersburg. Formerly, he had been a KGB intelligence officer in East Germany until the fall of the Berlin Wall.

On August 9, 1999, the largely unknown Putin was, to the great surprise of nearly everyone, put in charge of the Russian government. The surprises didn't end there, however. At the same time, Yeltsin announced that he hoped Putin would succeed him in the presidency in 2000 and Putin publicly stated he would run. This made Putin stand out compared to the four other prime ministers Yeltsin had gone through in the previous eighteen months. Russia was facing many challenges at the time, but the top priority for the new government was promoting Putin as the undisputed president in waiting.

Things moved very quickly after that. As many a head of state is aware, winning a war, or even just waging one, can be an excellent way to win reelection. This was essentially the scenario for Putin, who was Yeltsin's anointed successor and the head of

74

government. He was still completely unknown to the Russian public, however, and becoming the public face of a new war in Chechnya and hunting down the terrorists behind the apartment bombings was the best way to fix that. Over the next few months, Yeltsin practically disappeared from sight (not that unusual considering his serious health problems) and Putin was suddenly everywhere.

Although the supposed targets of the Russian offensive in Chechnya were the militants who had gone into Dagestan in August, the bombing campaign was enormous and indiscriminate. Within weeks, hundreds of thousands of Chechens had been forced to flee. In October, Putin announced a ground offensive and tens of thousands of Russian troops advanced toward Grozny. Cluster bombs and heavy artillery caused thousands more civilian deaths and countless more refugees. What was ostensibly an anti-terror operation turned into a scorched-earth campaign.

The campaign in Chechnya had the predictable effect on the other campaign: the one for president. To deny this would be to deny the obvious. The war, for all its ugliness, was popular among Russians, and even reformers like Anatoly Chubais toed the patriotic line by supporting the war effort. For a very brief moment even my own attitude was quite sympathetic to the government's actions.

True, innocent people were suffering, and the suspicion at the time that Russia was using excessive force and committing war crimes was later confirmed. The Russian press was largely controlled by Yeltsin's oligarch supporters who had also endorsed Putin, or you might say had created Putin, and gave a very rose-colored picture of unfolding events. The Russian public also bought the official story that Chechens were behind the terrorist attacks in Moscow and Volgodonsk in September, even though there was hardly any proof. (More on that in a moment.)

But even knowing what we know now, I admit that the support Russians gave their soldiers in Chechnya was not the result of brainwashing. Many of the Chechen rebels were bandits who plied their trade on Russian territory and whose methods could only be described as medieval. Nor were their activities constrained to the Caucasus and the occasional terror attack outside. Chechen criminal gangs were active all over the country, although it was clear that they would never have become as powerful and dangerous as they were without their reliable "business partners" in Moscow. For the majority of Russians the military crackdown in Chechnya was part of their desire to end the plague of corruption and criminality in cities where they lived.

Every day struggling Russians read about the new billionaires being created by cozy deals with the government. You didn't have to understand how things like privatization vouchers, loans-for-shares, and rigged auctions worked to realize there was a huge scam going on. Worried that reforms might be rolled back by conservatives, Yeltsin's reform team, led by Yegor Gaidar and Chubais, started selling things off at a frantic pace at absurdly low valuations. Mikhail Khodorkovsky and Boris Berezovsky, already two of the wealthiest and most influential oligarchs, acquired their huge energy firms, Yukos and Sibneft, for less than 10 percent of their real value.

Such sanctioned looting continued under Putin, of course, and continues today. The difference was that in the 1990s Russians could find out about it. The various political and business factions had warring media outlets, and while the press could be more than a little yellow, at least it represented many different sides so the truth could be found somewhere in the middle.

When I am asked if Putin was inevitable, this is why I say you have to start ten years before anyone knew his name. By the time Yeltsin made Putin the heir apparent, Russians were demanding stability and looking for a tough guy to stand up to the criminals and to the Western influences they'd been told were damaging the country and their pensions. To prevent Putin, or *a* Putin, from coming to power, the 1990s would have required a very different script with less appeasement of Yeltsin and his entourage and stronger support for democratic institutions.

As the election approached, my own view was that a faceless technocrat like Putin might just be what Russia needed at the time. I believed that the Russian government had to project strength and self-confidence and only then would it gain the popular support needed to follow through with painful economic reforms. After years of looting and capital flight it was getting harder and harder to scapegoat the West for how badly things were going. Yeltsin's approval rating was dismal once again, another reason he and his oligarch backers were eager to find a fresh face to show to the frustrated Russian people.

The apartment bombings that terrorized Russia in September convinced even those who thought Russia should have let Chechnya go its own way in 1991 that the Chechens deserved everything they got. Laying siege to a hospital, bombing the families of soldiers: these were inhuman acts, so the gloves were off. The public cheered Putin as their new gladiator and enjoyed the rough, even profane language he occasionally used when talking about what he would do to those who would threaten Russia. "We will find the terrorists anywhere," he once said, "and if we find them in their shithouses, we'll wipe them out in their shithouses."

This was a real transformation for a boring back-room bureaucrat, aided by the hasty publication of a campaign-ready biography that emphasized his deprived and difficult childhood and tough-guy credentials over anything that might prepare him for being a political reformer. This was no accident. The advantage of being faceless was that Yeltsin's chief backer and master conspirator, Boris Berezovsky, could apply whatever face was needed.

We were forced to contemplate just how far Yeltsin, Putin, and their backers might go to guarantee Putin's election on the night of September 22, when local police in the city of Ryazan interrupted what would have been the fifth apartment bombing of the month. Alerted by a resident, the police were too late to catch the perpetrators, but they found three fifty-kilogram sugar bags filled with white powder in the basement, connected to a detonator.

Chemical analysis on the scene the next morning detected the same military-grade hexogen explosive used in all of the previous bombings.

The next evening, the twenty-third, Putin made a televised statement praising local law enforcement and the alert citizens who had called them for averting a catastrophe. He also spoke briefly on the ongoing air strikes against Grozny. There was nothing to contradict the day's dramatic news that a terrorist attack had been foiled in Ryazan. The next day, something incredible happened. FSB director Nikolai Patrushev issued a statement saying that the planting of a bomb in the Ryazan basement had been a "training exercise" to test the vigilance of the local security forces and residents! He said that there had been no explosives at all and that the sugar bags had actually been full of sugar, not hexogen.

This fantastical story was required because law enforcement and the local FSB office in Ryazan had already detected and exposed extensive FSB involvement in the attempted bombing. Suspicious phone intercepts on the night of the bombing were traced back to FSB headquarters in Moscow. Two men arrested in Ryazan had been carrying FSB identity cards and were released into the custody of a senior official from Moscow. Patrushev was obviously trying to cover his agency's tracks, but there were far too many giant holes in his story.

Just to invoke the most obvious contradiction available at the time, if the bags were full of sugar why did the substance test as hexogen on the scene and why did the FSB rapidly take the bags away to Moscow for further testing if they knew it was sugar? More and more evidence and inconsistencies accumulated, enough to turn a nightmarish conspiracy theory about agents within the Russian government mass-murdering people for political purposes into a case that is very hard to refute on the facts. It was revealed, for example, that some soldiers had earlier stumbled onto sugar bags full of a "strange substance" on a nearby base, which turned out to be hexogen.

A deep investigation and analysis of the case were turned into a devastating book by former FSB agent Alexander Litvinenko, *Blowing Up Russia*. The same Litvinenko, who had become a fierce Putin critic, was assassinated in London in 2006 with the rare radioactive substance polonium-210. An independent FSB investigator of the case, Mikhail Trepashkin, was arrested a week before hearings began and jailed for four years. In 2000, the Duma twice rejected calls for a parliamentary investigation of what happened in Ryazan. All evidence and internal documents related to Ryazan were then sealed on the grounds of secrecy for seventy-five years. While I admit to possessing the healthy paranoia developed by most people born in totalitarian states, this all seems like an overreaction over three bags of sugar.

Of course any suggestion that the bombings had been a self-inflicted "false flag" operation to stoke outrage and fear was condemned by the government. The theory didn't make it into the mainstream inside Russia at the time; it was just too horrible to contemplate. The idea that a government would massacre its own people was too shocking in 2000. But by 2002, 40 percent of Russians believed the security forces were involved in the apartment bombings. By then we had more information about Ryazan and, more importantly, we had much more information about Vladimir Putin. The suspicion that the Putin regime had no allergy to Russian blood was confirmed by revelations about the scope of devastation in Chechnya, and then by the brutal government interventions in the Nord-Ost and Beslan hostage situations in 2002 and 2004.

Similarly, although the huge discrepancies in the official story on Ryazan were reported in the West, nobody wanted to hear the truth. This is a typical pattern of convenient cowardice. If you acknowledge the horrible truth you would have to act, so it's easier to ignore the facts and pretend it's "disputed" and say you're "concerned" about "the allegations." This charade is particularly important when you feel obliged to pretend the perpetrator is an ally and is operating in good faith. For example, European nations still don't want to admit Putin has declared war on Ukraine. Even when Russian forces apparently shot down a civilian airliner over occupied Eastern Ukraine, the EU representatives seemed as eager to deny Russian culpability as the Russians. Again, if they admitted the truth, they would have to act, and nobody wants to act.

And so Putin's popularity continued to rise. By October 1999, he was already polling ahead of opposition hopeful Yevgeny Primakov, one of the most successful of Yeltsin's many former prime ministers and backed by the Communist Party and the powerful mayor of Moscow, Yuri Luzhkov. The election was scheduled for June, but Putin wouldn't have to wait that long to sit in the president's chair.

━━━━

The December parliamentary elections came first, however, and at the time they felt like the first time Russians had gone to the polls the way other democracies did: simply to vote for the candidates who best reflected their views. All previous elections had taken place in a crisis atmosphere, especially Yeltsin's desperate battle for survival in 1996. The newly formed "Unity" bloc, assembled by the government only three months prior and endorsed by Putin, did quite well; well enough to prevent the Communists from controlling the Duma.

I felt optimism based on the relatively normal appearance of the elections. Efficient and expensive political campaigns, famous personalities, and sitting members of the Duma dominated the polls, and the public showed a healthy conservatism by staying with known devils. As I joked at the time, the appearance of aggressive TV ads and mudslinging showed that we Russians were quickly learning to live up to American campaign standards.

My concern was that the West still showed no sign of developing a long-term strategy for Russia. Was it going to treat the Russian people like adults capable of hearing the painful truth, or would Western leaders continue to speak over our heads? Aid and understanding over Chechnya were important, but not at the cost of appeasing anti-democratic practices and epic corruption.

Russia's terrible problems were not going to disappear overnight. Like most observers inside and out of Russia, I was primarily worried about the usual perils of corruption, inefficiency, and red tape that made it difficult for any government to forge ahead. Despite my hopes that the darker, more ideological challenges had been left behind us, I hinted at my doubts in the *Wall Street Journal* a few days after the elections. I wrote, "There is no guarantee that nationalism can be mastered and will not rise to overshadow liberal reforms. Mr. Putin's KGB roots and strong military backing could well turn out to be liabilities that are too heavy to overcome."

I had each point half right, as it turned out. Putin discarded the liberal reforms first, right out of the gate. He only revived nationalism as a political tool later when it served his purposes to do so. The military was never again the factor in politics it had been for so long, and Putin's KGB roots were what would define him and the future of Russia.

With the apartment bombings to fan the flames of vengeance, the assault in Chechnya gained force. By December the siege of Grozny had begun and would last for two months. When it was over, Grozny would be described by visiting journalists as looking worse than Berlin in 1945. Not a single building was undamaged, earning Grozny the dubious title of "the most destroyed city on Earth" by the United Nations in 2003.

The human destruction was no better. Refugees were scattered all over the region in abysmal conditions. Russian troops rounded up prisoners indiscriminately. Torture and murder of captives was routine. As described by the incredibly brave Russian journalist Anna Politkovskaya, who visited Chechnya every month during the second war, what happened there was "a clear, obvious, unbelievable worldwide betrayal of humanitarian values. The Universal Declaration of Human Rights, a little more than a half a century old, has fallen in the second Chechen war."

She was validated when the European Court of Human Rights began to issue rulings against the Russian government in favor of the families of some of the many thousands of Chechens who had been tortured or disappeared in military custody.

When Politkovskaya wasn't in Chechnya documenting the personal stories of families torn apart by violence and war crimes by the Russian military, or writing her reports for *Novaya Gazeta*, she was traveling widely to rally support for international humanitarian intervention that never came. After dodging death in the mountains for years, and being harassed and threatened from every possible direction, Politkovskaya was gunned down in her Moscow apartment building on October 7, 2006, Vladimir Putin's birthday.

The federal government of Chechnya was abolished in May 2000, when President Putin established direct rule. Fighting continued after Putin appointed Akhmad Kadyrov as the head of the local government and would continue as a guerilla conflict for many years to come. Terror attacks large and small by Chechen groups would continue around the country. And even when violence had been reduced to "tolerable" levels, the repercussions from what Russia had done in Chechnya continued to ripple around the world. Chechnya's main export became well-trained, well-armed radicalized fighters and terrorists.

Yes, I said "President" Putin. He had been inaugurated on May 7, 2000, a month before the election had been scheduled to take place. Yeltsin had another surprise up his sleeve and had suddenly resigned on December 31, 1999, making Putin the acting president and requiring an election in three months' time. Putin took care of the most important business immediately, ensuring the security and wealth of Boris Yeltsin and his family. A decree granting Yeltsin and all his relatives freedom from prosecution was signed the same day Putin took office, revealing the real reason Yeltsin had selected him for his successor: self-preservation.

5

PRESIDENT
FOR LIFE

Putin's sudden ascent to acting president eliminated any remaining doubts about the result of the election. Not only would he have three months as the most visible and powerful person in Russia, with the full apparatus of the state to promote him, but the election would come three months earlier than the competition had expected. Putin appeared on television constantly in the months before the March 26 vote, with one exception. Continuing a Yeltsin tradition, he declined to participate in any debates with other candidates.

Putin won with 53.4 percent, nearly doubling Zyuganov's tally and avoiding the runoff that would have been triggered had he failed to reach a majority. On election night I was watching the returns come in on television with several American guests curious to see the beginning of the post-Yeltsin era. One was Chris Cox, the congressman from California who had become a great advocate of Russian democracy and bilateral affairs, and a personal friend. Other guests that evening included James Woolsey, the former CIA director under Bill Clinton, and Alexander Haig, Ronald Reagan's first secretary of state. I remember watching Putin's numbers carefully that night. He was holding steady at around 47 percent when in less than an hour they jumped up to

53 percent and then never fluctuated again. It would have been embarrassing for Putin to have to undergo a second round. He was the chosen one and the time for uncertainty was over.

This is not to suggest Putin would not have won a completely fair election at the time. He would have. People were nervous and craving stability and strength, which is what Putin promised them. The various liberal reform groups, most notably the Yabloko ("Apple") party of Grigory Yavlinsky, who received my vote, were relegated to bystanders. The idea that greater centralized power could lead to a loss of civil liberties was far from most Russians' minds. We still had a mostly free media, with programs that openly criticized our politicians and their ideas. The brilliant satirical puppet show *Kukly* had raked Yeltsin over the coals for years on NTV. The government was not the sacred cow it would soon become.

Terrorism and physical security were not the only voter priorities. The 1998 financial collapse was still on everyone's mind. Although it was relatively short-lived, and the economy would rebound in 2000 to achieve its highest ever GDP growth of over 10 percent, there were serious concerns about how much we could trust the banks and other financial institutions, especially because of who owned them.

The oligarchs who had gotten unimaginably rich in the 1990s while allying with Yeltsin were the public faces of the corruption that infuriated the average Russian. We saw them on TV and in the papers, saw their ostentatious wealth while their gangsters and bodyguards fought battles in the streets of Moscow. A "law and order" campaign is one of the oldest clichés in the history of elections, but it had real resonance in Russia in 2000.

Another element in the mood on the street in Russia then was Soviet nostalgia. Not for Communism, but the vague sense that something had been lost. It's difficult to explain, but the 1990s failed to provide a new sense of purpose to fill that feeling of loss and failed to provide enough prosperity to distract Russians from thinking about the past. Putin and his air of regret over the collapse of the USSR were therefore appealing along these lines. It's a subtle but important distinction. People did not really want to return to the Soviet days; they just didn't want to feel bad about thinking about it.

Putin arrived mostly untainted by the corruption and financial ruin associated with the Yeltsin administration. The 1998 financial crisis had forced Yeltsin to clean house, and he swept out the good with the bad. The economic team led by Anatoly Chubais was demonized, fairly and unfairly. The purge also caught a young Yeltsinite on Chubais's team, Boris Nemtsov. Once treated by Yeltsin as a potential successor, Nemtsov would go on to become one of the strongest voices in opposition to Putin's rollback of democracy in Russia. Boris and I worked closely together for years in the anti-Putin opposition movement and I was horrified, but not surprised, by his assassination in Moscow on February 27, 2015.

Boris Yeltsin's needs were far more personal. Corruption accusations were rising around him and members of his family, and not just "the Family," as his closest circle of oligarchs and advisors were known, but his actual relatives. The 1998 government shake-up left Yeltsin rattled and aware of his vulnerability. Impeachment forces in the Duma were rising before he conceded and dropped Chernomyrdin for Primakov as prime minister. Yeltsin needed a presidential successor who would be grateful and loyal to him, without his own constituency, and who would be strong enough to stand up to Yeltsin's enemies if they came after him.

Yeltsin's younger daughter, Tatyana, was also his close advisor and was a major power behind the throne in the later years of his administration. She has been credited with influencing her father's choice of Putin. There is a historical twist here going back to 1933, when ailing German president Paul von Hindenburg was convinced by his son Oskar to name Adolf Hitler chancellor. Hitler seized all state powers for himself within hours of von Hindenburg's death in 1934. Ironically, in her blog in 2010, Tatyana Yumasheva (her married name) briefly and cautiously attempted to defend her father and his legacy against the Putin regime's attempts to rewrite the history of the 1990s.

The nonaggression pact between Putin and the Family has otherwise held up very well. In fact, I think Putin was cautious about completely demolishing Russian democracy up until Yeltsin's death. Despite his faults and fall from grace while in office, Yeltsin was a true freedom fighter. Had he felt obliged to speak out about Putin's dictatorial maneuvers it could have had real repercussions going into the 2008 election season. But after he died on April 23, 2007, Putin clearly felt no constraints.

Yeltsin deserves to be remembered for more than his drinking and for sitting atop a tank during the August coup attempt. In December 1991, the Western world watched with grave suspicion as Mikhail Gorbachev was forced to resign from office. Yeltsin got little credit for leading the revolution that finally swept away Communist institutions and broke up the Soviet empire. It was Yeltsin, not Gorbachev, who brought Russia out of the looking glass into the sunlight. During the painful transition period, Russians lost their illusions about a shining future just around the corner. Corruption, poverty, crime, and war in the North Caucasus made daily life in Russia quite ugly, and Yeltsin received most of the blame.

But who could have found an easy way out at the end of 1991, when the Soviet Union had collapsed and the mere survival of the Russian state and its people was the only relevant issue? Yeltsin's battering-ram power was sufficient to destroy the prison of the past, but he lacked the preparation and creativity to design the palace of the future.

Despite the challenges, by 2000 Russians lived in the same dimension as the rest of the civilized world, and we measured success and failure in our lives by the same standards. As did many of my compatriots, I always supported and voted for Yeltsin— with great expectations from 1989 to 1993, with hard feelings from 1994 to 1996, when his only great virtue was that he was an obstacle to Communist revanchism.

The growing disappointment of his last two years in office was due to Yeltsin's inability to carry forward necessary reforms and root out corruption from Russia's political and economic life. But, frankly speaking, we didn't have any real alternative. In judging the pros and cons of Yeltsin's rule, one may argue that he failed to root out the Communist and KGB seeds from Russian soil but at least he stopped them from sprouting on his watch.

Lenin still lies in Red Square, and the two bans (in 1991 and 1993) on the Communist Party marching under the banners of Lenin and Stalin were only temporary. As a dedicated anti-Communist, I'm the last one to excuse such softness on what's left of the criminal Soviet state. Yet I understand Yeltsin's unease about dealing the final blow to the regime that propelled him to the top of the nomenclatura.

Perhaps the most important thing Yeltsin did was something he did not do when he took power. After the blackest pages of post-Communist Russian history had been turned in October 1993, and after several bloody days in Moscow, Yeltsin declined to do what his opponents almost surely would have done: wipe out the other side. For the first time in all of Russian history the new ruler did not eliminate the losers to consolidate control. What's more, eventually they were integrated into the political process. Yeltsin called for immediate elections and accepted an independent parliament.

Out of nowhere, the career bureaucrat literally leapt to the front lines armed with an instinct for breaking down barriers and opening doors long closed. And yet Yeltsin's inconsistency was boundless. He allowed regional leaders to have more power but then dived into the tragic war in Chechnya. He waged battle against special privileges for the elites but later opened the flood-gates for the oligarchs to loot the country. He promoted free and fair elections, but in the end he couldn't accept that popular will could decide supreme power.

It was clear Yeltsin couldn't stay in power with fair elections and the abuses quickly mounted. From that point on the Putin police state was all but predestined. Putin had only to follow his own instincts and carry through what was already in motion. Yeltsin failed the final and most important test. The fragile democratic structures he allowed to form could not survive his own need for power and security. He failed to create lasting institutions. The structure relied on his leadership, and the freedoms that existed were there only because he allowed them. There was no way such a system could withstand the exit of the ruler who created it.

Worst of all, his collapse poisoned the minds of the Russian people against what they saw, incorrectly, as uncontrolled capitalism and democracy. The oligarchs who took power prevailed over the good of the people. Russians saw no benefits from the supposed blessings of elections and the free market. A new ruling elite was formed out of the old bureaucrats and the new technocrats, united in their indifference to the values of liberal democracy. The fights among them at the end of the 1990s to find Yeltsin's successor could have gone differently, but democracy was sure to be the loser. They quickly recognized that elections and a free media could only threaten their grip on power. It was no coincidence that Yeltsin's hand-picked successor came from the KGB.

Missed opportunities were inevitable considering the magnitude of the changes and problems that confronted Yeltsin. It's still early to analyze what he could have done better, but it is relatively simple to compare how things have gone since Putin took over in 2000. There was chaos, but Yeltsin never attacked individual freedoms. Putin has built his entire presidency to be the opposite of the Yeltsin years, with a great deal of success. The entire government has been brought under the direct control of the president. The parliament attempted to impeach Yeltsin twice; now it is a puppet show. The corruption of the oligarchs has been moved inside the Kremlin walls where it has expanded to staggering levels. The media, which was free to criticize Yeltsin, is entirely at the service of the Putin administration. The economy is where we see the biggest difference, although most of the credit must go to the simple fact that during Putin's tenure the price of oil went from $10 a barrel to over $100. And even with those untold energy riches the average Russian is seeing little improvement in his standard of living.

Boris Yeltsin had more than his share of faults, but he was a real person. He had virtues and vices in his flesh and blood. We exchanged him for a shadow of a man who wants only to keep us all in perpetual darkness. The long lines of Russians who waited to view Yeltsin's coffin and pay their respects at a Moscow cathedral demonstrated that despite his many failures people sensed the possibility for good in what he attempted. This is a stark contrast to what we got in his successor.

───

Fifteen years into his rule in Russia, there is still an impressively large industry of pundits discussing Vladimir Putin's true nature. Some guesswork is to be expected considering the lack of documentation about most of his early life and the conflicting reports and biographical portraits about him and about his career. Even his own autobiographical statements and interviews seem designed to obscure and mislead, which of course they are.

Putin's early life story is not the subject of my interest or this book. Investigating the hardships of his Leningrad childhood and trying to sort fact from fiction in his biography has been done elsewhere by those who find such things more rewarding than I do. I expect there is much to learn that will never be learned until Putin is out of power, if ever. So I will cite a few authors whose opinions and analysis I respect and move ahead to Putin's time in power. Russian journalist Masha Gessen knows as much as anyone can likely know about Putin and writes with her usual acuity on his character in her excellent 2012 biography, *The Man Without a Face*:

Like most Soviet citizens of his generation, Putin was never a political idealist. His parents may or may not have believed in a Communist future for all the world, in the ultimate triumph of justice for the proletariat, or in any of the other ideological clichés that had been worn thin by the time Putin was growing up; he never even considered his relationship to these ideals. . . . Like other members of his generation, Putin replaced belief in communism, which no longer seemed plausible or even possible, with faith in institutions. His loyalty was to the KGB and to the empire it served and protected: the USSR.

A new biography I haven't had a chance to really study is *Mr. Putin: Operative in the Kremlin* by Hill and Gaddy. This passage near the beginning caught my eye as an insightful explanation of Putin's behavior during most of his public life. It jibes well with my description of Putin as a poker player who was adept at reading his opponents. Keep this description in mind as we move into discussion of what other world leaders thought of Putin when they met. In all likelihood it was whatever he wanted them to think.

> Putin is less interested in presenting a particular version of reality than in seeing how others react to the information. For him, others are participants in a game he directs. He chooses inputs; they react. He judges. Their responses to his input tell him who they think he is—but by responding they also tell him who they are, what they want, what they care about. For his part, Vladimir Putin reveals very little in return. Indeed, he goes to great, often elaborate, lengths to throw other participants off track. As president and prime minister, he has presented himself as a myriad of different personas. Since 2000, Mr. Putin has been the ultimate international political performance artist.

I would add, however, that Putin's character and his performance have begun to merge under pressure over the last few years. When he was forced to switch from currying favor with the leading democratic nations to raging against them to stoke domestic support, the real Putin came to the surface and the layers of masks could come off. This wasn't only a matter of Putin acting on his nature, like the scorpion on the frog's back, but of being allowed to grow into and fulfill his nature.

That is the ultimate answer to the question of dictators being born or raised. As with most nature-nurture questions, it's both in varying degrees of balance. In 2000, Putin didn't know he wanted to be a dictator. (Unlike Hitler and Stalin, whose early writings and statements made their dreams all too clear.) Insider stories from 1999 even suggest Putin was alarmed by Yeltsin's proposal to resign early and thrust him into the presidency early.

Putin's instinct was to align himself with power and to bring power to himself. Anything he didn't control was something he couldn't trust. His solution was to try to control everything. Unlike the totalitarianism of the Soviet Union, which handed all control to the system, Putin aimed for the totalitarianism of one person: himself.

When Putin took over the presidency in 2000 he was surrounded by many other potent forces. Various Yeltsin advisors (including his daughter) and oligarchs still wielded power inside and outside of the Kremlin walls. These included Yeltsin's longtime éminence grise, Boris Berezovsky, and his collaborators Alexander Voloshin and Roman Abramovich. Berezovsky had been acquainted with Putin for years and is credited with lifting him out of the bureaucracy and into the prime minister's post.

While Yeltsin's reforms had weakened the Duma considerably relative to the presidency, it was still a factor and couldn't be completely ignored. The media was subjected to considerable government influence, but there were still many alternatives, and political reporting, while biased and vitriolic, was unrestrained.

Since I have often touted my prescience, I should give some time to my mistakes as well. Two days after Putin took office, I eulogized Yeltsin's tenure and tried to set an optimistic tone for the future under Putin. My January 3, 2000, op-ed in the *Wall Street Journal* made no mention of Putin's KGB background or horrific human rights record in Chechnya. My focus was Yeltsin's legacy and any predictions were difficult since Putin was still mostly an unknown. Plus, like any patriot I wanted the best for my country. Foreign support and investment were still very important for Russia, something I surely had in mind when I took to the pages of the newspaper. I wrote:

> I'm convinced Mr. Yeltsin genuinely believed in the necessity of making Russia a full-fledged democracy and wanted to be certain that a new strongman in the Kremlin would be able to protect precious democratic reforms. Only time will tell whether Mr. Putin can be a good president. But today we may state that, under the circumstances, Mr. Yeltsin bet on the right horse. . . . The obvious question is how Mr. Putin's team will cope with Russia's mounting economic problems, but undoubtedly they will be looking for a solution within the constitutional framework Mr. Yeltsin drew up. By doing so they will contribute to the final historical triumph of the first president of Russia.

Of course it turned out that Yeltsin wanted a strongman in the Kremlin to protect the precious wealth he and his family and associates had accumulated, not democratic reforms. And I simply could not imagine that the constitutional framework itself would be targeted so quickly and so brutally. Like most, I imagined Putin would favor his own friends and be more disciplined, not that he would immediately steer the entire country back toward totalitarianism.

Then we come to the forces outside of Russia, the Western administrations and investors that had practically given up on Russia as the decade came to a close. Instead of using their considerable leverage to back reforms and democratic institutions, the leading free world nations limited their investment to nuclear disarmament and other relatively easy cooperation. While it should already be clear that I do not subscribe to the myth of Russian humiliation, much more could have been done had there been a sincere interest in the West regarding the future of Russia.

George Soros was a participant in and a witness to many of the events around the attempts to reform and rebuild the Russian economy in the post-Soviet years. His investment fund was as important a factor in many ways as the International Monetary Fund. He was also very disappointed in the feeble and hypocritical engagement by the West in the late 1990s. By the time Putin arrived at the presidency, Soros saw the writing on the wall. Much earlier than most observers, he saw where Putin would take the country. In February 2000, the famous investor penned an article in *Moskovsky Novosti*. Most of it was dedicated to describing the battle royal behind the scenes between Chubais and Berezovsky, and criticizing the West for what he saw as its failure to support Russia adequately. In between, he had this to say about the future of the new Putin regime:

> But the state built by Putin will hardly be based on the principles of the open society. It will continue to use the feeling of fear that emerged after the apartment explosions. This state will try to establish its power over private life and it will struggle for the world superiority of Russia. It will be authoritarian and nationalistic. It is impossible to predict the development of events, but it is also clear that this perspective is emerging, and that it could have been avoided if the Western free society followed the principles of free society.

When it comes to getting Putin right, and getting him right early, the highest laurels must go to Andrei Piontkovsky. One of the sharpest minds in political analysis, Andrei also has one of the sharpest tongues. In January 2000, he called Putinism "the highest and final stage of bandit capitalism" and "the coup de grâce" to the head of the Russian nation. The article he penned in February 2000 in the *Russia Journal* deserves immortality for seeing very clearly what most of us only feared. He begins the article in

93

the World Economic Forum in Davos that January, where he was amused to watch a panel of Russian officials attempt to answer the question "Who is Putin?"

The distinguished gentlemen who in the corridors had been busy aggressively pushing their product under the brand-name "Vladimir Putin, next Russian president" were at a loss—none of them wanted to speak out in public, or they dared not to speak out in public. It was as when referring to the deceased—"one either speaks well of them, or says nothing at all." Only Putin is still very much alive and politically kicking.

He then relates how he answered the question himself on his own panel the next day. As ever, Andrei pulled no punches:

"Don't pretend you don't know who Putin is," was my answer. You are just not prepared to face the truth. I have no more knowledge about Putin than you have. But what I do know is enough for me to make my personal judgement as an ordinary Russian voter about this contender for the post of president—that this man is dangerous for my country and for the world.

This is a man who has shown a complete disregard for human life, cynicism and hypocrisy, and a willingness to use war and the deaths of thousands of Russian soldiers and innocent civilians as a PR instrument in his election campaign. This is a man who raised a toast on the anniversary of Stalin's birth, had the plaque commemorating former KGB head Yury Andropov restored to its place on the wall of the Lubyanka—Federal Security Service headquarters—and dreams of seeing the statue of butcher Felix Dzerzhinsky, founder of the Soviet secret police, stand once again in the center of Moscow.

Piontkovsky then referred to the plight of journalist Andrei Babitsky, who had been abducted by Russian military forces in Chechnya and who was later personally accused by Putin of treason for reports he felt were too sympathetic to the Chechen militants. Andrei concluded his article:

> This game is also full of political significance. It is not only Babitsky who is being tortured in filtration camps. We are all being held in one huge filtration camp outside the gates to the Brave New Putin-Stasi World. They are testing our fitness for this world that awaits. How much can we swallow in silence? How quick and how easy is it to break us? Those who don't make the grade will be ruthlessly cast off as rejects.
>
> Don't ask me who Putin is. And don't ask me for whom Putin tolls. He tolls for thee.

In 2005, a bust of Felix Dzerzhinsky was returned to its old place in a courtyard behind the Moscow Police Building at Petrovka 38. The towering statue of him in Lubyanka Square that was pulled down in 1991 still awaits its return.

======

Putin was inaugurated on May 7, 2000, faced with an array of outside influences, not to mention a shaky economy and an ongoing war in Chechnya. With impressive focus, Putin began work immediately to tame or eliminate everything and everyone that could limit his power. His first decree had been to provide protection to Yeltsin, as had no doubt been promised. Those that followed in quick succession over the next few days were dedicated either to strengthening the military or dismantling Russia's democratic institutions.

Oligarchs who had been on the wrong side of the power struggles quickly found out what it meant to lose to Putin. Vladimir Gusinsky, the media baron whose NTV had been the first independent channel in Russia, was considered too close to Moscow mayor Yuri Luzhkov, whose presidential ambitions Gusinsky had funded. Gusinsky was deemed untrustworthy and potentially dangerous by Putin and the consequences were swift. Within days of Putin's taking office, Gusinsky's media company was raided by police. In June he was arrested on a bizarre charge and spent three days in jail. After being released on bail he left for Spain, where later in the year he was briefly arrested due to an Interpol warrant filed by the Russian government. (An early example of this tactic, abusing international institutions for political persecution.) Gusinsky's media assets were eventually consumed by the state, a punitive form of renationalization that would also become a familiar pattern.

Berezovsky himself didn't last much longer. Now also a member of the Duma, he published a letter protesting Putin's proposed legislation that would demote regional governors and subject them to the authority of the central government, saying it was a threat to Russian democracy, which of course was the entire point. Six weeks later, on July 17, Berezovsky resigned from parliament, supposedly in protest over Putin's onslaught of anti-democratic legislation. After the two exchanged criticism and threats in the media, an old fraud investigation against Berezovsky was revived by federal investigators in October. That was the only hint he needed to stay out of the country, which he did, eventually settling in London. As with Gusinsky, Berezovsky's remaining Russian assets were stripped or he was forced to sell to oligarchs with higher loyalty ratings.

Putin may have simply deemed Berezovsky too powerful and too knowledgeable to keep around. The oligarch knew where lots of bodies were buried because he had buried many of them himself. He also controlled several very high-value targets, the oil company Sibneft and the TV channel ORT, later known as Channel One. Putin quickly realized that it was more effective to control the media completely than to censor it, so he cut out the middlemen.

Media outlets were taken over by forces friendly to Putin and his closest associates. This "takeover censorship" was accompanied by the more conventional kind, with its lists of non grata names and verboten topics. Media power was centralized in the same fashion as political power, and with the same purpose: looting the country without causing a popular revolt. The corruption of the Yeltsin era is burned into Russia's collective memory only because we learned about it in the press at the time. In the 1990s, the competing oligarchs waged war against one another in their media outlets. It was not a fight fought fairly or decently, but a preponderance of facts came to light and thousands of honest journalists worked to bring the truth to the Russian public.

Putin's obsession with the media boiled over after the accident that sank the *Kursk* nuclear submarine in the Barents Sea in August. One hundred eighteen sailors died, twenty-three of them after escaping the initial explosions and surviving for hours, maybe longer, in an isolated compartment awaiting a rescue that only arrived days later. The *Kursk* was the pride of the Russian fleet, launched in 1994 and deemed, like the *Titanic,* "unsinkable." Due to budgetary cutbacks the sub had seen very little activity and not much maintenance, just like the rest of the military at that point in time. Poor training and corroded equipment led to disaster when an old practice torpedo exploded on board, sinking the submarine in one hundred meters of freezing water.

Putin was on vacation in Sochi at the time and decided to stay there during the crisis. There was likely nothing he could have done to save the trapped men on the *Kursk*; there is no way he could have known that at the time. He accepted the navy's statement that a rescue was in motion with no debate. He admitted later that it looked very bad for him to be seen relaxing on the Black Sea while the disaster unfolded. For nearly a week no one was sure if there were survivors. The television reports switched back and forth between images of distraught families at the Vidyayevo Naval Base and the president's barbecues in Sochi. The Russian Navy rejected offers of help that came immediately from the United States, France, Germany, Norway, and others.

Only five days and many failed Russian rescue attempts after the disaster did Putin accept international aid. A Norwegian ship arrived on the nineteenth, a full week after the *Kursk* had sunk. It took two more days to penetrate the submarine and confirm that there were no survivors. The navy, including several of its highest officers, had begun to spin stories about the cause of the disaster almost immediately. Their favorite was that it was the result of a collision with a NATO submarine, a conspiracy theory for which there was not a shred of evidence. Officials continued to suggest the collision theory even after evidence of two internal explosions was confirmed beyond any doubt. (Russian state-controlled media sources still mention it as a valid theory today even though the 2002 official report verified that the explosion of a faulty torpedo was the cause.)

Russian media, especially Boris Berezovsky's television station, heavily criticized the response of the government as callous and bumbling, which was nothing more than the truth. Video of Putin and other unsympathetic officials being berated by grieving family members made Putin realize what a threat the media could be to his early popularity. Revealing that his totalitarian instincts were far stronger than any he had for reform, instead of reorganizing the military that had caused the horrible accident and botched the rescue, or publicly punishing the incompetent officers, Putin went after the media that reported on it.

So in less than six months after Putin's taking office, two of the most influential oligarchs in Russia were in exile, the constitutional power structure of the country had been shifted dramatically toward Moscow, and free media outlets were falling like dominoes. Six months! The main myth that was built up around these events was that Putin was just cleaning up the town like a good sheriff. The Russian people despised the oligarchs and viewed them as criminals who were above the law. And here was Putin, a strong man from the security services, showing everyone that this was no longer the case. Not bad! Even if he pushed the limits of legality to do it, what else could he do, went the refrain.

Never mind that Putin was taking the private assets of Gusinsky and Berezovsky and putting them in the hands of other, more loyal, oligarchs or putting them under direct state control. The Putin government wasn't cracking down on corruption, it was sanctifying it. It was a unique method of cleaning up the town that involved deputizing one set of "entrepreneurs" while demonizing another.

Make no mistake, I have little sympathy for the first generation of oligarchs that looted Russia as the USSR collapsed. They and their political and mafioso partners exploited Yeltsin's lack of control and combined to derail the best chance Russia had at a market economy and democracy. The epic levels of corruption made the already difficult job of reform impossible and pushed the minimum standard of living needed for economic stability out of reach just long enough for Putin, or someone like Putin, to be welcomed with open arms.

What I reject is the mythologizing by those looking to praise Putin relative to Yeltsin on grounds of progress on corruption, institutional economic reforms, and growth. When it comes to Putin fighting corruption, I don't think that legalizing theft and then boasting of a drop in crime should be considered progress. The actual crime rate in Russia kept increasing until 2002, when the revenue from skyrocketing oil prices began to have a broader impact. Putin would rely on a similar pacification maneuver in Chechnya when he gave official status and huge payoffs to a prominent warlord, Akhmad Kadyrov.

There is a practical argument to be made for these appeasement schemes, but I find it cynical and immoral, as well as harmful to the national interest in the long run. Reducing street violence and conflict by adopting one clan of the mafia while wiping out the others came at a huge cost. With no free media, no justice system to worry about, and no competition, Putin's preferred oligarchs were like vermin whose natural predators had been eradicated. The chosen winners had the full power of the state behind them and the Russian treasury opened wide.

Had Putin come in and threatened to do to all that he selectively did to a few—that is, had he applied the rule of law properly—it would have been a very different story. He could have ended the looting, told his friends and foes alike that the party at the expense of the Russian people was over. At first it looked like he might be making an example of Gusinsky and Berezovsky for just this purpose. After all, if he could kick out two of the most influential and wealthy oligarchs so quickly, the others would surely fall into line. Instead, Putin's message to the rest turned out to be that of a mafia don. Either you swore loyalty to the capo to steal within his system or your freedom and your assets could disappear overnight. As became increasingly clear during Putin's first year in office, what was good for Putin and his friends was far more important than what was good for Russia. That is still very much the case today.

The many business-related reforms that were passed were never applied as envisioned. The assertion that there were successful institutional reforms in the 2000s is inherently false, although this remains a fundamental legend of the systemic liberals to this day—many of whom, remarkably, are still in government. They tell us that important laws were passed that lowered taxes, made it easier to start up a business, and so on. However, in my view, "institutional reforms" are not simply paper documents: the Duma rubber-stamped whatever decisions came down from on high. In a dictatorship, the formal content of the law is not important. What is important is how the law is applied. Reforms are only institutional if they have a real effect on how people live.

And just in case it wasn't completely clear where Putin was steering the country, we come to one of those symbolic moments that can say as much as the legislation and persecution. In the fall of 2000, supposedly in response to complaints from Russian athletes that the new Russian anthem from 1990 was embarrassing them because it had no words for them to sing, Putin restored the old Soviet anthem. Not with the old original Stalinist lyrics, of course, or the updated ones from 1977 I remembered all too well. That is, instead of writing new lyrics for the Russian anthem, the old Soviet song was brought back and new lyrics were commissioned for it, and from the same author. And while I surely prefer the new "Our loyalty to the Motherland gives us strength" over "Barbarian invaders we'll swiftly strike down" from 1944 or "The victory of Communism's deathless ideal," in 1977, the symbolism of bringing back the Soviet music was both obvious and shocking. The words change, but the song remains the same.

THE SEARCH FOR
PUTIN'S SOUL

Anyone who says they are still uncertain about Putin's true nature at this point must be joking, a fool, or tricking us. There is no reason to waste time on jokers or fools, however useful they may be in Putin's marked deck of cards, but tricksters must be watched carefully. For at least a decade now, those who defend Putin either have something to gain from it or they are dangerously ignorant. People can be excused for letting optimism and diplomacy blind them for a while to Putin's character and ambitions. One of the strengths, and weaknesses, of liberal democratic societies is giving the benefit of the doubt even to one's enemies. If Putin really was an anti-democratic thug, he was going to have to prove it.

And prove it he did, year after year, as his Western defenders migrated from the "ignorant" camp to the "something to gain" camp one by one. From energy companies trying to get a piece of Russia's oil reserves to European prime ministers and chancellors willing to sell out their countries' strategic interests in order to do business on the side, Putin had no trouble expanding his international fan club despite his dictatorial turn in Russia.

As soon as Putin appeared on the international stage, every foreign leader and pundit was obliged to have an opinion about him. Reviewing this literature in news reports and memoirs to-day is a master class in the art of saying something nice without saying anything at all—while also engaging in that most critical of the political sports: covering one's posterior. Needless to say, the memoirs written with the benefit of hindsight are far more critical of Putin than the contemporary comments. Only a rare few have the honesty to admit they were mistaken about Putin, or worse, that he fooled them.

The cumulative impression is that everyone knew Putin had troubling autocratic tendencies but didn't believe it was worth making an effort to challenge those tendencies early on when it would have been much easier to do so. After all, Russia's rela-tionship with the West was already on the rocks and the Russians were looking for a strongman anyway, went their logic. So why not hope for a fresh start with the new guy?

It was a difficult position for Western leaders to be in. Putin spoke the language of reform and Russia's post-Soviet difficulties very well and he had none of Yeltsin's baggage or bluster. When they looked at his actions, however, the picture was very differ-ent. I recently asked my friend and US State Department veteran Steve Sestanovich what surprised or worried him most about Pu-tin in the early days. His reply is an excellent introduction to how the West struggled to understand the new Russian leader and what this meant for Russia:

From the very beginning "Putinism" was an uneasy package that honestly we didn't know how to handle. On one side there was the reformist talk of his campaign platform, and his blunt statements about how far Russia had fallen behind the West. All that seemed encouraging. But there was also the relentless shutting-down of independent media—and the scorched earth campaign in Chechnya. That was disturbing. Who was this guy?

I remember a conversation that Madeleine Albright had in her office in the spring of 2000 with a Russian visitor, one of the most influential figures of the Yeltsin era. She asked me to sit in. He said to us, "I want you to know that Russia now has the best successor to Boris Yeltsin we could have hoped for. We also have a president who is going to be rolling back some of our democratic achievements. He is going to attack press freedoms first. Here we who support him count on you to oppose him." I came out of that meeting thinking, how are we ever going to get this right?

I could essay a few good guesses as to the identity of that Russian visitor to US Secretary of State Albright's office that day, but there is no point. The guest was quite accurate in his assessment of what Putin was going to do and how the United States should react to what was coming. And you can easily see the dilemma Sestanovich and the entire administration could see forming in front of them, especially if you remember that Bill Clinton was still the president at the time.

Clinton's last year in office was already a complicated one. He had just survived impeachment related to the Lewinsky sex scandal, which had cost him much of his remaining energy and credibility. The Internet bubble burst in February, taking with it much of the optimism around the US economy. It was also an election year and Vice President Al Gore was battling George W. Bush over Clinton's legacy.

Foreign policy was also giving Clinton a headache. Every US president attempts to solve the Israel-Palestine problem in his last year in office and Clinton was no exception. After doing little since the 1995 assassination of Yitzhak Rabin had halted the Oslo Accords peace process, Clinton arranged the Camp David Summit between Ehud Barak and Yasser Arafat in July 2000. To the surprise of everyone who knew nothing about history, no agreement was reached. A few months later, the second intifada erupted after Ariel Sharon visited the Temple Mount. In a relative footnote at the time, al-Qaeda suicide bombers attacked the USS *Cole* in Yemen, killing seventeen.

In short, Clinton was in no condition to take any strong stands against a tough and complicated new Russian leader. The White

House continued to pay lip service to healing the atrocities in Chechnya, always at great pains to emphasize that "Chechnya isn't Kosovo," in the infamous phrase of British prime minister Tony Blair. Russia was still pained by the way the United States and NATO had run roughshod over Russian interests with the Serbs in 1999, something Putin would refer back to time and time again.

In Clinton's last visit to Moscow as president on June 3, 2000, the two leaders went through the usual US-Russia checklist of nuclear issues, trade, and American missile defenses, which would become one of Putin's favorite subjects over the years. The Clinton administration deserves credit for at least mentioning civil liberties during the trip. Madeleine Albright visited Radio Liberty, whose unvarnished Chechnya coverage had gotten its journalist Andrei Babitsky abducted.

Clinton gave an hourlong interview to Echo of Moscow radio, a member of the Media-MOST group then still owned by Vladimir Gusinsky, whose outlets had declined to endorse Putin. Clinton sounded surprised when he was asked if he had ever used police powers against critics or the media. "I have never done anything like that. It's illegal!" Exactly one polite week after Clinton left Moscow, Gusinsky was arrested.

Most of Europe was also eager to paper over concerns about the bloody mess of Chechnya and embrace Putin with no conditions. Two key European leaders, Tony Blair in the UK and Gerhardt Schröder in Germany, were constitutionally averse to confrontation, especially when there were deals to be made and so much Russian money coming into the markets. (Silvio Berlusconi, who would become Putin's most eager partner and staunchest defender, would return as Italian prime minister in 2001.) Some praise must go to Jacques Chirac in France, whose government strongly protested atrocities in Chechnya at the time, even receiving a representative of the Chechen president to the National Assembly. But this victory was excruciatingly brief, and by the time Putin visited Paris in October, Chirac was toasting

Putin and his wife Lyudmila with, "It's up to us to write a new page in Franco-Russian relations." How do you say "press the reset button" in French?

By then Blair had set a high bar for pandering when he performed the bizarre maneuver of making a sudden private visit to Putin in St. Petersburg on the eve of the Russian presidential election in March 2000. Human rights organizations and the British press attacked Blair for essentially endorsing Putin while "mass executions of civilians, arbitrary detention of Chechen males, systematic beatings, torture and, on occasion, rape" were occurring under Putin's command. Instead of discussing that, Blair and his wife visited the Hermitage Museum, the Tsarist Summer Palace, and "spen[t] a night at the opera, attending with the Putins the premiere of Sergei Prokofiev's *War and Peace*." Blair declined to meet with any other candidates or opposition figures on his visit.

Two thousand wasn't my best year either. I had a spent much of the latter half of 1999 launching a massive chess website, Kasparov Chess Online, which would arrive in the world just as the dot-com bubble was deflating. It was still an exciting time, and I'm proud of some of the projects we accomplished, but like so many other Internet ventures it flamed out after just a few years. In October, I had my first world championship title defense in five years, against my compatriot Vladimir Kramnik. I arrived in London in great shape, full of ideas and confidence. A month later I had been defeated in a title match for the first time, and without winning a single game. Kramnik had outprepared me and outplayed me and I was a victim of my own complacency after fifteen years at the top. It was a crushing experience and, at thirty-seven, I briefly considered retirement for the first time. But my desire to prove I was still the best player in the world was too strong and I would retain my number one ranking until I retired in 2005.

While licking my wounds and preparing for my comeback, I had plenty of time to survey the results of Putin's first year in office. Many of the thoughts below on Putin's first year were included in a January 4, 2001, *Wall Street Journal* op-ed titled "The Russian President Trades in Fear" which, to my dismay, still holds up very well today. I would much rather be able to admit to having been wrong in that one than in my optimistic article from a year earlier. Putin has the habit of making me into an accurate prophet, but a very disappointed Russian.

Boris Yeltsin's sudden resignation on December 31, 1999, had caused me to spend New Year's Eve writing about his role in Russian history. Since the outgoing president had named his successor (which in Russian politics meant guaranteed election), I had tried to predict the parameters of Vladimir Putin's politics. Unfortunately, my forecast, based on the assumption that a young pragmatic Russian leader would strengthen democratic processes inside the country, fight corruption, and level the curves of Boris Yeltsin's uneven foreign policy, turned out to have been wishful New Year's thinking.

I could be more clear-eyed with a year's hindsight. Putin had had every advantage a new president could wish for. His public-approval rating reminded us of the euphoric early days of the Yeltsin Kremlin—and back then the polls in Russia could still be somewhat trusted, unlike today. The staggering devaluation of the ruble after the default of August 1998 gave a boost to Russia's heavily export-oriented economy. And high oil prices created a hard-currency cushion not seen by any post-Communist Russian government.

And yet this huge credit was wasted. Putin's KGB roots sadly informed a style of governance that was neither reformist nor democratic. The common thread throughout his domestic and foreign policies was his effort to trade on fear—the fears of Russians that their country was under attack from hostile external forces (Chechens, NATO, or free marketeers; usually all of the above) and the fears of Westerners that if not for a strong, pragmatic leader, Russia would again become unruly, unstable, and potentially aggressive. Fifteen years later Putin's fearmongering tactics remain very similar, and equally effective.

Instead of beating down the real hostile forces in Russia—corruption, ignorance, a bloated state—Putin cleverly changed the rules of the game. Beneath the superficial success of Russia's economy, structural change had yet to take place. Some reforms to the tax code notwithstanding, painful domestic reforms were buried by powerful *nomenklatura* lobbies, the castes of entrenched bureaucrats and officials whose power depends on powerful patrons. Corruption flourished and the judicial system remained too ineffective to be a stabilizing force. Thousands of Russian soldiers perished in the Chechen conflict, which produced uncounted victims among Chechen civilians, made ruins of Chechen cities and villages, and sent hundreds of thousands of refugees scrambling for survival. Billed as an anti-terrorist operation, Putin's continuation of the war there turned out to be another business venture for Russian generals and their Chechen counterparts.

Putin's new policies toward the Russian regions represented a strange mixture of Soviet Politburo and the tsarist ruling of the Russian empire. To preserve the privileges of power, Russia's governors caved in to central authorities, gaining in exchange enhanced powers over traditionally weak municipal self-rule. Following in their footsteps, nearly all of Russia's political leaders jumped to the support of any presidential initiative. One example: Putin's idea to resurrect the old Soviet anthem received the support of more than 80 percent of parliament members. (Typically, Putin acted as though he was only following the will of the people. "The people and I can make mistakes" was his answer when challenged about the appropriateness of bringing back the Soviet song.)

Putin's foreign policy doctrine was essentially a broader version of the domestic strategy and it showed the opportunistic way he would operate for the next fifteen years. Both could neatly be summed up as "Rogue State Management, Ltd." Wherever there were trouble spots on the world stage or "threats" to Russia's domestic tranquility, the new president was there with a lever.

He was everywhere! Worried about the North Korea nuclear program? The Russian president had already established personal relations with Kim Jong-il and was ready to play a broker role on the Korean Peninsula. Saddam Hussein, Muammar Gaddafi, or Bashar al-Assad—Putin was ready to generously offer his assistance with all of these illustrious leaders. Whether he actually ever provided any assistance of value was another matter entirely.

On the familiar turf of Afghanistan, Putin offered the Russian military machine to assist in the quest for Osama bin Laden. Never mind that this presence allowed Russia's generals to retain control of the major drug routes from Afghanistan to Europe via the Central Asian states. As the main supplier of its conventional weapons and nuclear technologies, Russia held the keys to Iran's military ambitions, and Putin would repeatedly dangle those keys just out of the reach of American and European negotiators.

Putin's early strategy was based on his reading of history. The see-no-evil Western approach to the Russian Civil War in 1919 and Britain's Munich peace treaty with Hitler in 1938 paved the way for some of the most appalling tragedies of the twentieth century. In 1961, JFK recalled US airplanes from supporting anti-Castro forces, leaving them to be massacred by the Soviet-led Cuban army. Encouraged by this demonstration of weakness, the Soviet Union shipped nuclear missiles to Cuba. The Cuban missile crisis of October 1962 brought mankind to the verge of nuclear Armageddon.

There were also more recent examples of the limits of Western involvement at crucial points in the development of a crisis: the initial passive approach to Saddam's aggressive plans in 1990 and support for Yugoslav territorial integrity in 1991, to name two. In each, the moral of the story was the same: a timely response to such dangerous games instigated by the foes of democracy dramatically reduces the price to be paid for deterrence.

Putin's December 2000 trip to Cuba to reinvigorate Russia's friendship with the Castro dictatorship demonstrated his geopolitical strategy and knack for tactics. The year after his visit, having provoked worry in Washington, Putin announced the closure of the Lourdes spy base in Cuba, the largest foreign Russian military base in the world. Putin desperately needed to cut expenses and this was another chance to gain points with the new Bush administration while doing what he needed to do anyway. Putin did the same thing by closing the Cam Ranh Bay base in Vietnam in 2002, a base that annoyed both the US and Russia's soon to be priority patron, China. (In July 2014, when Putin was looking for a way to antagonize the US over its support for Ukraine, he returned to Cuba to forgive 90 percent of the country's unpaid Soviet debt and to announce the Lourdes base would reopen.)

Despite Russia's demonstrable weaknesses, Putin would poke a finger wherever he could, especially in weak spots and old wounds. He regularly made threats and promises no one was sure he could keep, even if he wanted to. Russia still had its seat on the UN Security Council and often found an ally in China when looking to thwart American initiatives. I believe it was Andrew Ryvkin at the *Guardian* who cleverly referred to this technique of Putin's as a "photobombing" foreign policy.

Some of Putin's early maneuvers could simply be seen as shrewdly playing a weak hand, but they also reveal his real priorities in those first years. Foreign policy was secondary, almost irrelevant, to consolidating power at home. Putin couldn't afford to lose time or influence dealing with external pressure. Making friendly overtures to the powerful leaders bought him the time he needed by exchanging real power abroad for more liberty to crack down at home. Closing the military bases annoyed Russian Communists and nationalists, but they were not yet much of a political factor and Putin soon brought many of them inside the tent. With a shaky domestic economy and a broken-down military there was little more Russia could do at the time, but it was effective in making Russia look and feel like a power on the world stage again.

Nuisances left unattended grow into real problems. The surge in oil prices would continue for seven years, putting trillions of dollars at Putin's disposal; money he would use to crack down at home, buy influence abroad, and upgrade the armed forces. Strengthened by his friendly association with the leaders of the world's great democracies, Putin became the de facto leader of nations that had chafed under uncontested US dominance in the 1990s. The window of opportunity to reshape the world order to favor democracy was closing. Putin, left unchecked, consolidated power at home and then graduated from photobombing to real bombing.

The two most significant phone calls of the twenty-first century were made on September 11 and 12, 2001. Both were made by Vladimir Putin to George W. Bush after the al-Qaeda attacks on the World Trade Center and the Pentagon. The first call, just a few hours after the attacks, was received by Bush's national security advisor Condoleezza Rice in a bunker under the White House, since Bush was unreachable on *Air Force One.* This is Rice's description of the call from her 2011 memoir, *No Higher Honor:*

> I asked to speak to Sergei Ivanov, but Putin got on the phone. "Mr. President," I said, "The President is not able to take your call right now because he is being moved to another location. I wanted to let you know that American forces are going up on alert." "We already know, and we have canceled our exercises and brought our alert levels down," he said. "Is there anything else we can do?" I thanked him, and for one brief moment the thought flashed through my head: *the Cold War really is over* (italics in the original).

Putin reached Bush the next day. Here is Bush's description from his 2010 book, *Decision Points:* "When I talked to Vladimir the next day, he told me he had signed a decree declaring a minute of silence to show solidarity with the United States. He ended by saying, 'Good will triumph over evil. I want you to know that in this struggle, we will stand together.'"

With two phone calls probably totaling sixty seconds of his time and costing him absolutely nothing, Putin had cemented himself with the Bush 43 administration as a friend and ally. Bush's comment three months earlier about looking Putin in the eye and getting a sense of his soul had put him in an awkward position rhetorically, but this was real solidarity. Or at least it was accepted as real, and that perception is why it mattered, and mattered more than any actual cooperation ever could.

Putin saw the opportunity for exactly what it was. The first call was the most important despite not having reached the president. It etched Putin into the moment, into Bush's mind, and forever into history as "the first foreign leader to call Bush on 9/11." In the second call, the famously cold KGB man also spoke in terms the emotional and sympathetic Bush would most appreciate at the traumatic moment. Solidarity, struggle, a moment of silence, good and evil. . . . It was a perfect performance and it paid untold dividends over the next seven years.

Contemporary reports of the calls and their supposed significance for the new world order were no less enthusiastic. "The Cold War really was over" and now the historical enemies would unite in this new great war, the war on terror; that was the consensus. Putin was the first to realize how valuable an ill-defined, never-ending war could be, although others would catch on soon enough.

Putin jumped at the chance to portray 9/11 as another front on the war on terror Russia had been fighting in Chechnya for so many years. The fact that there was never evidence that the Chechens were a part of any global jihad didn't prevent the Kremlin from claiming so routinely. Bush and Rice had both spoken out strongly against human rights abuses in Chechnya previously, but all that ended after 9/11. Mikhail Kasyanov, who was Putin's prime minister at the time, later said that it was like a magic bullet that made all criticism disappear.

Putin's promise of aid was real in this case, and Russia had the local expertise and connections to be useful to the American effort against the Taliban. So did several Central Asian auto-crats, who were nearly as quick as Putin in realizing that this was a chance to escape US pressure over their own woeful human rights records. As al-Qaeda and the Taliban melted away in Af-ghanistan and the Bush administration's eyes turned to Saddam Hussein and Iraq, Putin resumed his usual obstructionism.

━━━━━━

What's so wrong with solidarity and cooperation against a com-mon foe after a horrible disaster? Nothing, of course. Nor do I think the Bush administration was too naïve to realize that Putin was always seeking advantages for himself. As the Bush admin-istration suggested at the time—and its members have made this clearer in their high stack of memoirs—it was a matter of prior-ities. If Putin would help with Afghanistan and provide intelli-gence that might save American lives, then that was far more important than pressuring him on civil liberties in Russia.

It's hard to imagine many people disagreeing with this stance, and if this trade-off were the only possible option I would agree with it myself. The problem is that it is a fallacy to say that any cooperation with despotic regimes requires overlooking human rights. Nor does a moral foreign policy preclude pragmatic action in a time of crisis. A moral foreign policy means your positions on certain matters are clear no matter what, and that you won't forget about them when it's convenient. This is essential because otherwise human rights and moral issues become just another chip on the geopolitical gaming table. Not coincidentally, that's exactly how Putin and other dictatorships treat human rights. They jump at every chance to gain leverage, to be helpful in the short term in order to better consolidate their repressive regimes and escape international censure. The free world must hold itself to a higher standard if it hopes to encourage others to do so.

A related fallacy says that taking human rights off the bar-gaining table weakens foreign policy, or even imperils national security. To take the bigger picture first, let us agree that the more liberal democracies there are in the world, the safer we all will be. "Never" is a risky word in any argument, but it's safe to say that healthy democracies almost never make war on each other. In the long run, policies that promote the creation and success of more democracies improve national security. It is fundamentally flawed to believe you can achieve the ends of moral policy with the means of moral compromise. You cannot go north no matter how small the steps you take south.

The year 2014 was the twenty-fifth anniversary of the death of the great Soviet physicist and human rights beacon Andrei Sakharov. Rediscovering some of his lectures and articles at the time, I was tremendously impressed with his clarity of thinking on this cloudy topic. I knew he was a very brave man, of course, and he spoke as someone who had faced the most difficult moral battles anyone could face. The "father of the Soviet H-bomb" became an important voice for nuclear anti-proliferation. A hero of the Soviet Union became its prisoner and its most effective critic. His premature death in 1989 changed the course of the world, as I very much believe his presence would have guided Russia toward a better path than what we achieved without him. Sakharov was our Mandela figure, and without him it was too easy to pretend we could put the crimes of the Soviet Union behind us without ever truly facing them.

The three years of freedom Sakharov had before his death were largely owed to just the sort of moral stand he advocated. In the October 1986 Reykjavik summit between Mikhail Gorbachev and Ronald Reagan, the American president disappointed Gorbachev by staying firm on American commitment to the Strategic Defense Initiative (SDI). A series of bold proposals and counterproposals to drastically reduce, even completely eliminate, their nuclear arsenals fell apart. Reagan was criticized by many at the time, and was even distraught about the result himself, but as we know in hindsight this refusal to give an inch in Reykjavik was a serious blow to Gorbachev's hopes to save the Soviet Union.

Gorbachev returned home realizing that if Reagan wasn't going to throw him a lifeline, dramatic reforms in domestic policies were the only way the USSR could survive. Perestroika began. One of Gorbachev's first acts, heavy with symbolism, was to call Andrei Sakharov to release him from six years of internal exile and abuse. Sakharov was elected to the new parliament in March 1989, but died of heart failure just nine months later.

Sakharov was not a pie-in-the-sky idealist. He championed universal principles but was well aware of the limitations of trying to influence the Soviet regime. When he wrote a letter entreating the US Congress to pass what ultimately became known as the Jackson-Vanik amendment, in 1973, Sakharov stayed with the matter at hand—Jewish emigration from the USSR—instead of making grand speeches. He was a crafty verbal tactician. Knowing he couldn't openly call for legislation that was seen as punitive toward his home country, Sakharov wrote that the USSR had been "developing under conditions of intolerable isolation" and made the case that the amendment would alleviate that isolation, and thus was actually beneficial to the USSR.

This was a clever and ironic maneuver, since the Jackson-Vanik amendment was devised to pressure the Soviets into relaxing emigration controls by tying them to trade relations, and was clearly a tool of isolation of the Soviet *regime*, not engagement. But it engaged the Soviet *people* and held out the hand of friendship and freedom to them directly, a critical distinction. What could be a more effective criticism of the Soviet Union than millions of its citizens yearning to be free? When discussing the amendment in his memoir, Soviet ambassador Anatoly Dobrynin wrote that any demand for emigration was "a reproof to our socialist paradise" and "that anyone should have the temerity to want to leave it was taken as a rank insult!"

Sakharov's letter to Congress also made use of the dissident tactic of "civil obedience," demanding that the Soviet government respect its own laws and international laws. "The amendment does not represent interference in the internal affairs of socialist countries, but simply a defense of international law, without which there can be no mutual trust." The anti-Putin movement adopted this tactic as well. Our protests were often based on demands that the government abide by the Russian constitution, which, in theory, guaranteed rights of assembly and speech that the Putin regime routinely violated.

Sakharov's letter was published a few days later on a full page in the *Washington Post*, leading to Leonid Brezhnev's rage and the bizarre statement that the letter was "not just an anti-State and anti-Soviet deed, but a Trotskyist deed." Ironically, the administration of Richard Nixon was just as angry about it.

Sakharov was an opponent of détente, a word he and other dissidents accurately saw as a euphemism for appeasement. His fellow dissident and collaborator Natan Sharansky summed up the resistance to their movement from the "realist" camp led by Nixon's secretary of state, Henry Kissinger, who saw the Soviet dissidents as troublemakers who threatened to derail his carefully balanced realpolitik. Sharansky writes, "Kissinger saw Jackson's amendment as an attempt to undermine plans to smoothly carve up the geopolitical pie between the superpowers. It was. Jackson believed that the Soviets had to be confronted, not appeased."

Sharansky, who has himself spoken and written with great eloquence and authority on moral policy, goes on to cite his friend: "One message [Sakharov] would consistently convey to these foreigners was that human rights must never be considered a humanitarian issue alone. For him, it was also a matter of international security. As he succinctly put it: 'A country that does not respect the rights of its own people will not respect the rights of its neighbors.'" Putin's Russia is a perfect example of this truth.

The moral policy view was shared by another well-known dissident, exiled author Aleksandr Solzhenitsyn, who used the American founding fathers to illustrate the point. At a lecture in New York City on July 9, 1975, Solzhenitsyn said, "The men who created your country never lost sight of their moral bearings. They did not laugh at the absolute nature of the concepts of 'good' and 'evil.' Their practical policies were checked against that moral compass. And how surprising it is that a practical policy computed on the basis of moral considerations turned out to be the most far-sighted and the most salutary."

If I may take the liberty of boiling Solzhenitsyn's prose into an aphorism, the most moral policy also turns out to be the most effective policy. Believing otherwise leads to false trade-offs that imperil liberty without enhancing our security.

After discussing it for years, when the United States moved to finally revoke Jackson-Vanik in 2011, I complained about the timing of the move. The borders of Russia were open, so the original purpose of the amendment was obsolete. But to lift this landmark piece of human rights legislation while Vladimir Putin was returning Russia to totalitarian darkness was a terrible idea. More than anything, the measure confronted the USSR instead of appeasing it and said very loudly and clearly that individual freedom mattered. Jackson-Vanik was a relic of a past era, but it was a powerful symbol. To repeal it without putting something in its place would send a message that either the United States no longer cared about these universal rights or that America believed Putin's Russia was not an authoritarian regime.

In 2011, I joined the global campaign launched by Bill Browder to promote the Magnitsky Act, partly as a way of replacing Jackson-Vanik by once again connecting American (and later European) foreign policy with human rights abuses in Russia. I gave several lectures in DC and wrote op-eds urging Congress and the Obama administration not to reward Putin for destroying Russian civil society and for persecuting those who exposed his crimes.

It was while preparing these speeches that I became a big fan of Henry "Scoop" Jackson, the Washington State senator who was the primary force for a moral American foreign policy in the 1970s. I could happily fill several pages with Jackson's powerful statements on why America had to live up to its ideals of freedom and democracy by actively promoting and defending them abroad. My favorite is the conclusion of his impassioned September 27, 1972, speech on the Senate floor to advocate for the amendment that would bear his name: "We can, and we must, keep the faith of our own highest traditions. We must not now, as we once did, acquiesce to tyranny while there are those, at greater risk than ourselves, who dare to resist." Jackson also quoted Solzhenitsyn's 1972 Nobel Prize–acceptance lecture, "There are no INTERNAL AFFAIRS left on our crowded Earth!"

When I was invited by Hillsdale College to speak about Russia at an event in Jackson's home state of Washington in 2013 I jumped at the chance. Hillsdale is a very politically conservative institution, the "conservative Harvard," so I enjoyed playing the contrarian by invoking Jackson as well as his fellow Democrat Harry Truman in my lecture. Both were strong advocates of using American power and moral authority to defend people around the world from dictatorship. Unfortunately, with a few notable exceptions this stance has been completely abandoned by the current generation of Democrats. After my lecture, I was approached by an elderly local woman who had clear memories of supporting Scoop Jackson (and maybe Truman!), calling him "the only Democrat I've ever voted for!"

The Bush 43 administration openly promoted a "freedom agenda" (aka the Bush Doctrine), an agenda of which Scoop Jackson would have been proud. It recommended actively promoting liberty abroad—an agenda I supported in nearly every aspect, by the way. But they still fell into the trap of inconsistency and trade-offs when it came to Russia. Rice's "the Cold War really is over" when getting off the phone with Putin on 9/11 says it all. The Cold War had been over for a decade!

This comment reinforces what Rice once said on the *Charlie Rose* show, in 2009 I believe, about "Russians being better off than in the USSR," again making it sound like the 1990s had never happened. Arguing degrees of repression in a theoretical or historical debate is one thing, but doing it when people are being jailed and killed is immoral. Even if the water has receded, a few feet is still enough to drown in, especially if your hands are tied.

Yes, the Cold War was over, but Putin was already fighting the next war and it wasn't in Chechnya or against terror. Putin's war was against Russian democracy and anyone who might stand in the way of his mission to destroy it. Those 9/11 phone calls to Bush were preemptive strikes, a targeted maneuver by Putin to undermine potential American influence against his crackdowns at home.

Unfortunately, the tactic worked quite well and it wasn't until Putin invaded Georgia in 2008 that Bush and his administration admitted as much and stiffened their policies. By then Bush was on his way out, and Russian democracy was on its deathbed and beyond the help that foreign pressure could have provided when Putin was still vulnerable at the start of the decade.

━━━━━━━

Looking at what happened inside Russia after 9/11 is also a good way to examine one of the most critical patterns of Putin's rule: the less pressure he felt from the outside, the more dictatorial he became inside Russia. Despite his tough-guy persona and rhetoric, Putin, especially in the first few years in office, was sensitive to external pressure over civil liberties and other abuses. It was only later, when the oil money was rushing in and all his potential domestic rivals had been destroyed, that Putin would go out of his way to flaunt his immunity to outside pressure.

During the dark days of the USSR the world understood that people like Andrei Sakharov, Sergei Kovalev, and Natan Sharansky were heroes for their nonviolent resistance. The modern Putin style of oppression is different and it has many advocates in the West, who refuse to distinguish between Putin's regime and the Russian people it oppresses. For example, after I appeared on a panel discussion on BBC television in 2006, on a show recorded in Moscow but of course not aired in Russia, a British viewer wrote in amazed at how freely we said things that, he said, would have led to our execution not long ago. This attitude, that Russians are "better off now" and should count our blessings, has been very harmful to our democratic cause. It validates repression with absurd relativism.

The Cold War and the threat of nuclear destruction focused everyone's attention very well on every move Russia made. As soon as that threat faded, Western leaders preferred to keep their heads in the sand and to pretend everything was fine, especially when they had more urgent and visible problems to deal with after 9/11. It took a generation of an existential threat and the real and imagined menace of Communism to produce an active moral foreign policy constituency in the West. It only took a few years for governments to outsource human rights to NGOs like Amnesty International. Human rights were no longer government business.

Meanwhile, with nothing more to worry about from the outside, for Putin the coast was clear. He continued to "consolidate" the media by shutting down independent television stations and making it clear to the press that certain topics were off limits. The harassment of the political opposition became increasingly routine. Even for established politicians and successful businesspeople it was no longer possible to oppose Putin's principles or policies without taking on considerable risk of losing your career, your freedom, or your life.

Any doubts about the Putin regime's willingness to spill blood were erased in the 2002 hostage crisis at the Dubrovka Theater in Moscow. A small army of Chechen militants took nearly 850 people prisoner for four days in what would become known as the "Nord-Ost" siege, for the name of the Russian musical play that was being performed on the night the attack began, October 23.

There is no need to recount every grisly detail of the siege, especially since nearly every detail is disputed. I especially wish to avoid any appearance of sympathy with the hostage-takers despite my focus on the response of the government. Terrorists are scorpions; we know their character and condemn them for it in good conscience. The true nature of the Putin regime, however, was still somewhat in doubt and is the subject under discussion.

The hostage-takers demanded the immediate withdrawal of all Russian troops from Chechnya and said that they wanted to "bring a taste of what is happening in Chechnya every day to the people of Moscow." They were heavily armed with machine guns, grenades, and improvised explosive devices. The first night they released a large group of hostages, between 150 and 200, mostly children, women, Muslims, and foreigners. The next day, the terrorists accepted negotiations with quite a few public figures, including opposition politician Boris Nemtsov and journalist Anna Politkovskaya, the long-time war correspondent in Chechnya.

Despite every conversation resulting in the hostage-takers confirming that they were there to die, they released another large group of hostages, mostly foreigners. On the twenty-fifth they accepted food, juice, and medicine from the Red Cross for the hostages. The leader of the terrorists, Movsar Barayev, gave interviews to the press, reiterating their willingness to die and that "we are here with the specific purpose to end the war." With such a large and well-prepared group of experienced militants and so many hostages, it looked like it was going to be a long standoff.

I was still playing chess professionally then, and at the end of October I was leading the Russian team to the gold medal for the last time at the Chess Olympiad in the Slovakian city of Bled. The news of the hostage crisis at the Dubrovka Theater shocked all of the participants, but most of all, of course, those of us who were born in the Soviet Union, and for whom the word "Chechnya" was more than just an unfamiliar geographical term.

I remember well the heated discussions of this tragic situation in the halls, when, looking one another in the eye, people would express the same hope: "The government won't decide to use force. They won't let hundreds of people die."

On the morning of the twenty-sixth, Russian special forces stormed the theater. Simultaneously, a toxic gas was pumped into the theater. According to survivors and a frantic call from one of the hostages, they and the terrorists were aware of the gas and some of the assailants had gas masks. The terrorists fired at the Russian forces instead of executing the hostages, another fact that only became clear later and that was contrary to initial official reports that most of the dead had been shot.

All 40 hostage-takers were killed in the raid along with over 130 hostages: all but one of the hostages were either killed by the gas directly or indirectly by choking to death while unconscious and failing to receive medical care in time. Local hospitals were flooded with poisoned hostages they didn't know how to treat because officials refused to identify the type of gas that had been used. Immediately afterward, officials said the attack was provoked by the terrorists beginning to execute hostages. This statement was revealed to be false only a few days later when other officials said the attack had been scheduled and planned since the first day.

Despite controversial reports that at least one of the hostage-takers was a known FSB operative, there is no way to know if the special forces knew that most of the explosives in the theater were fake, meaning the gas wasn't really necessary before storming the theater. The Russian parliament declined to launch an investigation of the government's conduct during the siege, which is why there are so many unknowns to this day. The government's policy after the attack, of stonewalling or spreading misinformation about every facet of the operation, makes it difficult not to think the worst.

It is easy to cynically state that a few hundred innocents killed at the hands of the government is better than seven hundred dead at the hands of the terrorists. The mathematics are unassailable, even in hindsight. There is no way to know what would have happened in the alternate universe where negotiations continued. The only clear conclusions to come out of the horrible tragedy were that the war in Chechnya wasn't over, no matter what Putin said, and that the Putin regime had no greater regard for human life than the terrorists did—a point it seemed the government wanted to make.

If the goal of the rapid and lethal intervention was partly to send a deterrent message to the Chechens that there would be no negotiations, it was a failure. Two years later, the Beslan school siege would result in an even more violent and catastrophic military intervention against Chechen hostage-takers, resulting in the deaths of nearly 400 people, including 186 children. (One result that can definitely be attributed to the Nord-Ost siege was the end of NTV's quasi-independence after Putin was displeased by its coverage of the crisis.)

Putin's Russia does not consider the deaths of its own citizens to be a serious crime worth punishing guilty officials for. And yet, having quietly decorated and promoted many of the organizers of the storming of the Dubrovka, the Putin regime went even further by issuing an indefinite indulgence to carry out any of his immoral orders. Lacking organized pushback from society, the soft authoritarian regime spent the next decade gradually acquiring the sinister traits of a fascist dictatorship.

Sandwiched between the Nord-Ost and Beslan sieges was another landmark event in establishing the reach and grasp of state power in Putin's Russia. On October 25, 2003, the richest man in Russia, Mikhail Khodorkovsky, was arrested and charged with fraud. In a scheme that would prove to be a model for future behavior, Khodorkovsky was convicted and his company, the oil giant Yukos, was promptly chopped up. Its assets were handed out to companies controlled by Putin's closest buddies at bargain prices. By the time he was released in December 2013—after a second conviction that was even more preposterous than the first—Yukos was no more.

As I said earlier, it was difficult to find many Russians willing to express sympathy for the oligarchs who had made their vast fortunes in the early days of privatization. If the saying "Behind every great fortune is a great crime" is valid in the relatively transparent market economies of the West, it was doubly the case in the Wild, Wild East of 1990s Russia and the other post-Soviet republics. They were considered unscrupulous entrepreneurs at best and predatory criminals at worst, people who had used political connections to amass untold fortunes while average Russians struggled. And, well, this was largely true, with the caveat that it's not constructive to blame the winners for breaking the rules in a game that had barely any rules at all.

Many of the persecuted oligarchs were also Jewish, and anti-Semitism, usually subtle and coded in the media and unsubtle and blatant from the nationalists, played a part in the political and public campaigns against them. That a few of Putin's most loyal oligarchs were also Jewish blunted this line of criticism of his purges, but there is no question their Jewishness was used against those who came under state attack.

This revival of another wretched Soviet tradition hardly surprised me. Despite my many sporting successes for the glory of the motherland, my ethnicity occasionally appeared in questions about my loyalty during my rivalry with Karpov, who was of "respectable stock" from the Russian heartland while I was an "explosive combination." And ever since I became active in the anti-Putin movement there has been a dramatic increase in the number of times I have been called "Weinstein," my father's name, which was exchanged for my mother's Armenian family name not long after my father died when I was seven.

I'm not sure if it's ironic or just disgusting that the anti-Semitic chorus has again raised its voice beyond the gutters of the Russian Internet since Putin began his war on Ukraine in 2014. According the Kremlin propaganda, the new democratic government in Kyiv is full of fascists and Nazis, as is required of anyone declared an enemy by Russia, and Russia had to intervene to protect not just ethnic Russians, but the poor Jews! In response, the Association of Jewish Organizations and Communities of Ukraine responded with an open letter saying that President Putin's assertions about the rise of anti-Semitism in their country "did not match reality" and "might have confused Ukraine with Russia where Jewish organizations registered a rise of anti-Semitism last year." Ukraine also has a lower rate of anti-Semitic incidents than nearly every other country in Europe where statistics are recorded, including France and Germany. At the same time, stories about Jewish oligarchs "running Ukraine" have also been part of the Kremlin information war, apparently in an attempt to provoke Russia's fellow Slavs in Ukraine to rise against them, or perhaps to let Putin do the job.

These perverse accusations led to a good joke that I heard when I visited Ukraine in December 2014. A Russian watches the TV news and calls his Jewish friend in Ukraine in a panic: "Moishe, is it true your country has been taken over by fascists and ultranationalists?" "Yes," his friend replies, "our synagogue is full of them!"

Returning to 2003 and Khodorkovsky's arrest, it was presented as a blow for justice, reform, and as retribution for the common people. In fact, it was exactly the opposite on all three counts. At the time there weren't many questions as to why it was happening in 2003 if the crimes he was accused of had supposedly taken place in the 1990s. A look at Khodorkovsky's activities both inside and outside of Yukos at the time reveal the true motives behind his captivity.

Gusinsky and Berezovsky had been chased off two years before Khodorkovsky's arrest. They were both clear and present dangers to Putin due to their media holdings and political influence. In contrast, Khodorkovsky and his oil company had thrived in the first years of the Putin government. Yukos was ready to exploit the skyrocketing price of oil to modernize the aging Soviet equipment it had inherited and to explore international partnerships on its way to becoming the first big Russian company to become a true multinational. That was a threat in Putin's mind. He intended to ensure that the oil and gas giants, the "national champions," were brought under firm Kremlin control.

Khodorkovsky also committed the sin of getting personally involved in politics and civil society, but wasn't interested in swearing loyalty to Putin or trying to compete with him directly in the rigged electoral game. Khodorkovsky founded the Open Russia foundation and used it to sponsor dozens of programs and charities across the country, all while refusing to seek approval for these activities from the Kremlin. He even publicly declared he would support opposition candidates, while other oligarchs brought briefcases of cash to support Putin's political causes.

Russian State University for the Humanities (RSUH) is very big in Moscow and they signed a contract with Yukos to receive $100 million in educational grants. After Khodorkovsky was arrested, there was suddenly new leadership in RSUH, and the new rector refused to take the money from Yukos. Khodorkovsky wasn't using his wealth to buy a soccer club in England, as Putin's buddy Roman Abramovich had done with Chelsea in June that year. Even if he was doing it partly to bolster his reputation, Khodorkovsky was investing in Russia and those activities made him a legitimate threat to Putin; legitimate in all ways. He wasn't a man Putin could control.

Khodorkovsky was also brave to the point of foolhardiness in 2003. His close business partner, Platon Lebedev, was arrested in July and there was no doubt who was next on the list. Another partner, Leonid Nevzlin, did the sensible thing and moved to Israel that summer. Instead of leaving or shutting up, Khodorkovsky spoke up even more, publicly condemning the state and corporate corruption that was holding Russia back. The consequences were swift.

Khodorkovsky was indicted on multiple charges of fraud and tax evasion, the usual Kremlin recipe. His trial was all the proof one needed to demonstrate that in the Putin regime, no proof was needed. Ironically, Yukos had paid more taxes per barrel than any other oil company. I'm not going to claim to be an expert on all the financial and legal chicanery that went on during the 1990s a few dozen people into billionaires in record time. But obviously there were few clean hands by the standards of the rest of the world. Khodorkovsky wasn't much different from all the others at the start. But his vision of the future was so radical that he scared not only Putin but the other oligarchs as well. Had every oligarch been audited and held accountable, it could have been a healthy result for law and order in Russia.

Instead we got a show trial against someone Putin considered a personal enemy. If the ad hoc nature of the trial itself wasn't enough to confirm this, it's worth noting that many other people connected to Yukos and the trial itself were also persecuted and prosecuted. Lebedev was convicted and abused in prison despite his serious illnesses. Many other Yukos employees were harassed and indicted. Even Khodorkovsky's defense lawyer, Karinna Moskalenko, was threatened with disbarment by the prosecutor's office. This became Putin's mafioso calling card: if you challenged the power vertical, he wouldn't just go after you and your assets, but also your employees, friends, family, and anyone who dared to defend you.

In May 2005, Khodorkovsky and Lebedev received nine-year convictions and were shipped off to prison camps. The response from the rest of the world was the typical mush about "concerns" over the independence of the Russian judiciary and "urging" the Russian government to observe certain standards. By that point I'm pretty sure the US State Department had a form letter expressing such concerns so it could just change the names and dates each time. That letter, usually issued quietly by a low-level functionary, would get a lot of use in the coming years as Putin's abuses in Russia piled up while the leaders of the free world insisted on embracing him warmly on the international stage.

The arrest led to a revealing comment from America's ambassador, Alexander Vershbow: "We hope there will be a fair trial, *by Russian legal standards*" (italics added). When a *Financial Times* article criticized the practices of the Russian attorney general's office, the Russian minister of finance, Vice Prime Minister Alexei Kudrin, waved it off, saying there were "some irregularities."

For American and Western European ears, I should enumerate some of these "irregularities": searching the offices of lawyers who had visited their clients in jail; searching the offices of members of parliament; and refusing to allow members of parliament to visit Khodorkovsky in prison, which is a violation of Russian law. No court in the West would have accepted the case for trial because the evidence was obtained by illegal means, but these are "Russian legal standards." As with two of Putin's favorite expressions, "managed democracy" and "the dictatorship of law," it's a revealing oxymoron.

Along with removing a critic and rival from the scene, Khodorkovsky's jailing was a warning to the rest of the Russian business world: play by the Kremlin's rules and don't get into politics. It was a turning point in Russia where the government officially gave up pursuing lawbreakers and instead became one itself. It changed from rogue elements with connections in high places abusing government power to steal into a state-run initiative of harassment, incarceration, and looting that targeted anyone disloyal to the center.

The Khodorkovsky-Yukos case represented how Putin's regime established ties between property rights and power. Unless you were in power you couldn't control your property. This in turn signaled the end of democracy. The elections were doomed to be rigged by those in power because if they lost political authority they would lose their assets. By the time 2004's presidential election came around, Putin and his cronies had far too much to lose to risk getting kicked out of the Kremlin by something as easily fixed as a vote.

The end of Russian democracy and total centralization of power in the Kremlin were in some ways only side effects of the mundane primary objective of theft. The attack on Yukos was aimed at redistributing property in favor of the oil companies owned by Putin's cronies. Instead of old-fashioned socialist redistribution it was "take from the rich and give to the richer." The entire vast nation was turned into an asset vacuum cleaner that used the power of the state to pull everything to Moscow, where it was portioned out to well-connected allies and companies with just enough invested in the government to keep people out of the streets and the country from falling apart. There was always plenty in the budget for propaganda and internal security forces.

The brutally efficient way Yukos was broken up and plundered made the rigged auctions and shell company tricks of the 1990s look amateurish. The Putin regime would soon expand its consolidation operation to the rights of the average citizen. If the Russian people had been robbed in the 1990s, the 2000s showed us that we hadn't seen anything yet.

In 2009, with Khodorkovsky's scheduled release on the horizon, Russian prosecutors filed new charges against him, even more absurd than the original ones. He was essentially charged with stealing all the oil he was accused of not paying taxes on the first time. Cases like this are why Russians and other people living under totalitarian regimes do not see the writings of Gogol, Kafka, and Bulgakov as fantasy, or even surrealism. The state doesn't have to be logical or reasonable, it just has to achieve its ends.

Dictatorships feel the perverse need to fulfill protocol, to have elections and trials even though the conclusions are foregone. The free world often rewards these charades with willing suspension of disbelief. Russia pretends to have elections and a justice system; the free world pretends right along with it, occasionally expressing their token concerns, citing irregularities, and attempting to shame the shameless. The dictators take all these background noises as the pathetic appeasement they are, and go on about their business. In the words of that keen observer of the totalitarian mindset, the Polish writer Stanisław Jerzy Lec, "Is it progress if a cannibal uses a fork?"

The conclusion of the new trial in November 2010 gave Khodorkovsky the opportunity to present a powerful closing statement on the state and future of Russia. It stands as an indictment of its own, an important document for the moment and for history. I will quote only a few parts of it here, but please find and read the entire document.

I am ashamed for my country.

I think all of us understand perfectly well—the significance of our trial extends far beyond the scope of my fate and Platon's, and even the fates of all those who have guiltlessly suffered in the course of the sweeping massacre of YUKOS, those I found myself unable to protect, but about whom I remember every day.

Let us ask ourselves: what must be going through the head of the entrepreneur, the high-level organizer of production, or simply any ordinary educated, creative person, looking today at our trial and knowing that its result is absolutely predictable?

The obvious conclusion a thinking person can make is chilling in its stark simplicity: the siloviki bureaucracy can do anything. There is no right of private property ownership. A person who collides with "the system" has no rights whatsoever.

Even though they are enshrined in the law, rights are not protected by the courts. Because the courts are either also afraid, or are themselves a part of "the system." Should it come as a surprise to anyone then that thinking people do not aspire to self-realization here, in Russia? . . .

Hope—the main engine of big reforms and transformations, the guarantor of their success. If hope fades, if it comes to be supplanted by profound disillusionment, who and what will be able to lead our Russia out of the new stagnation?

I will not be exaggerating if I say that millions of eyes throughout all of Russia and throughout the whole world are watching for the outcome of this trial. They are watching with the hope that Russia will after all become a country of freedom and of the law, where the law will be above the bureaucratic official.

Where supporting opposition parties will cease being a cause for reprisals.

Where the special services will protect the people and the law, and not the bureaucracy from the people and the law.

Where human rights will no longer depend on the mood of the tsar. Good or evil.

Where, on the contrary, the power will truly be dependent on the citizens, and the court—only on law and God. Call this conscience, if you prefer.

I believe this is how it will be.

I am not at all an ideal person, but I am a person with an idea. For me, as for anybody, it is hard to live in jail, and I do not want to die there.

But if I have to, I will not hesitate. The things I believe in are worth dying for. I think I have proven this. . . .

Everybody understands that your verdict in this case—whatever it will be—is going to become part of the history of Russia. Furthermore, it is going to form it for the future generation. All the names—those of the prosecutors, and of the judges—will remain in history, just like they have remained in history after the infamous Soviet trials.

Your Honor, I can imagine perfectly well that this must not be very easy at all for you—perhaps even frightening—and I wish you courage!

The words and dreams of a great man, regardless of his past sins or future activities. Five weeks later the judge extended the sentences of Khodorkovsky and Lebedev to 2017, which was later reduced to 2016 and then to 2014 on appeal. But of course Putin had yet more tricks up his sleeve.

Three years later Putin surprised everyone, including Khodor-kovsky, by announcing he would release him, which he did on December 20, 2013. It was likely due to a combination of German pressure—Khodorkovsky thanked former German foreign min-ister Hans-Dietrich Genscher for helping get him released—and Putin's desire to tidy up loose ends before the Winter Olympics began in Sochi in February 2014. Khodorkovsky was drawing too much attention, having been declared a prisoner of conscience by Amnesty International, and the Olympic spotlight would have found him a tempting subject. It was also an opportunity for Putin to play his favorite role of the "good tsar," showing mercy to a fallen foe and a chance to get something in exchange for the small cost of releasing him eleven months early. It also avoided the hassle of starting a third trial that would have to have escalated to crimes no less than murder to justify keeping Khodorkovsky imprisoned.

Khodorkovsky left for Germany on the day of his release to visit his ailing mother. He kept a fairly low profile upon his re-lease, but soon he began to speak against the Putin regime and has reopened his Open Russia program.

There is no epilogue to Khodorkovsky's story yet. As with so many Russian stories it cannot be written as long as Putin is still in power. As for Khodorkovsky's ambitions, when I spoke with him not long after his release he said to me, quietly but confi-dently, "If I were Putin, I wouldn't have let me go."

7

OFF THE BOARD, INTO THE FIRE

There's a very long list of things my hardline Soviet Communist grandfather would never have believed would happen in my lifetime, and my becoming the world chess champion doesn't even make the top ten. Giving a speech on the importance of the "American values" of capitalism and liberty to a black-tie audience in Manhattan would be high on the list. So would my wearing a borrowed cowboy hat in Wyoming after lecturing there on the threat of Putin's Russia.

The likely number one, however, took place on August 17, 2012, at a Moscow courthouse. Not even inside the courthouse, but outside of it. That was the day I was arrested and beaten by the police while protesting the sentencing of Pussy Riot, three members of the all-girl punk group that had been convicted for filming an anti-Putin protest inside a Moscow church. Their sentencing took place in the same Khamovnichesky court that had held Mikhail Khodorkovsky two years earlier. Unable to enter through the crowds, I was standing on the sidewalk outside speaking calmly with a few journalists when the police came over and literally carried me away.

By law, at least in theory, the police must inform you why you are being arrested. There were plenty of witnesses and even videos of my abduction to show that this never occurred. Instead, they show me, legs in the air, shouting, "What am I being charged with? What are the charges?" (As well as a few other words I would not want to explain to my young daughter.) They tossed me into the waiting police van and closed the door. But they didn't lock it.

In a move I would quickly have reason to regret, I opened the door and demanded again to know what I was being charged with. My words were cut off as I half fell and was half pulled into the crowd of police outside the van. My arms were twisted and several blows came down on my head and body before they lifted me back into the van and shoved me to the rear. A Dutch photographer was quick enough to get a shot of me pinned against the van's back wall by two cops, one bending my arm back and the other pressing against my throat.

I'm not objective about the events of that day, but I don't think that an unarmed chessplayer nearing his fiftieth birthday presented such a terrible danger to an army of riot police. But while I was bruised for quite a while, I was lucky not to suffer any permanent injuries. My spirits were good enough that I could laugh when the police issued a statement that they were considering filing additional charges against me for biting one of the officers on the finger during their assault. Well, I am by no means a vegetarian, though as I turned fifty a few years ago I have had to cut back on red meat on my doctor's advice. But I can say with certainty that were I to acquire a taste for human flesh, the way Bengal tigers are said to do, I would never bite anyone under the rank of general.

Knowing that witnesses and all the evidence in the world wouldn't matter inside a Moscow courtroom, my friends and I scrambled to put together as many photos, videos, and testimonies as we could and publish them widely before my trial. Our hope was that if it was totally obvious to the entire world that I had violated no laws, it would be too embarrassing for the government to convict me on the charge of "participating in an unsanctioned protest." That was 2012, when it was still possible to imagine the Putin government being embarrassed by anything.

I am quick to admit that in this I am very lucky to have a certain amount of protection because of my famous name. The news picked up the story and footage of my arrest and beating in minutes. Thanks to the power of social media, thousands of people could help my friends and me look through hundreds of photos and videos to prove that the officer who was going to charge me with assault had sustained the cut on his finger before my arrest. Unlike most Russians who are abused the way I was, or worse, I had the knowledge and resources to mount a defense campaign.

A week later, after nine hours in court, I was acquitted, to the great surprise of everyone, myself included. It was perhaps the first time ever in Putin's Russia that someone had been acquitted of those charges in this way. Ironically, I had been one of the first people convicted under the draconian new anti-protest laws when I was jailed in 2007. In my statement after the acquittal, I thanked everyone who had expressed support and pleaded for those who had helped me to stay involved.

"This result demonstrates the power of solidarity. This means more than donating money and your voice. It is a shared sentiment that freedom matters everywhere, for every person, not only in your own country. It is essential to stay involved. The more people pay attention and bring pressure from the grassroots, the more cases will end the way mine did and the fewer will result like that of Pussy Riot. Find a way to make a difference!"

It was a bittersweet moment. While I was being arrested outside along with many others, the three young women of Pussy Riot inside had been sentenced to two years in a prison colony. Maria Alyokhina, twenty-four, Nadezhda Tolokonnikova, twenty-two, and Yekaterina Samutsevich, thirty, had performed a brief "punk prayer" inside Moscow's Cathedral of Christ the

Savior, mentioning Putin by name in the video they made of it. You can guess which was considered the greater act of sacrilege by the authorities.

I will return later to these brave women and their story, which became an international sensation that confirmed to the entire world that Putin's regime had finally turned the corner into irredeemable despotism. But I would first like to explain how I came to be standing outside that courthouse and getting tangled up in ways that my grandfather would never have believed. For that we have to leave Moscow and go to Spain, and to the small Andalusian town of Linares.

In 1975, at the age of twelve, I played my first individual major chess event at the national level, the Soviet Junior Championship. Ten years later in Moscow, I became the youngest world champion in history. On March 10, 2005, in Spain, I played my last serious game of chess, winning the Linares supertournament for the ninth time. After three decades as a professional chess player, the last two of them as the number one ranked player, I decided to retire from professional chess.

It's not common, in our age, for someone to retire while still at the top, but I'm a man who needs a goal, and who wants to make a difference. My accomplishments and contributions are for others to judge, but I felt that I was no longer playing an essential role in chess. Reclaiming the unified world championship was out of reach due to political chaos in the chess world, so I was reduced to unfulfilling repetition.

I have always set ambitious goals, and I have been lucky enough to attain most of them. I had achieved everything there was to achieve in the chess arena. Meanwhile, I felt that there were other areas in which I could still make a difference, where I could set new goals and find new channels for my energy. My new projects included working on a book on decision making, called *How*

Life Imitates Chess, as well as lecturing and giving seminars on the topic. Another was the promotion of chess in education. The US-based Kasparov Chess Foundation (KCF) supports chess in schools and was working on a blueprint for teaching chess in the classroom. KCF now has centers in Brussels, Johannesburg, Singapore, and Mexico City with thousands of participating schools and a wide variety of events and training programs.

But all of those things could have waited. The main reason for my decision to leave chess when I did, and so completely, was of course politics—or what passes for politics in an autocracy. For many years I had been an ardent supporter of democracy in Russia, and at times I had participated in political activities back when campaigns and endorsement and votes actually mattered. By 2005, those things were already largely irrelevant to the power structure in Russia, but we still had hope. Thanks to a two-term limit, 2008 would bring the end of Putin's presidency unless he wanted to risk becoming a pariah by abrogating the constitution completely. With Putin not running, our goal was to build enough momentum to bring a real democratic alternative to the ballot. I wasn't sure how it was going to happen, but I knew I had to try.

As I wrote in the *Wall Street Journal* a few days after my retirement, my plunge into political activism was also personal:

> When I look at my eight-year-old son I know the stakes of this battle could not be higher. Many well-off Russians are sending their children to foreign schools, far from the dangers created by our authoritarian leadership. Most of my compatriots don't have that option. I do, but I want my son to grow up in the country in which he was born. I don't want him to have to worry about military service in an illegal war or fear the repression of a dictatorship. I want my son to live in a free nation and to be proud of his country, and of his father. . . . There are millions like me in Russia who want a free press, rule of law, and fair elections. My new job is to fight for those people and to fight for those things.

My son Vadim is now eighteen and has no knowledge of what it is like to live in a free Russia. What he has seen of democracy and civil liberties he has learned the way I did as a teenager in the USSR, from traveling abroad and reading foreign news. At least he and his generation have the Internet, which is still relatively free in Russia. Two thousand five was also the year of my third marriage, and my wife Dasha continues to play a vital role in making this new phase of my life a happy and successful one. Our daughter Aida and our son Nickolas were born in and are growing up in a free country. But contrary to how I'd envisioned it, that country is the United States, not Russia.

A few months prior to my retirement, the Beslan school hostage crisis shattered the global conscience. I place it here, outside of the chronology, because of the impact it had on my decision to leave chess and because of my personal experience visiting the site in 2005.

On September 1, 2004, Chechen separatists took over eleven hundred hostages at a school in North Ossetia, a Russian region of the Caucasus bordering Georgia. It was what we call "First Bell" or Knowledge Day in Russia, the start of the school year when parents and other family members accompany their children to school. Thirty very heavily armed terrorists took over the school and herded the hostages into the gymnasium. The building was mined with IEDs (real ones, unlike at Nord-Ost) and a number of hostages were killed immediately.

The situation outside the school was predictably chaotic as disparate groups of regional and national security forces and political forces formed separate camps. Parents and other locals refused to leave the area, many because they wanted to prevent any military assault on the school. Memories of Nord-Ost were still very fresh. The attackers' demands were similar to 2002: withdrawal of Russian troops from Chechnya and recognition of

Chechnya's independence. Other reports said they also wanted United Nations recognition of Chechnya.

They also demanded the presence of several regional politicians to serve as intermediaries, including North Ossetia's president, Aleksander Dzasokhov, and the president of neighboring Ingushetia, Murat Zyazikov. Neither came to Beslan. Dzasokhov later said that he had been forcibly prevented from coming and told *Time* magazine that "a very high-ranking general from the Interior Ministry told him, 'I have received orders to arrest you if you try to go.'"

Anna Politkovskaya, the journalist who was one of the few Russians trusted by the Chechens, was also invited. She immediately set off for Beslan but never arrived. Her tea was poisoned during the flight, putting her into a coma, and after coming close to death at a small medical center in Rostov, she returned to Moscow to recover. She stated that she was sure Russian security forces "neutralized me because they knew I was going to Beslan to set up talks."

The despised leader of the Chechen independence movement, Aslan Maskhadov, who had a $10 million price on his head from Moscow, condemned the attack through his spokesperson and sounded ready to personally intervene. Dzasokhov later said he had been ready to negotiate, to offer safe passage for the terrorists and to release some imprisoned guerrillas, in order to guarantee the safety of the remaining hostages.

But as negotiations proceeded, the unthinkable happened. On September 3, the third day of the siege, two explosions shook the gymnasium just as medical workers were approaching the building to remove twenty bodies outside. One of the explosions started a fire on the roof. It is telling that, once again, there are a half-dozen theories about the origin of the initial explosions and even more about the ensuing battle, half of the theories coming from the same officials, whose stories changed by the day. Some reports said that some of the terrorists' explosives had gone off by accident. Others that a Russian sniper had shot a terrorist, who detonated a bomb.

Equally confusing is the story of who was in charge outside, and who gave the orders to fire and when; and it has all only become more confused as time has passed after the tragedy. As firing of all kinds erupted inside and outside the gym full of hostages, many of them too dehydrated and weak to run, armed civilians participated alongside of local police forces and heavy military weaponry. It was deadly chaos. Only after neighbors found enormous shell casings on nearby roofs was it revealed that the military had fired flamethrowers into an auditorium full of children.

Practically as soon as the battle ended, bulldozers and dump trucks came in and removed debris (including some physical remains) and everything else that could have served as evidence with which to reconstruct the horrific events of the day. Testimony from locals outside and hostages inside repeatedly contradicted government statements about what had happened. The authorities were caught lying so many times about easily disproven claims, such as which weapons were used and when, that it is impossible to accept any of the official statements in good faith.

Unlike after Nord-Ost, there would be several official investigations of Beslan. One was completed in 2005 by a member of the North Ossetian parliament who was actually on the scene the day the school was stormed. The federal parliament produced two extensive reports in 2006. The Duma was controlled by United Russia, Putin's party, and the report controlled by their representative became the official one. Another was done by Yuri Savelyev, a member of the Russian nationalist party Rodina ("Homeland") and, coincidentally, a recognized expert in rockets and explosives. Savelyev's report fits much better with the testimony of witnesses outside and the hostages inside regarding the weapons used and the order of events. He and another colleague filed their own report and refused to sign off on the official one. In 2007, they broke their silence to denounce it as a cover-up.

A 2006 article by David Satter looked at the evidence:

The version of the Beslan parents was supported by the findings of a commission of the North Ossetian parliament. In a report released on November 29, 2005, the commission concluded that the first explosion was produced by either a flamethrower or grenade launcher fired from outside the building.

The most powerful confirmation, however, came in a report released by Yuri Savelyev, a member of the federal parliamentary investigative commission and a highly regarded expert on the physics of combustion. . . . Savelyev concluded that the first explosion was the result of a shot from a flame thrower fired from the fifth story of a building near the school at 1:03 P.M. The second explosion came 22 seconds later and was caused by a high explosive fragmentation grenade with a dynamite equivalent of 6.1 kilograms shot from another five story building on the same street. The explosions, according to Savelyev, caused a catastrophic fire and the collapse of the roof of the school gymnasium, which led to the deaths of the majority of the hostages. The order to put out the fire did not come for two hours. As a result, hostages who could have been saved were burned alive.

Even the casualty records are disputed and were regularly revised for weeks. Interviews with family members and survivors helped fill in the gaps in the official records. The final numbers are 334 dead hostages, of which 186 were children. Over 700 were injured, with many requiring amputation from shrapnel wounds. Many of the killed had burned alive. The number of hostage-takers alive and dead is also disputed. The official numbers say that there were 32 attackers of whom one survived. Other reports say that there had been many more attackers, up to 75, many of which escaped. At least 10 members of the security forces were killed, including all three commanders of the assault group.

Credit for the Beslan attack was claimed by Chechen commander Shamil Basayev, who claimed he had originally hoped to target a school in St. Petersburg or Moscow. He also promised more such attacks, although this did not happen and Basayev died in an explosion in 2006. Once again, no one was sure exactly how he died, but in this case precious few people cared as long as he was dead.

The government was the only available target for the grieving Beslan families. You cannot demand answers from terrorists or from the dead. The one captured hostage-taker, Nur-Pashi Kulayev, was quickly convicted and disappeared into the Russian prison system. The Mothers of Beslan advocacy group supported appeals for him in the hopes of gaining information about the attack during a public trial. While they got very little government accountability for their tears, there were indeed dramatic governmental reforms after Beslan. Unfortunately, there was little in them related to greater security for the Russian people.

Just two weeks after Beslan, Putin brought together all eighty-nine of the nation's governors along with his cabinet and spoke with them for several hours. After some opening remarks about Beslan, Putin said that the response had to be greater effectiveness and unity in the government and the country. Those words are red flags to any student of dictatorship, and this was no exception. Aside from a few natural responses about strengthening laws against terrorism and expanding law enforcement powers, the reforms were mostly aimed at further diminishing democratic institutions in Russia. Putin would now directly appoint governors: no more elections. Duma elections changed from a direct vote to a party vote, guaranteeing that established figures could keep their seats forever. Other reforms attacked the foundations of the democratic system, making it more difficult to register parties. Of course these things had nothing to do with Beslan or fighting terrorism or anything other than Putin seeing an opportunity to centralize more power into the Kremlin.

As a famous individual I had advantages in my new career as a political activist, but there were also drawbacks. I was vulnerable to accusations of being a neophyte, a dilettante who wouldn't be interested in the hard work of building alliances and listening to people. I was determined to refute this perception as much as possible, and so I set off on a tour of Russia to hear what people thought of the state of the country and to spread the message that a different future was possible.

Also keep in mind that the opposition had no access to the mass media, so we had to be seen in person to be heard at all. A famous sportsman quitting to enter politics would have been big news just about anywhere else. But since my views about Putin were already well known, my retirement was covered from a purely sporting perspective. In contrast, several famous Russian hockey stars, including Fetisov and Tretiak, publicly endorsed Putin and received a great deal of attention. There was no chance for me to get on TV and discuss my future plans. Not only wasn't I invited in the first place, but live television had been practically banned already in order to avoid any awkward political content.

I knew it wasn't going to be easy. I was already being subjected to the attention every prominent opposition figure received from the Kremlin's thugs and their proxies. These groups ranged from annoying pranksters to dangerous criminals, all on the payroll of those in charge of making sure any grassroots opposition movement met with immediate and heavy resistance. Youth groups we nicknamed the "Putin-Jugend" after their Nazi predecessors assigned members to heckle and throw things at me wherever I went to speak, and of course these groups were never bothered by the police. In April, I was bashed over the head with a wooden chessboard by a young man at an event in Moscow. And of course I was followed and recorded by more serious members of the security services at all times. That is the confidence of a totalitarian system.

But I wasn't going to give up so easily. It was also important for me to travel because of how heavily the opposition world was weighted toward Moscow, and to a lesser extent St. Petersburg. Putin's support was far greater outside of Moscow's ringed roads, out in the regions where the economy was more likely to depend on the government and where the only sources of news were the Kremlin-controlled television channels. I visited Vladivostok in the east, sixty-two hundred kilometers from Moscow. I went to Rostov and then south into the Caucasus. I spoke with fishermen, railway workers, and students. And I went to Beslan.

I first visited the cemetery, or the New Cemetery as the people there had named it. There was still construction going on there, ten months after the attack. I put flowers on every grave, walking through the cemetery in a state of shock from my proximity to the horror that the people there had suffered and that the survivors lived with every day. Imagine row after row of graves, each with the same date of death: September 3, 2004, September 3, 2004, September 3, 2004, over and over 330 times. Row after row with birth dates in the 1990s and some in the 2000s. It was the most painful day of my life.

Yet I was still supposed to give a lecture in town, so I collected myself as best I could and headed to the local house of culture. Unsurprisingly, it was locked tight and every light was off. This was part of the usual package of harassment and isolation employed against opposition figures. Everywhere I went, meeting halls would suffer strange electrical or plumbing problems. Our plane wouldn't be allowed to land and buses would arrive at incorrect locations. Locals would let me know they'd been threatened with harm or the loss of their jobs if they came to hear me speak. And so I spent much of my speaking time outdoors, in the street, or in lobbies and restaurants. Even hotels would be instructed not to give rooms to my colleagues and me.

This happened even in Beslan, a place that deserves peace and sanctity if any place in the world does. For that reason I had not wanted to come, but at the same time I felt that I had to. I had come not to make politics, but to see with my own eyes what had happened and to demonstrate to the families that they had not been forgotten. At this point, nearly everyone in the town blamed the government for caring more about killing the hostage-takers than about saving the lives of the hostages.

The Russian journalist Masha Gessen accompanied me on this leg of my journey and I have relied on her reporting of my visit to refresh my memory, which is clouded with the overpowering emotions of the day. Here I will quote two paragraphs directly, the first to show I'm not exaggerating about the juvenile harassment and the second to save myself more pain from reliving that day.

Just then there was a dull pop, very much like a gunshot, and the women screamed, "Garry! Garry!" The crowd broke apart, and Kasparov's bodyguards tried awkwardly to shield him while keeping people from trampling one another as they rushed off the porch. A young man standing in front of the building suddenly turned out to be holding a bottle of ketchup, which he shook up violently and then aimed at Kasparov and squeezed. Kasparov was presently covered: his head, his chest, and the right shoulder of his blue sport coat were stained sticky red. The porch was empty now, save for a clear plastic bag with several broken eggs in it that had hit the roof of the porch before landing: that was what had made the popping sound. An old woman, now standing on the porch with us, tried to clean Kasparov's face with a handkerchief. "Forgive me, forgive me," he whispered over and over again, apologizing for triggering this incident in a town that was already racked with grief.

The crowd gradually grew as people came out of the houses and apartment blocks along the way to join the walk. They entered the school through the giant holes in the walls of what used to be the gymnasium. . . . Kasparov gasped when they entered the gym. "Oh my God, oh my God," he whispered. The women walked to different corners of the ravaged space and began wailing; soon the hall was filled with a muffled, high-pitched sound. Kasparov looked stricken: his eyes red, mouth slightly open, head shaking. It was clear that it would not be possible to talk in here: the room was oversaturated with grief. He asked to be given a tour of the school, and as he walked around with the crowd, now grown to about a hundred people, he talked: "I'm walking through this school, thinking: How do people in Moscow keep walking around, saying something, continuing to lie? Among them, there is someone who gave orders to open fire. If that person gets away with it, we will all be to blame!"

Only three officials were ever charged over what happened at Beslan. All three were local North Ossetian police officers who were charged with negligence for failing to protect the school. Perhaps this was too much of a blatant scapegoating attempt even for Putin's court system to abide, and all three were granted amnesty. When the judge read out the amnesty order in May 2007, a group of twenty-five Mothers of Beslan tore the courtroom to pieces. These officers could hardly be responsible for what had happened, but they were the only targets for the impotent rage of the families.

Here is the point at which we can divide our horror and our rage between those responsible—the terrorist murderers who conceived and carried out the attack—and those who failed in their duty to protect and preserve life, and then refused to produce accountability for those failures. Confusion, mistakes, outrages, and cover-ups occur in democracies, too, of course. Humans make mistakes and humans do horrible things all over the world; sadly, we seem unable to prevent these kinds of tragedies from happening in the first place (although one can certainly argue that treacherous dictatorships engender more of them). That is why the true test of our institutions is how they deal with these mistakes and horrors in order to maintain trust and to improve security.

The government's responses to the terrorist attacks of Nord-Ost and Beslan and their aftermaths showed very clearly that the Putin regime had no interest in the trust or security of the Russian people. Putin didn't need the people or their trust. He had oil, gas, total control of the media and the government, and a rapidly expanding security force. Unlike in democracy, where the loss of people's faith in your administration will quickly cost you your job, being a dictator means never having to say you're sorry, or even addressing the matter at all.

━━━━━━━━

The other motive for my tour was to make contact with other activists around the country. There were still various opposition parties and NGOs struggling against the tide of increasing marginalization. As Putin tightened his grip on civil society, no group was too small or too innocuous to be persecuted. Ever on the alert against any "orange" activity, laws were passed to limit foreign funding of NGOs and increase penalties against protestors. A raft of "anti-extremism" bills went into effect, with language so broad and vague that any criticism of the government could be deemed an extremist act punishable by years in prison.

The Russian opposition in 2005–2008 was a jumble of liberal politicians, young activists of every political stripe, and old-guard human rights defenders. Several of the politicians were exiles from the Putin regime, including his former prime minister, Mikhail Kasyanov, and economic advisor Andrei Illarionov. There was Boris Nemtsov, Yeltsin's former first deputy prime minister, and Vladimir Ryzhkov, one of the last surviving independent members of the Duma. Georgy Satarov was a former Yeltsin aide who had helped devise the new Russian constitution. It was a fairly high-powered group, except for the fact that they had absolutely no power at all.

In a more distant orbit there were the "respectable" politicians of the Yeltsin era attempting to cling to relevance in government as the political world crumbled beneath their feet. These individuals, such as former presidential candidates Irina Khakamada and Grigory Yavlinsky, founder of Yabloko, attempted to protest from within while staying on passable terms with Putin. Eventually they realized Putin had no use for them, even as loyal opposition. Some gave up and joined in Putin's democracy charade for a paycheck while others left politics altogether. A few joined us, the "radical" or "external" opposition.

The human rights cadre included the venerable Ludmila Alek-seeva, a founding member of the Moscow Helsinki Group and one of the few Soviet dissidents still active. Lev Ponomaryov was one of the founders of Memorial, one of the first Russian human rights organizations. The "young guns" included Sergei Udaltsov, chairman of the Vanguard of Red Youth, and Ilya Yashin, a charismatic youth activist on the liberal side. A few years later, former Yabloko activist Alexei Navalny would become the most prominent of us all thanks to his sharply penned and well-researched anti-corruption investigations finding a huge audience online.

Then there were the "disloyal nationalists," the radicals, mostly young, in groups like writer Eduard Limonov's National Bolshevik Party, which wasn't as scary as the name sounds by the 2000s but was still more than enough to scare off the respectable liberal opposition. But they were willing to march against Putin for free speech and fair elections, and that was all that mattered to me.

Along with the politicians, organizers, and activists, there was substantial intellectual firepower in the wings among the countless Russian writers, journalists, and intellectuals disillusioned by Russia's return to the dark ages. There were big-hearted lawyers who put in long hours of work defending protesters and activists from spurious charges for little or no pay. Political directors and staffers of a dozen or more opposition groups, including my own United Civil Front, organized protests, training seminars, and communications for little reward and often at great personal risk.

And suddenly there I was, dropped into the middle of it all. I felt at home with the liberals like Nemtsov and Illarionov, who shared my ideology of free markets and close alignment with Europe, but I also realized that opposing Putin had little to do with ideology by that point. It mattered little what policies you supported when there was no chance at all you would ever have the chance to enact those policies. The debates among opposition candidates were a like a group of starving people with no money arguing about what to order at a fancy restaurant.

I was already doing what I could on the international front, speaking at foreign parliaments and writing editorials to encourage Western leaders to increase pressure on Putin over his anti-democratic ways. In Russia, I hoped to use my lack of political affiliation as an advantage by bridging the gaps between the disparate opposition movements so we could unite to solve the only problem that really mattered: ending Putin and Putinism as soon as possible.

Before my retirement from chess I had helped form the Free Choice 2008 Committee and the All-Russian Civic Congress in 2004. I had been observing the dissatisfaction of the activists on every side. They were tired of dancing to Putin's tune while watching their party leaders cut deals for paltry handouts. The Civic Congress was conceived as a unifying platform, but it fell short when forces from both sides of the political spectrum were unable to leave behind the Yeltsin-era civil war mentality and work alongside their traditional ideological adversaries.

In 2005, I formed my own small social action group, the United Civil Front, so that I would have a base of operations and an address. Then I went to work looking for strategic targets on the calendar where the opposition could make the most of our limited resources. It was important to have clear targets so we would have a feeling of purpose and hope. When I first entered the Russian political arena full time I had the feeling of sitting down to a chess game in progress, with my side facing checkmate in every variation. I realized that our first task as an opposition force was simply to survive, to get out our message that we existed, that we opposed the Putin regime, and that we were fighting. With every television station and major newspaper under state control it was a very difficult task, as you might imagine.

The opposition was in disarray, but the one thing we all had in common was the knowledge that democracy was our only salvation. By 2006, liberals, human rights activists, even the

Communists—they all agreed that given a choice in a fair election the Russian people would reject Putin's attempt to turn our country back into a totalitarian state. It didn't matter that afterward we would be sitting on opposite sides of the floor. First, we needed to rescue our democracy.

This mixing of opposition groups also had several positive side effects. The leftists and those still mourning the Soviet Union came to recognize the importance of liberal democracy and political freedom now that they'd been cut out of the picture. The liberals, which in Russia refers to those like me who favor free markets and an open, Western-leaning society, learned to accept the need for the social and economic stability programs touted by the left. Unity not only stiffened the opposition to the Putin government, but has also clarified and advanced the specific goals of our member groups. This isn't to say it was all one big happy family, but at least we were together.

To have a real impact, I felt it was necessary to unite on the core issue: you were either working with the Kremlin or dedicated to dismantling the regime. It was clear by then that there was no way to change anything from the inside. In a way, the key step was taking a page out of the Kremlin's book: a nonideological movement. Forces from across the political spectrum came together. In the summer of 2006 we had enough momentum to go on the offensive, hosting The Other Russia Conference in Moscow in advance of the July G8 meeting in St. Petersburg.

The conference brought activists from all over Russia to share ideas and support. We also invited the international media and speakers from all over the world who were not afraid to speak strongly for democracy in the shadow of the Kremlin. My Civic Congress co-chairs and I wrote countless letters of invitation, calling in favors and twisting arms when necessary. Eventually many prominent figures contributed statements of support, although few G8 administrations had the courage to openly endorse us. We chose the name, The Other Russia Conference, to tell the world that the stable, democratic Russia Putin presented was not reality.

The Russian authorities made efforts to harass us at every turn; perhaps we were irrationally optimistic, but we interpreted this as a sign of progress: "We have them worried!" If this was truly a measure of success, I should have been proud that my humble United Civil Front offices were raided by security forces a few days prior to our December 16 march in Moscow, the first of a series of what would come to be called the Marches of Dissent. Thousands came out in peaceful support under our WE DO NOT AGREE banners despite being outnumbered five to one by police.

It led to an even bigger, and more contentious, March of Dissent in St. Petersburg on March 3, 2007. We had been denied permission to hold a rally, but over six thousand people defied the ban in the largest political protest of the Putin era up to that time. That sounds like nothing, I understand, but this was new and risky and it felt like a huge wave of energy. In democratic nations protests are routine, the kind of thing you might do for social reasons even if you don't feel all that strongly. But coming into the streets in Russia was associated with upheaval and drama. It was a very big step for many of the participants to "radicalize" in this way, walking through OMON (paramilitary riot police) cordons and chanting "Russia Without Putin!"

I felt the energy in the street myself, and I liked it. When I retired from chess I had been told that my fiery, undiplomatic nature would make me unsuitable for political activism. I had been an aggressive attacker at the chessboard and a fractious rebel in the chess world even as world champion, so how would I adapt to the subtle world of alliances and diplomacy? I would like to think that in this I met politics halfway. I listened and showed respect— half the time. I argued with colleagues who knew more and who had done more because I wanted to push us all to a new level of cooperation and confrontation. It was the only way to build a coalition that included former prime ministers and would-be Bolsheviks. And when it came time to march, my loud voice and hard head were assets, not weaknesses.

Dozens of marchers were attacked by the riot police that day, the only violence that took place. It is very important to emphasize that over the course of many marches there was not a single overturned car or broken window. But of course we were demonized in the Kremlin-controlled media as violent hooligans and reporters focused their cameras on the few clashes with police, which of course had been provoked by the police. Around a dozen Marches of Dissent took place around the country in 2007, though the majority were in Moscow and St. Petersburg.

In November I was arrested at a Moscow rally and this time I was sentenced to five days in jail under the new anti-demonstration laws. It wasn't pleasant, although I enjoyed a relatively gilded jail experience, signing autographs for guards and police and generally hearing a lot of sympathetic remarks from them about the state of the country. My old world championship rival, Anatoly Karpov, even tried to visit me. He was turned away, but I very much appreciated the gesture, especially since we were as opposed politically as we were in chess style.

As the rift between Putin's Russia and the governments of the United States and Europe became increasingly apparent, a new diplomatic position was slowly adopted in the West. After years of trying to accept Putin as an equal, they started to say that while there are differences between Russia and our Western counterparts, these differences are minor, and "within an acceptable range," in the words of one European Union official.

For me and for a dozen of my colleagues marching for democracy, that "acceptable range" was 120 square feet. That's the size of the jail cell several of us occupied for five days as punishment for "disobeying the orders of a police officer" at the opposition rally in Moscow. That was the charge a Moscow district court added after the fact, a charge not mentioned in the handwritten testimony of the arresting officers. That was the least conspicuous of the many illegal aspects of my arrest and trial.

After our rally of several thousand people we attempted to meet up with another group, a meeting led by well-known human rights leader Lev Ponomaryov. From there we intended to deliver a petition of protest to the office of the Central Election Committee (CEC). The police had blocked the underground pedestrian passageways so we had to cross the broad street instead and we were soon blocked by more police. When they moved in close I spoke with commanding officer Major General Vyacheslav Kozlov, whom I had met previously. He warned us to turn back, saying we would not be allowed to approach the CEC offices. I offered to send a small delegation of twenty people to present the petition and he again told us to turn back, which we did.

Of course it is inaccurate to say that the police commander was the one in command. FSB officers in plain clothes were clearly in charge even at the police station, and the arrest itself was as choreographed as the trial to come. When the OMON special security forces pushed in past everyone else to arrest me, we could all hear "Make sure you get Kasparov" on their walkie-talkies.

From the moment of our detention we were not allowed to see our lawyers, even when we were charged at the police station. Three hours into the trial the judge said it would be adjourned to the following day. In fact, ten others were held at the police station without counsel for two days prior to their hearings instead of being released, as should occur with an administrative charge. But the judge then left the bench and returned to say that we had misheard her and that my trial would go forward! No doubt another example of what we call "telephone justice" in Russia. That is, before delivering the verdict the judge goes into the back not to deliberate, but to get a phone call from the powers that be.

As in the street and at the police station, the FSB agents and OMON forces were in control. The defense was not allowed to call any witnesses or to present any materials, such as videos and photos taken of the march and the arrests. After this show trial was over I was taken to the police jail at Petrovka 38 in Moscow and there the procedural violations continued. Not with regards to my treatment, which was respectful and as hospitable as a small box with metal furnishings and a hole in the floor for a toilet can be. I wasn't allowed a phone call and all visitors were refused access. Even my lawyer Olga Mikhailova and Duma member Vladimir Ryzhkov were forbidden to visit me despite having the legal authority to do so.

My other concern was food, since it was out of the question to consume anything provided by the staff. (Nor would I fly Aeroflot unless I had no choice, and when I did I brought my own food and drink. Paranoia long ago became an obsolete concept among those in opposition.) On Sunday, thanks to growing external pressure, they allowed me to receive food packages from my mother.

In a fitting conclusion, even my release was handled illegally. Instead of letting me out at the jail into the waiting crowd of media and supporters, many of whom had themselves been arrested and harassed while picketing, I was taken secretly to the police station where I was first charged. From there I was taken in a colonel's automobile all the way to my home. This may sound like good service, but it was obvious the authorities wanted to avoid the festive scene that would have occurred outside the jail upon my release.

When I had been arrested the previous April and fined $40, some people poked fun at the trivial amount. And five days in a Moscow jail is hardly the worst fate that can be imagined. Some commenters even suspected I wanted to provoke my own arrest for publicity, a chessplayer's far-sighted strategy. First off, the penalty was not the point: the principle is. Were we to have the rule of law in Russia or not? Secondly, I had no intention of becoming a martyr or in leading an opposition movement from prison. I had no illusions before, and afterward I could confirm it was not a pleasant place to be even for a brief stay.

And this was not chess, with its cold-blooded calculations. This fight was about honor and morality. I could not ask people to protest in the streets if I was not there with them. At the rally on Saturday I had said our slogan must be "We must overcome our fear" and I was obliged to stand by these words.

It is also essential to point out that these arrests were only the tip of the iceberg, the small fraction that can be seen. Such things were taking place all over Russia on a daily basis. Opposition activists, or just those who happened to be in the way of the administration, were being harassed and arrested regularly on false charges of drug possession, extremism, or the latest trend: for owning illegal software.

During my five days in jail I had the chance to speak with many of the "ordinary consumers" of Kremlin propaganda. They were generally sympathetic and showed no signs of believing the many lies the Kremlin and the youth groups it sponsors have spread about the opposition. For them I was still the Soviet champion and the idea that I was an "American agent" sounded as ludicrous as it was.

So why was Mr. Putin so scared if things were going so well? He is, or at least he still was back then, a rational and pragmatic person, not prone to melodrama. He knew the numbers, so why the brutality and heavy-handed campaigning if he knew he and United Russia were going to win easily?

The answer is that he was becoming aware of how brittle his power structure was. Instead of sounding like the tsar, high above the crowd, he was starting to sound like just another paranoid autocrat, surrounded by enemies. As George Bernard Shaw wrote, "The most anxious man in a prison is the governor."

And so demagoguery it was and demagoguery it continued to be. A violent pro-Putin youth group, Nashi, had already released a poster celebrating Putin's "crushing victory" in the December 2 parliamentary elections. It also warned against the "enemies of the people of Russia," me included, attempting to disqualify the results. These terms jibed nicely with Putin's own rhetoric of threats and fear. The ground was being prepared for greater oppression.

Along with our public protests, The Other Russia also worked to establish a communications structure beyond the long reach of the Kremlin. We wanted to expose the daily crimes that were occurring and get this information into the hands of the right people in the press and the governments of the free world. As time went on, and the crackdown on civil society and public protest got stronger and stronger, I came to believe that this international outreach was the most promising avenue of attack. Putin benefited so much from economic and political engagement with the West that he was practically unassailable at home. Cutting him off from that foreign embrace was a priority. Unfortunately, the leaders of the world's so-called leading democracies showed little interest in living up to their professed ideals.

———

Nothing symbolized the lack of will to stand up to Putin than the G8 Summit in St. Petersburg held July 15–17, 2006. The G7 was an informal club more than an organization, a strangely casual group that brought together the leaders of the seven largest industrialized democracies. (Britain, Canada, France, Germany, Italy, Japan, and the United States, as first met in 1976. Brazil and India have recently surpassed Canada and Italy on the GDP list, or will soon.) Boris Yeltsin was invited as a sort of honorary participant in 1998, a tradition that was carried over to Vladimir Putin. Russia hosting the meeting in 2008 represented its official entry into the club, which many had already called the G8 for years, instead of the awkward "G7+1."

This was the cast: Stephen Harper, Canada; Jacques Chirac, France; Angela Merkel, Germany; Romano Prodi, Italy; Junichiro Koizumi, Japan; Tony Blair, United Kingdom; George W. Bush, United States. The president of the European Commission was also usually invited and José Manuel Barroso attended the summit at the Constantine Palace in St. Petersburg.

It was a grand moment for Putin and an equally dismal one for Russian democracy. Putin loved to see and be seen with these paragons of democracy as much as he despised what they supposedly stood for. It had been a nice gesture to invite Yeltsin to attend in the hope that all additional engagement with Russia would be good for everyone. Instead, the G8 became a perfect example of the damage engagement could do. Putin exploited every photo-op and handshake to flaunt these democratic credentials at home. It was difficult enough to communicate the opposition message of democracy to the Russian people without their seeing Putin on every channel being embraced as an equal by the leaders of the free world. I maintained the hope that the West would find its collective backbone and that Russia's participation would be made contingent on our actually being a democracy. Instead, it took Putin's invasion of Ukraine in 2014 to finally get Russia's G8 membership suspended.

While President Bush was in St. Petersburg he met with a group of Russian NGO directors and opposition figures—at least that's what he was told. Whether he was aware of it at the time or not, every participant at the meeting had to be preapproved by the Kremlin. No one there would have qualified as an opposition figure in my view, except perhaps for Alekseeva, the former Soviet dissident. As ridiculous as this charade was, Tony Blair wouldn't even make that token effort and was upstaged by his wife, Cherie Blair, who met with a group of NGO heads during the summit.

When observing the West's conciliatory dealings with Russia during this period, a favorite quotation from Winston Churchill comes to mind: "However beautiful the strategy, you should occasionally look at the results." For five years, President Bush had been talking about maintaining an open dialogue with Putin and about how hard he had worked to convince the Russian leader that "it's in his best interest to adopt Western-style values and universal values." This sounded quite reasonable, but we didn't have to go on theory. We had a track record to scrutinize and it was already clear that the strategy of discourse and appeasement toward Russia had failed.

By the time the G8 meeting came around it was long past time for Western leaders to take a harder stance if they wanted their rhetoric about the promotion of democracy in Russia to have any credibility at all. The St. Petersburg summit offered the visiting heads of state a chance to see for themselves how bad things had become. If they had opened their eyes, the leaders who talked so often about receiving "mixed signals" from Russia would have seen that the only mixture that mattered was that of oil, money, and power.

Bush and Europe's leaders apparently believed it was best to disregard such things for the sake of getting Russia's cooperation on security and energy. But as Solzhenitsyn foretold, this cynical and morally repugnant stance has also proved to be an entirely ineffective one. Just like old times, Moscow has become an ally of troublemakers and anti-democratic rulers around the world. Nuclear aid to Iran, missile technology to North Korea, military equipment to Sudan, Myanmar, and Venezuela, making friends with Hamas; this was how Putin repaid the West for keeping its mouth shut about human rights in Russia for eight years.

And yet the G7 leaders refused to acknowledge that it was absurd to come to Russia for help with Iran, North Korea, or Hamas when the high energy prices the Putin administration required to keep its hold on power were driven by the tension that comes with every North Korean missile launch and each Iranian nuclear threat. Russia continued to block UN sanctions against these rogue states; the only mystery is why the West continued to treat Putin's Russia like an ally.

The Europeans in particular also pretended Putin was some species of democrat in order to promote their nations' business interests. Of course you can expect leaders to support their national interests to a certain extent. In France, Sarkozy promoted Renault and the oil company Total. In Germany, Merkel promoted Mercedes-Benz and Deutsche Telekom. And of course Berlusconi promoted the companies of . . . Berlusconi.

Economic engagement kept the billions coming in that Putin needed to expand his repression at home. Instead of these contacts helping to liberalize and modernize Russian business practices, the flow went the other way. Russia's biggest export was corruption, not oil or gas. Putin's oligarchs invited foreign investors and companies to partake in sweetheart deals in Russia and cleaned their money in London and New York IPOs with the help of eager Western banks and politicians looking for a cut.

After six years of crackdowns going uncontested, Putinism was reaching its second stage. When he took power in Russia in 2000, the question was "Who is Putin?" By 2007 it had changed to "What is the nature of Putin's Russia?" His regime had been remarkably consistent throughout its stay in power, and yet foreign leaders and the Western press still acted surprised at Putin's total disregard for their opinions. He needed Western aid and support while he was still consolidating power in Russia. When that task was completed, Putin no longer had to pretend to care about what the rest of the world thought.

Again and again we heard cries of "Doesn't Putin know how bad this looks?" When another prominent Russian journalist was murdered, when a businessman not friendly to the Kremlin was jailed, when a foreign company was pushed out of its Russian investment, when pro-democracy marchers were beaten by police, when gas and oil were used as political weapons, and when Russian weapons and missile technology were sold to terrorist sponsor states like Iran and Syria, "Putin has blundered!" the Western leaders would say. Why? Unlike politicians in democracies, Putin didn't care how something looked as long as he knew nobody would act to stop him. The only image he cared about was looking tough at home, and blatantly ignoring the feeble complaints of Western leaders only helped him in that regard.

What needed to be asked was what sort of government would continue such behavior, and where such a government would end up. Putin's regime operated on an amoral scale, something entirely different from that of the Western nations struggling to understand what was happening behind the medieval red walls of the Kremlin. By 2007, I had become a full-time Putin explainer in my articles and lectures.

Putin's government during that transitional period from fragile democracy to full-blown dictatorship was unique on the historical timeline. It was part oligarchy, with a small, tightly connected gang of wealthy rulers. It was partly a feudal system, broken down into semiautonomous fiefdoms in which feudal payments were collected from the serfs, who had no rights, and the smaller lords pay the bigger lords. Over all of that there was a democratic coat of paint, just thick enough to earn Russia entry into the G7 and keep the oligarchy's money safe in Western banks.

As I wrote in the *Wall Street Journal* in July 2007, if you really wished to understand the Putin regime in depth, you had to go to the bookstore. Not to buy the works of Karl Marx or Adam Smith. Nothing by Montesquieu or Machiavelli, although the author you are looking for is of Italian descent. Skip Mussolini's *The Doctrine of Fascism* for now (but hold on to it for later . . .) and the entire political science section. Go directly to the fiction department and take home everything you can find by Mario Puzo. *The Godfather* trilogy is a good place to start, but do not leave out *The Last Don, Omerta,* and *The Sicilian.*

The rise of Vladimir Putin and his St. Petersburg clan has been described as Machiavellian, but it is better described by the achievements of Don Vito Corleone: the web of betrayals, the secrecy, and the blurred lines between what is business, what is government, and what is criminal—it's all there in Puzo's books.

A historian could look at the Kremlin in 2007 and see elements of Mussolini's corporate state, Latin American juntas, and Mexico's pseudodemocratic Institutional Revolutionary Party machine. A Puzo fan sees the Putin government more accurately: a strict hierarchy, extortion, intimidation, a tough-guy image, a long string of convenient deaths among leading critics, eliminating traitors, the code of secrecy and loyalty, and, above all, a mandate to keep the revenue flowing. In other words, a mafia.

As long as you are loyal to the capo, he will protect you. If one of the inner circle goes against the capo, his life is forfeit. Once Russia's richest man, Mikhail Khodorkovsky, wanted to go straight and run his Yukos oil company as a legitimate corporation and not as another cog in Putin's KGB Inc., he quickly found himself in a Siberian prison, his company dismantled and looted, and its pieces absorbed by the state mafia apparatus of Rosneft and Gazprom. Private companies were absorbed into the state while at the same time the assets of the state companies moved into private accounts. State and corporate power merged. It became a perverse combination of Adam Smith and Karl Marx in which the profits were privatized and the expenses were nationalized.

Alexander Litvinenko was a KGB agent who broke the loyalty code by fleeing to the UK. Even worse, he violated the law of omertà by going to the press and even publishing books about the dirty deeds of Putin and his foot soldiers. Instead of being taken fishing in the old-fashioned *Godfather* style, in November 2006 he was killed in London in the first recorded case of nuclear terrorism. The Kremlin refused to hand over the main suspect in the murder and eventually Britain shelved the case, only to reopen it in 2014 when Putin's invasion of Ukraine finally persuaded the British that engagement with his regime was no longer a possibility.

For seven years, from Putin's election until the moment of the Litvinenko assassination, the West tried to change the Kremlin with kind words and compliance. They believed that they would be able to integrate Putin and his gang into the free world's system of fair trade and honest diplomacy. Instead the opposite happened. The Kremlin was not changing its standards; it was imposing them on the outside world. The mafia corrupts everything it touches. Bartering in human rights begins to appear acceptable. As an added benefit, Putin and his cronies received the stamp of legitimacy from Western leaders and businesses while making those same leaders and businesses complicit in their crimes.

With energy prices so high, the temptation to sell out to the Kremlin was almost an offer you couldn't refuse, and many didn't even try. Schröder and Berlusconi could not resist and found themselves entirely compromised. Then we saw the spectacle of Nicolas Sarkozy boosting the interests of French energy company

Total in the Shtokman gas field. There, too, we tried to warn everyone that foreign companies and investors were not immune. Shell found this out when the Kremlin pushed them out of the Sakhalin 2 gas fields in 2006, and British Petroleum learned the hard way in 2008 when its CEO fled Russia in fear for his life. Of course both of them soon came running back for more. If you want to invest in KGB Incorporated you should remember that they are very, very active shareholders.

In case you have forgotten the tale of Gazprom, Gerhard Schröder, and his dear friend Vladimir, its details are worth recalling. Not because anyone should care how Schröder spends his days, but because of the Kremlin methods the deal exposed to the world without an ounce of shame. What was one more small step for Putin was one giant leap for corruption in the West. When Putin invaded Ukraine in 2014, it was deals like these and thousands more that made it nearly impossible for Europe to disengage itself from Russia, let alone lead an effective boycott.

Just days after being pushed out of office as chancellor of Germany in November 2005, Schröder made sure he wouldn't add to the high rate of unemployment he left behind. He accepted a top post with Russian energy giant Gazprom, which was the company in charge of a controversial gas pipeline project that Schröder actively supported as chancellor. The dubious ethics of this move and the speed with which it was made led to many obvious questions about whether or not Schröder abused his office to set up the deal, especially as he was trailing badly in the polls for most of the campaign against Angela Merkel. But the groundwork for Schröder's new job was laid out in advance as part of a well-organized operation that brought in capital before personnel.

Matthias Warnig, as head of Russian operations for Germany's Dresdner Bank, first brought in a deal to purchase 33 percent of Gazprombank in August. (Dresdner also helped the Kremlin pick the bones of Yukos.) Accordingly, Warnig was given a top position at the North European Gas Pipeline Company. Finally everything was ready for the arrival of Mr. Schröder.

The deal also kept everything in the family as Warnig was a spy for the East German secret police, the Stasi, at the same time Putin was running agents for the KGB in Dresden. As Putin himself has said, there is no such thing as a former KGB agent. In reality this was the lesser story: that Germany's most powerful politicians and businessmen could be purchased the way a Russian oligarch might buy an aristocratic Bavarian estate to gain entry to high society. The larger and darker picture was how Putin has made the nation's energy resources the center of his ruling clique. They completely erased the lines between public and private power and assets.

In Russia everyone was wondering, "Does the state run Gazprom or does Gazprom run the state?" Putin made a priority of tightening the unholy bond between his regime's internal and external goals and the company that provides most of the natural gas to Central and Eastern Europe. They are not state-run companies; they are the state. Gazprom's chairman at the time was Dmitry Medvedev, who had recently been named first deputy prime minister. Putin's deputy chief of staff Igor Sechin headed the other Russian energy goliath, Rosneft. But that wasn't the only reason Rosneft wasn't investigated for its shady takeover of Yukos's prime asset, Yuganskneftegaz, in a bogus auction. Taking *la famiglia* literally, Sechin's daughter was married to the son of then–Russian attorney general Vladimir Ustinov.

So Schröder didn't just join a Russian company; he joined the Putin administration. For Schröder's price, Gazprom and Putin's regime bought legitimacy in the eyes of the West. Deals like that one also provided Putin with priceless propaganda fodder. He could trumpet this coup of putting a former German chancellor in his pocket while at the same time the state-controlled media presented it as an example of how the West was only after money and oil.

Totalitarian regimes everywhere love to tell their citizens that for all their professed interest in democracy and human rights, Americans and Western Europeans are just as corrupt as their own leaders. It does tremendous damage to the pro-democracy cause in Russia, and elsewhere, when a figure like Schröder, the former leader of the third-largest industrial democratic nation, enthusiastically allies himself with authoritarian thugs. Using energy as a political weapon is a tried and true tactic, and the hiring of Schröder allowed Gazprom to act with even more impunity.

This was the new Kremlin strategy: to co-opt and quiet the West by recruiting prominent individuals. When everyone is guilty, no one is guilty, goes the logic. We already had seen the price paid for these see-no-evil policies on civil liberties and in Chechnya. With this new tactic, Western leaders had to resist the calls of their bank accounts, not only the calls of conscience. Everyone was engulfed in the same toxic cloud of oil, gas, politics, intimidation, and repression.

Those of us in the Russian opposition had been saying for a long time that while Putin was our problem, soon he would be the world's problem. Our warnings went largely ignored. After years of rumbling warning signs, when the threats materialized in 2008 in the form of Russian tanks entering Georgia, the leaders of the free world were totally unprepared to deal with it. Engagement had failed but they didn't know any other tricks to try. Expelling diplomats and limiting official visits was not going to have an impact. My suggestion then was the same as it is today: simultaneously curtail engagement and use the economic leverage of existing engagement to pressure its beneficiaries in Russia.

Ironically, Putin's elites liked to keep their money where they could trust in the rule of law, and after the G8 lovefest in St. Petersburg, Putin and his wealthy supporters had every reason to believe their money was safe in the West. Limiting that access, or even threatening to do so, would have had a dramatic deterrent effect. Instead, it was business and appeasement as usual. The central myths of engagement are that it (1) liberalizes the unfree states and (2) provides leverage over them if they don't liberalize. The first has proven false. The second has failed because the free world refuses to exploit its leverage the way dictatorships are so eager to do.

I have never called for a boycott of Russia, by the way. The free world also does big business with China, Saudi Arabia, and other autocracies without providing their leaders with democratic credentials the way they did with Putin. And it's hard to imagine the elites who run another belligerent rogue state living in luxury in Western capitals. The minions and the oligarchs are loyal to Putin because he is the *capo di tutti capi* and he offers them protection. They can do as they like in Russia, and as long as they stay loyal they can get rich and take their money to America, to London, wherever. This is why I pushed for legislation to cut off that pipeline and damage Putin's ability to protect his gang—and it's why Russia fought so hard to prevent such legislation from gaining ground.

There was no reason to cease doing business with Russia. The delusion was that it could ever be more than that. The mafia takes and takes, and it only gives with many strings attached.

8

OPERATION
MEDVEDEV

Boris Yeltsin died on April 23, 2007. I already eulogized him and his legacy in chapter 5, but I would like to focus on an overlooked aspect of his passing. As was likely required by both his health and his peace treaty with Putin, Yeltsin had kept a very low profile after leaving office on December 31, 1999. The only time I can recall his name in the news after that was when he and Mikhail Gorbachev publicly, if mildly, criticized Putin's power-grabbing reforms after Beslan.

Putin also seemed to uphold his side of their bargain. No member of Yeltsin's family, or his extended "Family" of allies and cronies, has ever been pursued by Putin's government. Although Yeltsin stayed out of the limelight, I think his presence weighed on Putin's mind. Putin may have become the Godfather, but Yeltsin was the founding father of Russian independence and democracy. Destroying Yeltsin's legacy completely while the man was still alive might have been risky even for Putin. With Yeltsin gone, another of the thin restraints holding Putin back from totalitarianism was severed. Yeltsin had limited himself to two terms and surely would have expected his successor to leave power as well.

This mattered because in 2007 Putin was faced with the biggest decision of his life. His second term as president was coming to an end the next year, and according to the Russian constitution he couldn't run again. The election would take place on March 2. First there was the matter of the Duma elections on December 2, 2007. It was a foregone conclusion that Putin's United Russia Party would win overwhelmingly, but we did our best to track the "irregularities" that took place anyway. The art of rigging an election, you see, lies in making the election itself entirely meaningless. You don't have to worry about who votes, or even who counts the votes, if you control the entire process and who appears on the ballot to begin with.

United Russia, with the sitting president at the top of its list, enjoyed every imaginable advantage, both legal and illegal. Opposition groups, including our own Other Russia coalition, were denied access to the ballot by meticulous new election laws designed for exactly that purpose. The alternatives left for voters on Sunday were mostly Putin supporters or parties that had made deals not to oppose Putin if they were allowed to stay in the parliament or on the ballot.

In the first category there was "A Just Russia," whose first move after the election was to propose an extension of Putin's presidency. Some opposition! In the second category were the Communists, who received, or you might prefer "were allowed," 11.6 percent of the vote (around 20 percent according to an independent count), for 57 of 450 Duma seats. This low number angered Communist leader Gennady Zyuganov, who rumors said had been promised at least 90 seats by the Kremlin for his loyalty. Zyuganov started making charges of election anomalies. As I joked in an article after the election: "I hate to say it, Gennady, but I told you so!" As the joke going around had it, the difference between democracy and the Putin system was like the difference between two chairs: one leather and one electric.

Not that it really mattered, but the most damning of all were the official statistics in places like Chechnya and Dagestan where there was little monitoring at the polls. With an outlandish 99.5 percent voter turnout, 99 percent of Chechen votes went to

United Russia. Do not forget this is a party led by Putin, the author of the second Chechen war that razed the Chechen capital Grozny to the ground. As usual, the truth is visible in the actions of lackeys who are too eager to please their Kremlin masters. My wife commented darkly that the only ones who didn't vote in Chechnya were those who died on election day.

One can only imagine what the United Russia bosses thought of Hugo Chávez losing a referendum by a measly 1 percent on the same day. What an amateur! Meanwhile, despite the absence of real alternatives on the ballot and with all the chicanery included, United Russia barely topped 50 percent in St. Petersburg and Moscow. It's no coincidence that the residents of these cities had much greater access to news not provided by the Kremlin thanks to greater Internet penetration and Echo of Moscow, the one radio station where a variety of views was still heard.

It was a clear indication that Putin considered these elections important when he gave several frenzied speeches to get out the vote. The vicious language he used could barely be called coded as he warned against "enemies within" and "jackals" supported by the West. It was less Russian than what we might call Putinese, with a vintage Austrian-German accent.

Why bother making such an effort when the Kremlin's control was apparently so absolute already? First we should recall that even Stalin held elections in 1937 during the Terror. The results on that Sunday weren't in any doubt either, confirming our return to the rule of an all-powerful single-party state. But the elections were important to Putin's regime for several reasons, starting, of course, with financial ones: Putin's. Putin's close relationship with Western leaders served as a guarantee to his ruling oligarchs that their money was safe. Had he discarded the last vestiges of democracy too blatantly at that stage this cozy situation might have ended, a risk Putin was not yet ready to take.

The first indications were bad. Nicolas Sarkozy had touted himself as a tough guy but seemed to have gone weak in the knees after a few drinks with Putin. The French president wasted no time in calling his counterpart to congratulate him on his big win. Putin always watched these signals from the West carefully, looking for signs of any real pressure. Most comments about the blatantly fraudulent elections weren't favorable, especially in the media, but how much danger could there be if Sarkozy and Putin's old buddy Tony Blair called him?

The other purpose of the Kremlin campaign was to provide the regime with pseudodemocratic cover for whatever machinations they were going to come up with to keep their hold on power after the March 2 presidential elections. Putin couldn't run again, or at least the constitution said he couldn't and he had promised not to change it—if you wished to value the promise of a KGB lieutenant colonel.

After eight years blessed with record oil prices and a compromising West distracted by the "war on terror," the Putin regime had reached its crisis. The Kremlin's presidential candidate had to be named soon. Would it be a feeble puppet, leading, by "popular" demand or maybe a health emergency, to Putin's return? Or could they find someone foolish enough to step in and risk taking the blame when the neglected Russian infrastructure and economy finally collapsed? Or would they change the system, eviscerating the constitution in some way so Putin could keep power in some new role?

After Putin's friendly visit to Iran in October 2007 I wrote in an article that perhaps he was considering a new title for himself, one above the petty responsibilities of prime minister or even the old grandeur of the general secretary of the party. "Supreme Leader Ayatollah Putin" had a nice ring to it, I wrote, and I was sure he had always dreamed of running things from behind the scenes, without the petty annoyances and appearances of the presidency. My joke was closer to the mark than I could have imagined.

I was tempted to reproduce in this book a sort of protest that I employed in an article I wrote on the state of Russia in 2009 by not mentioning the name of Dmitry Medvedev even a single time. Ignoring him completely would be a fitting treatment of the man who held the presidency of Russia from 2008 until 2012, when he handed it back to Vladimir Putin like a dog bringing a stick back to its owner. There is no sense obscuring this story for the sake of personal protest, but I will keep my remarks on him brief.

Medvedev the human being was, and is, completely irrelevant. But the idea of *a* Medvedev, the idea of a young liberal president who might turn the country back toward the path of modernity, that was very, very useful. You can almost envision Putin and his inner circle in a laboratory, designing the ideal Medvedev. He had to be fresh-faced and bright-eyed and capable of spouting reformist jargon for the intelligentsia and keeping a straight face while politely acknowledging that things in Russia weren't all great, but were definitely going to improve. The Medvedev also couldn't have any mind, ambition, or power base of his own, just in case. Finally, he also needed to be shorter than Putin and with even less charisma, a very rare combination indeed. Fortunately for Putin, he happened to have one on hand right in his own cabinet.

On December 10, 2007, Putin made a big fanfare of endorsing his first deputy prime minister, Dmitry Medvedev, to succeed him in the presidency. He was quickly nominated by United Russia and its puppet parties, and a week after receiving Putin's blessing Medvedev was officially the candidate. His first priority was to announce that, should he be so lucky as to win the election, he would make Vladimir Putin his prime minister. Putin graciously accepted and that was that. (Medvedev also resigned as the chairman of Gazprom in order to run for president, leading to jokes about his being demoted to the presidency of Russia.)

One response from the Western leaders to the news will serve as an example of nearly all of them. The day after Putin's endorsement of Medvedev, Secretary of State Condoleeza Rice had a round-table discussion with the editorial board of the newspaper *USA Today*. They covered Iraq, Iran, and then moved to Rice's former area of expertise, Russia. She made several solid remarks about how "democratic processes have taken a step backward in Russia" and "it's not an environment in which you can talk about free and fair elections." But then she went on to say that she knew Medvedev, and that he was "intelligent" and "of another generation," as if any of that would matter, true or not.

The most revealing moment in Ms. Rice's comments came when the topic of Mr. Medvedev as the next president was first broached. The official transcript reads:

SECRETARY RICE: Well, I guess, they're still going to have an election in March. (Laughter.)

I'm sure everyone there had a good laugh about referring to Medvedev's inevitable installation as president as an election. And, to be fair, our elections were laughable. But why wasn't the next question to Rice, "So why is Russia still in the G7 if Russian elections are such a joke?" Or "Why has the Bush administration invested so much time, blood, and treasure in trying to build democracy in Iraq and elsewhere while virtually ignoring what Putin has done to the world's largest oil-exporting nation, which also has the world's largest nuclear arsenal?" Not that anyone advocated or expected Bush to invade Russia, of course, but a little consistency wasn't too much to ask of a man who so actively promoted what he called the "US Freedom Agenda."

A few days before the Rice interview, *Time* magazine named Putin its 2007 Person of the Year. They took obvious pains to explain that the award was "not an endorsement" and that it went to the person who made the most news "for better or for worse." But the article nonetheless praised their selection for restoring his country to prominence in the international arena, dispelling "anarchy," and recovering national pride. The magazine did express concern about his "troubling" record on human rights.

The exact same things could have been said about Adolf Hitler in 1938, when he took his turn as *Time*'s Man of the Year. "Fascism," *Time* wrote then, "has discovered that freedom—of press, speech, assembly—is a potential danger to its own security."

Again these words applied equally well to 2007's winner. Most of the criticism leveled against Putin regarded "alleged" abuses or came directly from known critics. In my opinion this abdicates the journalist's role to report the facts as facts. And consider the timing of this announcement, coming right after fixed parliamentary elections that crowned Mr. Putin's steady record of eradicating democracy across Russia.

Of course the *Time* article was trumpeted by Kremlin propaganda as another endorsement of Putin and his policies. The focus was on the myth that Putin had built a "strong Russia," when in fact he and his cronies had hollowed out the state from within.

On March 2, Medvedev's coronation as the king of nothing was completed and the last remaining element of democracy in Russia, the transition of power, was destroyed. As expected, the election itself was a complete sham and the Kremlin didn't even bother to cover its tracks. Opposition candidates were forced out of the race. The state-run media promoted Medvedev while either slandering or just not mentioning the other candidates. Several overenthusiastic precincts reported Medvedev receiving over 100 percent of the vote in the initial returns.

Medvedev's 70 percent fell just short of Putin's 71 percent in 2004, an additional indicator of who was really in charge, in case one was necessary. You may wonder why they bothered rigging the results when they already possessed so many unfair advantages. It was a designed display of loyalty by the regional politicians and bureaucrats to prove they could, and would, produce the results demanded by the Kremlin. This is not the way a democracy works, but it is very much the way a mafia works.

We in the Russian opposition waited anxiously to see what the rest of the world would say about Russia's return to outright despotism. Now, at long last, surely the leaders of the free world would have harsh criticisms after they had allowed Russia to join the G7 and had treated Putin as a democratic equal. Of course they would be outraged at having been played for fools. Perhaps, we hoped, enough external pressure would mount over this scandalous transfer of power to help weaken the Kremlin's stranglehold in Russia.

What happened instead could not have been more devastating. Western administrations lined up to applaud Medvedev on his outstanding victory, although most handed off this distasteful task to spokespeople. One or two statements managed to work in a few words about unpleasant "incidents" during the Russian election process.

France's Nicolas Sarkozy showed no such qualms. He telephoned Medvedev to congratulate him and to invite him to France. (I take for granted that Putin's long-term business partners Silvio Berlusconi and Gerhardt Schröder sent personal notes.) The West's acceptance of Medvedev as a democratically elected leader was another turning point. The last hurdle to Putin retaining power forever had been cleared. It signaled that the United States and the European Union would play along with even the most absurd charade in order to avoid confrontation.

For the Russian opposition the Western reaction was a disaster. Our coalition of nationalists, leftists, and liberals had little in common beyond a belief in the power of the democratic process. With no access to mass media and under constant persecution, our members attempted to spread the word about the importance of these principles. In one stroke, the free world announced that democracy was a scam, a cover-up for business as usual, just like Putin and his allies always said it was.

Five months later, in what I called then the culmination of Putin's feeling of impunity, Russian forces invaded neighboring Georgia in August when given the first hint of an excuse in South Ossetia. Putin had no reason to believe there was anything to fear over something as minor as punishing a neighboring nation led by his personal enemy, Georgian president Mikheil Saakashvili.

Putin was always good at reading other world leaders and, once again, he was right.

The world order has rules, but they are mostly based on the honor system and are infrequently tested. Putin has learned that the brutal methods of his KGB world are equally effective on the global stage. Violence returned on cue to the Caucasus, where Putin made his reputation as a strongman when he first came on the Russian political stage in 1999. Maybe it was a present for Medvedev. A war is always useful to build up a new Russian president's domestic reputation.

The real catastrophe, the one that gave Putin the confidence to shed blood across an international border, took place on March 3, 2008, the day after the election. That was the date on which the international community of free nations had a chance to sound the alarm about the Putin dictatorship, a chance to send an unambiguous message that democracy mattered. No alarm sounded. The election wasn't important. The world's reaction was.

As the worst of the violence between Russia and Georgia over South Ossetia wound down, I was reminded of a conversation I had had in 2005 in Moscow with a high-ranking European Union official. Russia was much freer then than it is today, but Putin's onslaught against democratic rights was already picking up speed.

"What would it take," I asked the official, "for Europe to stop treating Putin like a democrat? Maybe if all opposition parties are banned? Or what if they started shooting people in the street?"

He shrugged and replied that even in that case there would be little the EU could do, adding that "staying engaged will always be the best hope for the people of both Europe and Russia." I expect the citizens of Georgia and Ukraine would disagree. Russia's invasion of Georgia was the direct result of nearly a decade of this combination of helplessness and self-delusion in the West. Being left unpunished over Georgia invited Putin into Ukraine six years later.

In response to the Russian invasion of Georgia, the EU held its first emergency summit since the outbreak of the Iraq war. It quickly postponed meetings on the partnership agreement with Russia until the Kremlin moved its troops back to pre–August 7 positions. The EU statement, additionally weakened by a proud Silvio Berlusconi, included the phrase "We expect Russia to behave in a responsible manner, honoring all its commitments," in addition to the evergreens "gravely concerned" and "strongly condemn." How Putin and his billionaire and KGB buddies must have laughed at such quaint language.

On May 7, Dmitry Medvedev was sworn in as the president of Russia, behind closed doors. Putin was asked if he would, following tradition, hang a portrait of the new president on the wall of his office. Putin balked, but the joke going around had it that he would indeed have one: a portrait of Medvedev in the president's office looking at a portrait of Putin. According to the Russian constitution, Medvedev was now the one in charge. But as there was never any actual evidence of his independence and authority, it was safe to assume that Medvedev still needed Putin's permission to use the Kremlin lavatory. The real "smooth transition of power," in the ironically perfect phrase of German chancellor Angela Merkel, was its move with Putin from the presidency to the prime ministry.

———

I've made well over a thousand international media appearances in the last ten years, nearly all of them to discuss Russia and Putin. Often a show's producers will ask you in advance what title you prefer to be called on the air and what you'd like to appear next to your name on TV. Sometimes they do not ask. I have a long and complicated résumé, so I'm used to hearing all sorts of things in these situations. It's similar with the introductions I receive at my business and political lecture events. They are always kind and usually flattering, but often they contain all sorts of spurious information about me gleaned from a quick Google search. I often have to follow up with a quick set of corrections and joke that I'm always interested in these introductions because I learn so many new things!

"Garry Kasparov, Russian human rights activist and former world chess champion" shouldn't be too hard, no? I am also chairman of the New York–based Human Rights Foundation and a senior visiting fellow at the Oxford Martin School, where I regularly have lectures and seminars. I'm also very proud to be the chairman of the Kasparov Chess Foundation, a global education nonprofit, and of being a modestly popular author and speaker. But that is all too long to put on TV.

The one title I truly dislike is one I hear quite often: "Garry Kasparov, former Russian presidential candidate." This is not only inaccurate, but it is misleading in a damaging way. Yes, the Other Russia and other opposition groups held internal primaries in order to put forward candidates in 2008 and I was a participant. Yes, we had online and in-person voting to select candidates and I was one of the winners. Yes, several of us attempted to register to become candidates and I was one of them. But was I really a candidate for president?

When people from democratic countries talk to me about polls, platforms, campaigns, and other normal elements of elections in a free country, I have to stop them short. None of those things ever really existed in Russia—not in 2008 and even less so now. In Russia the opposition isn't trying to win elections; we're trying to *have* elections. We had started out optimistically in 2004, hoping that Putin's departure might open the door to a contested election. By 2007, after the crackdowns on the Marches of Dissent and our other activities grew worse and worse, we realized there was little hope of that. Until Putin and Medvedev made their little announcement on December 10 we weren't sure exactly how the ax was going to fall, or when, but we knew it was very sharp and right over our heads.

Putin anointed Medvedev with what a Mexican friend called "*el dedazo*," the endowing touch of a finger akin to the god of Michelangelo's Sistine Chapel giving life to Adam. At that point the result of the election was no longer in question. The system could never allow anyone so designated to do anything other than win by a huge margin. It was also very clear that the Kremlin did not want the presidential ballot to be cluttered with too many names. The campaigns of the opposition candidates became a strange game of forcing the authorities to figure out different ways to disqualify us.

There was no shortage of hoops to jump through and the Central Election Commission (CEC), run by Putin's henchman Vladimir Churov, was dedicated to making sure nobody but the approved candidates made it. The main obstacle was practically insurmountable on its face. An independent candidate had to collect 2 million signatures in just five weeks, and only 40,000 could be from a single region. So in Moscow, no matter how many you got, only 40,000 counted. So you needed signatures from fifty regions, minimum. Then, two weeks out of the five-week window was a general holiday. Lastly, when you came up with the signatures you could submit only 2.2 million, no more, and if 10 percent were disqualified for any reason you were out of the game.

Even to reach that stage would also turn out to be difficult. Each candidate was required to hold a nominating convention with at least five hundred supporters under one roof to sign a declaration with a representative of the Ministry of Justice there to observe in person. But as during my travels around the country, it turned out no venues in Moscow were willing to rent me a hall for this purpose. Well, that's not completely true, since we did sign a contract for a hall for December 13 and even paid our fee up front. But two days before, we were informed that "for technical reasons the hall is not available on that date." Of course on December 14 the very same hall was ready and waiting to host a nominating convention for the Kremlin's new stooge candidate, Bogdanov.

And so I did not even get as far as being nominated by the deadline in order to have the pleasure shared by a few other opposition figures in having their paperwork dismissed by Mr. Churov. Former prime minister Mikhail Kasyanov pushed the hardest, appealing to the supreme court after the CEC decided that too many of his nominating petition's signatures were forged. Of course his appeal was denied.

That left the usual suspects on the ballot once again: the token nationalist nutcase, Zhirinovsky; the token Communist caveman, Zyuganov; and Putin, represented by his shadow, Medvedev. For a little flavor they also let Andrei Bogdanov appear on the ballot as a faux liberal alternative. He was even permitted to receive 1.8 percent of the votes before disappearing whence he came.

The Other Russia and other opposition organizations had held internal primaries in an attempt to foster and share a real democratic experience in a country that had very little of it. Volunteers set up polling places wherever they could, in gymnasiums, pubs, and homes, and often they had to do it in a hurry before police came to shut them down and confiscate their equipment. We had policy statements, platform arguments, even online and offline debates. All these things existed completely outside of the official political processes at any level.

Our other goal was to expose the official elections for the mockery they were as clearly and loudly as possible. Enough of Western observers and foreign ministries lamely regretting "reported irregularities" and "media bias" in Russian elections. Putin had become a dictator, full stop, and it was time to say it. He wasn't a president or a prime minister or anything else that connoted legitimacy or democracy. We knew this wouldn't be reported by Russian media or pointed out by Russian politicians.

Tragically, it wasn't much better outside of Russia. Heads of state had no interest in challenging Putin; that had been obvious for quite a while. It was less obvious, and it still is, why the majority of the free world's most important media institutions also go along with the charade. Once again we heard about "flaws in the system" and "uneven access to the media" from observers and the foreign press. The Council of Europe was critical but declined to condemn the elections. Even when the chairman of the delegation of European members of parliament called them "still not free and still not fair," he added that it "broadly reflected the will of the people." Yes, the will of a handful of people in the Kremlin.

That "will of the people" remark is a good place to present a series of arguments that I could recite from memory after refuting them dozens of times in media appearances. I call it "The Myths of Putin's Russia," and at the top of the list is "Putin Is Popular."

Now that Putin has been in power for fifteen years, has invaded his second European country in six years, and goes on TV to snarl about Russia's nuclear weapons, it may be difficult for some to recall how differently he was seen not so long ago. Until 2010 my harsh opinions about Putin were still regularly met with surprise from reasonably educated consumers of international news.

"But Russia is a democracy and he was elected, wasn't he?"

"Okay, maybe the elections are rigged, but Putin is very popular and he would win anyway."

"Well, Russians love a strongman anyway, and he did crack down on crime and improve the economy, didn't he?"

The crime and the economy we've already discussed. Putin only cracked down on those who would not be loyal to him; those who were loyal were brought into the system as partners. He made it clear that either you were going to steal with him or you were against him. It is notoriously difficult to accurately measure the economic activity of a nation slowly dismantling a stagnant and corrupt socialist paradise. But before Putin took power, the Russian GDP was expanding at a steady rate as the painful market reforms took effect. Soviet industry was in no way able to compete directly with the West, or the Far East, but there was still a lot of industrial capacity in operation. By 2000, GDP growth was over 10 percent, even higher than the typically high rate of the former Soviet Bloc nations undergoing the transition to market economies.

Also important is that the price of oil in 1999 had gone as low as $13 a barrel, so the new Russian export industry was as yet far from being a powerhouse. The strength of the Russian economy under Putin is best seen not in GDP figures but in a graph showing the price of oil. Starting almost exactly when Putin took power, that price shot up to over $100 a barrel, dipping only during the 2008–2009 financial crisis.

Russia is the largest oil producer in the world, despite only minimal modernization of the Soviet infrastructure. It is this flood of oil wealth, transforming Russia into a dictatorial petro-state, that has enabled Putin to create the illusion of stability at home and to buy off or threaten his critics abroad. To those who say the source of money makes little difference as long as the pensioners and police receive their checks, that is exactly what the Kremlin seemed to believe—for a while.

Without a growing industrial or technology sector, without a vibrant business community and entrepreneurship, without a tax base of middle-class citizens, Russia is hollowing out demographically. Those who don't have the connections or resources to thrive either struggle or leave the country. The bright city centers of St. Petersburg and Moscow stand in stark contrast to the increasingly impoverished outer regions. Add a total lack of political accountability to the equation and the result is a growing social crisis.

Putin and his gang have proven reluctant to manage a real economy and incompetent when they try. The last thing they will do is what is really needed: loosen the strict controls so that Russian business can experience real capitalism instead of the crony variety. Khodorkovsky was just the biggest example of what happens to business owners who try to do this without getting state approval, but there are many thousands more like him.

As for Putin being popular, I still hear this one all the time. Are you sure? Then why has he spent so much time and effort dominating the media, eliminating rivals, and installing a complicated system of rigging elections large and small? If Putin is so popular, why not have free and fair elections and a free media? Persecuting bloggers and arresting a single protestor standing in the town square holding an anti-Putin sign does not strike me as the behavior of a popular ruler.

The entire definition of approval and popularity of a democratic leader has no application in an autocracy. When there is only one restaurant in town and it has only one item on the menu, and no other restaurants are allowed to open, is it popular? Fifteen years of propaganda have created a powerful cult of personality that says Putin is the only person who can lead and protect Russia. It says that all his critics are dangerous traitors who should be jailed or murdered. (As they often are.) Anyone who might rise as a rival is demonized and cut down.

This leads into another of the myths, that the opposition was simply not competent or charismatic enough to challenge Putin. Who knows? I bring this up not to defend my own role or my own standing, but to illustrate the absurdity of talking about the Russian opposition as if it were a small, inept party in a real democracy. Our members were banned from the media, slandered, prohibited from holding meetings and rallies, frequently physically assaulted, raided and harassed by the police, and blocked from appearing on ballots. What brilliant and coherent message, what transcendent leader, would have led us to power under those circumstances?

As was increasingly obvious after 2008, the only way Putin was going to leave the Kremlin was feet first, either in a box or dragged out by a mob. As long as he enjoyed economic engagement with the free world and could prevent a million Russians from rioting in Red Square, he wasn't going anywhere. That first ingredient, engagement, was important for the second. As long as the money kept rolling in to buy Russia's vast natural wealth—oil, gas, metals, timber—Putin could afford the salaries, benefits, and armies of riot police that kept people at home.

As for polling, Russia is not the United States or France. When an anonymous voice calls an ordinary Russian at home and asks his opinion of the man who dominates the country, it takes great courage indeed to report anything less than enthusiastic support. Honestly, it is a testament to the courage of many of my compatriots that Putin does not receive the 99 percent approval scores that Saddam Hussein and Muammar Gaddafi received—up until the minute they no longer had the power of life and death over their own citizens.

Now that Putin's approval numbers have climbed into the 90 percent range during the Ukraine war and the fascist personality cult propaganda has been turned up to the maximum, I wonder if the foreign media will finally stop citing these figures so credulously. The despotic ruler of Kazakhstan, Nursultan Nazarbayev, in power since 1989, was just "reelected" in April 2015 with 97.7 percent of the vote. (With a 95 percent turnout, of course.) I'm glad to say that a glance at the headlines about his remarkable electoral feat finds that very few Western media outlets give much credence to Nazarbayev's overwhelming popularity with his people. Will Putin also have to top 98 percent before his supposed popularity gets the same skepticism?

That the Nazarbayevs, Putins, and Khameneis of this world still bother to hold elections is a worthwhile puzzle to ponder. Today's dictators have learned the lessons of their predecessors and combined them with modern methods of information and image control. They understand the symbolism of the vote even if they have no desire to submit to its authority. That they feel the need to hold elections at all, however blatantly fraudulent, speaks to a degree of successful pressure from the outside as well as a longing for legitimacy, to be seen as a member of the club of lawful leaders.

The leaders of these countries—we might call them "hypocracies," or use the term of a man who had great experience in covering Putin's Russia, German journalist Boris Reitschuster's *democratura*—are only partly concerned with duping their own citizens with the illusion of a voice in their government. A pervasive security force and domination of the mass media serve the dictator's purposes well. Few people in Russia really believe in the electoral charade at this point. The polls are for the benefit of the international community and for the predetermined winners themselves.

I repeat my early example of Sarkozy's shameful, or shameless, phone call to "warmly congratulate" Medvedev after his victory in 2008. The Russian media made a great fanfare about this call and the other encomiums from abroad, another indication of the importance the charade has for Putin and his allies.

There is more than ego and invitations to summits at stake, of course. The ruling oligarchy maintain their assets abroad and a chill in the cozy relationship between Russia's leaders and the West could put those countless billions in assets at risk. Sarkozy aggressively promoted French companies like Alcatel, Total, and Renault in Russia, with some success. With that in mind, Sarkozy's phone call was possibly one of the most lucrative in history.

So, no, I do not consider myself a former Russian presidential candidate. It was a civil rights protest, a corruption awareness campaign, and a way of helping people discover what real democracy could feel like. You can't have real candidates without real democracy.

———

"How come I am still alive? When I really think about it, it's a miracle." Those were the words of Anna Politkovskaya, the Russian investigative journalist who for years fearlessly dug into the deepest depths of war-ravaged Chechnya. She is seen speaking the fateful lines in the documentary film *Letter to Anna* by Swiss director Eric Bergkraut. The film premiered in the United States on June 26, 2008, at the Human Rights Watch Film Festival in New York City, a convenient moment in our chronology to again mention her work and her courage. She was as much of a crusader and partisan as a journalist, no doubt, and she didn't try to hide that. Her passion made her work all the more essential and unforgettable.

Politkovskaya's reporting on the atrocities in Chechnya usually took the form of conversations with families who had been ripped apart by war. She also served as a sort of confessor for Russian soldiers, even officers, who were ashamed of what was being done in Chechnya in Russia's name. This sort of work made her enemy number one to a long list of powerful people and groups who had already shown their brutality many times over. It was still a heartbreaking shock when the forty-eight-year-old was murdered in October 2006.

For the sake of objectivity, here are two reviews, one from the KGB and the other from a famous dissident. Two days after Mrs. Politkovskaya's death, President Putin, when asked at a press conference in Germany (not Russia, of course, where such a question would never be permitted), asserted that "her death caused more damage to the Russian government than her writings." Former Czech president Václav Havel, at the film's award-winning Prague appearance in March, stated, "It would be good if many people could see this film. Especially politicians who kiss and embrace Russian politicians, almost dizzy with the smell of oil and gas!" It may be difficult to find the film—I found it on You-Tube in German and Russian but could not find it in English—but it is well worth tracking down. It's a rare glimpse of an extinct species. By the time of Anna's murder, independent journalism of the kind she produced was already cold in the grave in Russia.

At the World Russian Press Congress in Moscow on June 11, 2008, Medvedev pledged to "support media freedom." Would there be any changes? The signs were not good. He touted the need for a "Cyrillic internet" and criticized the closing of Russian-language media enterprises in former Soviet states, where local languages were reasserting themselves after Soviet-era restrictions. Medvedev also added that Russian television is "one of the highest quality in the world."

Kremlin paranoia about who and what appeared on Russian television had reached new heights by then. Vladimir Posner, president of the Russian Academy of Television, confessed that he submits a list of guests he would like to have on his own show to Channel One management, who then let him know whom he can and cannot invite. Needless to say, people like Nemtsov, Navalny, and myself have never appeared on his show.

The Kremlin's subjugation of the Russian press was, along with the rise in oil prices of over 700 percent, the biggest reason behind the perceived success of Putin's regime. The oligarchs of the 1990s may have been robbing Russia blind, but at least we could find out about it in the news. Those days are over and the elite circle of oligarchs around Putin have power and riches beyond the dreams of Yeltsin's entourage. In 2000, when Putin took charge, there were no Russians on the *Forbes* magazine list of the world's billionaires. By 2005 there were thirty-six. In 2008 there were eighty-seven, more than Germany and Japan combined, in a country where 13 percent of our citizens were under a national poverty line of $150 a month. Putin and his defenders abroad bragged about Russia's rising GDP, but it was like taking the average temperature of all the patients in a hospital.

According to the 2015 numbers, even after a year of Western sanctions and plunging oil prices, there are still eighty-eight Russian billionaires on the *Forbes* list, which still doesn't list Putin or several of his closest cronies. I find it impossible to believe that a man like Putin who holds the power of life and death over eighty-eight billionaires is not the richest of them all. The occasional leaks about mysterious Black Sea mansions and enormous bank transfers to nowhere add more circumstantial evidence to the case that by now Putin is likely the richest man in the world.

———

On October 25, 2011, I gave a lecture on Russia at the Heritage Foundation in Washington, DC. Georgia was under great pressure from the United States and others at the time to allow Russia to join the World Trade Organization, despite two large pieces of Georgian sovereign territory still being occupied by Russian forces, as they had been since the 2008 invasion. Many in the media and even some governments still refer to Abkhazia and South Ossetia as "disputed territories," not occupied, ignoring the fact they were taken by military force from Georgia by Russia.

Despite heavy pressure from Russia after the invasion, including economic boycotts, tiny Georgia had remained defiantly pro-democratic and pro-Western under Saakashvili, and yet it was clear that getting Russia into the World Trade Organization (WTO) was of greater importance to Europe and the US than protecting the rights and territory of an ally. Putin's administration liked to boast about how they had kept Georgia and Ukraine out of NATO during the Bush 43 administration and that WTO membership would be another feather in their cap.

As part of my presentation, I put up a slide with an image of a set of folders, labeled like KGB case files. First came the folders for OPERATION YUKOS and OPERATION KADYROV. Khodorkovsky's case has been well covered already. Ramzan Kadyrov is the Chechen warlord who boasted of killing his first Russian soldier at the age of fifteen and was put in charge of the devastated region by Putin in 2007. Kadyrov's agents have assassinated Putin's enemies in other Russian cities as well as on foreign soil. It is hard to compare what Putin has done to the Russian Caucasus to anything else anywhere. He is not interested in attempting to better integrate these peoples, who are, after all, Russian citizens. Kadyrov is still in charge in Chechnya and has become Putin's most loyal soldier. How long that loyalty would last if the flow of money from Moscow dried up is yet to be seen.

The next folder was labeled OPERATION MEDVEDEV. I described it as Putin's most successful operation of all. It was a variation of the old Soviet game, letting the West think there was a chance of promoting moderates, or of a possible rift in the hierarchy. Everyone would scramble to figure out what was happening inside the Kremlin, wasting their time and energy. Putin's inevitable announcement that he would be reclaiming the presidency in 2012 made it clear that Medvedev was never anything more than the hoax many of us had said he was, that he had never been anything more than a shadow. But the United States spent considerable time trying to strengthen the imaginary "Medvedev faction," dreaming about a split between Putin and Medvedev, and fantasizing about liberal reform despite all evidence to the contrary.

I briefly met President Bush in September 2008 at a lunch he hosted for global dissidents in New York City. He had strong words about Putin then, but this was right after Russia's invasion of Georgia in August, which by all accounts, including his own, had infuriated Bush. In his memoir, *Decision Points*, Bush writes, "My biggest concern was that the Russians would storm all the way to Tbilisi and overthrow the democratically elected Saakashvili. It was clear the Russians couldn't stand a democratic Georgia with a pro-Western president. I wondered if they would have been as aggressive if NATO had approved Georgia's MAP [Membership Application Plan] application."

The answer is almost certainly no, though we have little way of knowing for sure, since Western leadership has consistently avoided even trying to stand up to Putin. And yet the mistake was repeated six years later in Ukraine, the other country on Putin's hit list that had failed to gain MAP status in 2008 thanks to opposition from Germany and France, who were quite open about saying it was because they didn't want to anger Russia. (In another memorable remark in the book, Bush writes, "At a G-8 dinner in St. Petersburg, most of the leaders challenged Putin on his democratic record. Jacques Chirac did not. He announced that Putin was doing a fine job running Russia, and it was none of our business how he did it." Clearly the French president was a greater fan of *fraternité* than of *liberté*.)

Later in his book Bush dedicates considerable time to the freedom agenda and his various disappointments and satisfactions. He concludes the section with, "I met with more than a hundred dissidents over the course of my presidency. Their plight can look bleak, but it is not hopeless. As I said in my Second Inaugural Address, the freedom agenda demands 'the concentrated work of generations.'"

It most definitely does, but any hope for bold American support for human rights and democracy abroad ended abruptly with the result of the 2008 American election.

9

THE AUDACITY OF
FALSE HOPE

Berlin is an ideal place for an American president, even a would-be president, to speak to the world about freedom and shared values. The visit of presidential candidate Barack Obama on July 24, 2008, evoked the famous speeches there by his countrymen John F. Kennedy and Ronald Reagan, speeches that defended the line, real and metaphorical, against the Soviet Union and the tyranny it represented in Eastern Europe. Although the line, the Wall, and the USSR itself are now gone, nuclear-armed dictatorships still pose dangers, something the senator declined to mention in Berlin.

The stage for Obama's performance had been set several weeks earlier when the Illinois senator rejected his opponent Senator John McCain's proposal to eject Russia and exclude China from the Group of Eight. Obama's response suggested that it was simply impossible to work with Russia and China on economic and nuclear nonproliferation issues while standing up for democracy and human rights at the same time.

Not only is this false, but it has repeatedly been shown that the exact opposite is true. Commercial agreements, arms control, and other mutually beneficial projects can be pursued without tacitly endorsing dictatorship. Senator Obama spoke of enlisting

China to help write the "international rules of the road." This is the same twisted logic that led the United Nations to place China, Cuba, Russia, and Saudi Arabia on its Human Rights Council. Do we really want to live under rules created with the approval of such regimes?

While Obama talked about the importance of receiving Russia's help in containing Iran's nuclear ambitions, Reuters reported that Tehran was acquiring advanced S-300 surface-to-air missiles from the Kremlin. If that was the level of cooperation the West earned by including Russia in the G8, it is difficult to imagine what Obama feared would occur should Russia be expelled. In a serendipitous echo, right now in April 2015, Iran's nuclear program and Russian S-300 missiles to protect it are again in the news. Alarmingly, Obama the president doesn't seem any more concerned about them today than he was as a candidate in 2008.

In Berlin, Obama repeatedly mentioned the 1948 Berlin airlift. And in a previous interview he had said he would like to "bring back the kind of foreign policy that characterized the Truman administration with Marshall and Acheson and Kennan." It was a strange statement, since President Truman, a great hero in my estimation, fought against giving up even an inch to the Communists on any front around the world. And the "Man from Missouri" was facing down no less a brute than Josef Stalin, who was making no secret of his desire for global dominance. Not only did Truman save West Berlin, but South Korea, Taiwan, and Western Europe also have much to thank him for. (In the light of current events it is also worth noting that Truman also forced Stalin to end the Soviet occupation of Iran in 1946.) Contrast that hard line to Obama's campaign advisors Madeleine Albright and William Perry, secretaries of state and defense under Bill Clinton, who also criticized McCain's proposal to respond to human rights abuses by major powers with more than lip service.

Also in his Berlin speech, Obama asked if the West would stand for "the human rights of the dissident in Burma, the blogger in Iran, or the voter in Zimbabwe." Commendable, but what of the political prisoner in China and the convicted blogger in Russia? Both Mugabe and Medvedev came to power in blatantly fraudulent elections. The hypocrisy of condemning weak dictatorships while embracing strong ones destroys American and European credibility and undermines any attempt at global leadership; in fact, it seems to encourage smaller autocracies to aspire to greater ambitions. Great leaders are formed only by taking on great challenges. Those of us living behind the Iron Curtain were grateful Ronald Reagan did not go to Berlin in 1987 to denounce the lack of freedom in, say, Angola.

Other than Obama's stance on Iraq, the candidate of change sounded a lot like he would perpetuate the destructive double standards of the Bush 43 administration. Meanwhile, the supposedly hidebound John McCain wasn't too old-fashioned to suggest that if something is broken you should try to fix it. Giving Russia and China a free pass on human rights to keep them "at the table" has led to more arms and nuclear aid to Iran, a nuclear North Korea, and interference from both nations on resolving the tragedies in Darfur and Zimbabwe. Would all of these things have occurred anyway had the United States and Europe threatened meaningful reprisals? We can't know, but at least McCain wanted to find out.

In 2008 and today there are wheeling-and-dealing capitalists and nationalists running the Kremlin and China's National People's Congress instead of Communist ideologues. They do not represent the existential threats faced by Presidents Truman, Kennedy, and Reagan. And yet Obama is still reluctant to confront the enemies of democracy to defend the values he touts so convincingly in his speeches. The Cold War ended and democracy became the global standard not because Western leaders merely defended their values but because they projected them aggressively.

On September 11, 1858, another Illinois politician soon to run for president, Abraham Lincoln, said, "Our defense is in the preservation of the spirit which prizes liberty as the heritage of all men, in all lands, everywhere." Not where it's convenient. Not in countries lacking large energy reserves and nuclear weapons. Everywhere.

Obama's biggest applause in Berlin came when he suggested that the unilateralism and military adventurism of the Bush 43 era would come to an end under his presidency. By that point in the campaign no one doubted Obama could deliver a great speech. But the reactions of the Berlin audience, and the US electorate, made it clear it was as much an anti-Bush rally as anything else. In 2008, Americans and the rest of the world were exhausted after two long military campaigns in Afghanistan and Iraq; campaigns without clear goals or visible finish lines.

To be fair, Obama was representing his constituents. Even the firmest supporters of the Bush 43 freedom agenda understood that their cause was severely damaged by the extraordinary cost and duration of wars in Afghanistan and Iraq and the never-ending nation building and security operations that followed. America's human and financial capital had been spent, but even more importantly, so had its political capital.

The deepening catastrophe in Iraq distracted the world's sole superpower from its wider goals and weakened the United States politically as well as militarily. With US congressional leadership threatening to make the same mistake by failing to see Iraq as only one piece of the puzzle, it was time to return to the basics of strategic planning.

Thirty years as a chessplayer ingrained in me the importance of never losing sight of the big picture. Paying too much attention to one area of the chessboard can quickly lead to the collapse of your entire position. America and its allies were so focused on Iraq that they were ceding territory all over the map. North Korea got nukes, an arms race erupted in Latin America, and the petro-dictatorships of Russia, Venezuela, and Iran were riding high on the surging price of oil. By 2006, even the vague goals of President Bush's ambiguous war on terror had been pushed aside by the crisis in Baghdad.

It was time to recognize the failure of America's post-9/11 foreign policy. Preemptive strikes and deposing dictators may or may not have been a good plan, but at least it was a plan. If you attack Iraq, the potential to go after Iran and Syria must also be on the table. Inconsistency is a strategic deficiency that is nearly always impossible to overcome. The United States found itself supervising a civil war while helplessly making concessions elsewhere. This dire situation was a result of the only thing worse than a failed strategy: the inability to recognize, or to admit to yourself, that a strategy has failed.

Within four years after the invasion of Iraq in March 2003, North Korea tested a nuclear weapon. Iran was openly boasting of its uranium enrichment program while pouring money into Hezbollah and Hamas. A resurgent Taliban was on the rise in Afghanistan. Nearly off the radar, Somalia was becoming an al-Qaeda haven. Worst of all, America was failing at its basic mission, the mission at the root of all these engagements: to make its people safer than they were before.

As is often the case, the seeds for this widespread catastrophe were sown in the one real success the West had. The attack on the Taliban and al-Qaeda in Afghanistan had succeeded so well in its original goal of routing al-Qaeda and its Taliban sponsors that the United States and its allies failed to understand all the reasons why. Almost every player on the world stage benefited from the attack on Afghanistan. The rout of the Sunni Taliban delighted Iran. Russia and China had no love for religious extremism near their borders. India was happy to see the US launch a direct attack on Muslim terrorists.

Only Pakistan was put under uncomfortable pressure, although even there President Musharraf was able to play both sides well enough to appear to be an essential ally to the West while terrorists and arms crossed his borders freely. Musharraf perfected the formula of holding himself up as the last defense against the extremists in order to gain immunity for his dictatorship, a ploy used by many Arab autocrats as well.

Not only was there a confluence of world opinion aided by sympathy for the United States after 9/11, but the proverbial bad guys were undoubtedly bad, and we knew where they were. As subsequent events showed, effectively bombing terrorists is a rare opportunity.

The allies fell victim to what I call the gravity of past success. Learning from our defeats is obvious, but too often we fail to appreciate the reasons for our successes; we take them for granted. The US charged into Iraq without appreciating the far greater difficulty of the postwar task there and how it would be complicated by the increasingly hostile global opinion of America's military adventures. What would have been relatively easy in 1991–1992 was much harder twelve years later without united global support.

This is the lesson of the initiative. The saying in chess is that if the side that has the initiative—the attacking momentum in the position—fails to use it, then the other side's counterattack is inevitable and will be very strong. The free world had overwhelming momentum after the fall of the USSR in every conceivable way, especially psychologically. Had the freedom promotion agenda of George W. Bush existed from 1992 to 1999, when the bad guys were already in disarray, it would have had a tremendous positive effect.

By 2008, Obama's promises to bring the troops home, and keep them home, was only telling the American people (a majority of them, anyway) what they wanted to hear. This of course is a small part of a politician's job description, but these days it is actually the only relevant part of a candidate's job description.

There is no doubt the election of Barack Obama as the new president of the United States had a real impact on how many in the rest of the world perceived America. Obama represented a new generation of leadership and he both sounded and looked very different from his predecessors.

In Russia, Obama's appearance—he became the first black leader of any world power, not just America—got the most attention. His victory marked the end of the view of America still promoted by many in Russia, a line used in the Soviets' patented what-aboutism to counter accusations of repression. "Ah, but in the US they lynch Negros!" It is practically conventional wisdom, and not just in Russia, that "in America the rich WASPs and Jews exploit the poor Blacks and Latinos." Suddenly it was as if everyone could see that the world was undeniably round.

The window of opportunity Obama had to take advantage of the world's curiosity and goodwill was very small. The crises we faced in 2008 were too big to give the new president much of a grace period.

Obama's other advantage was simply not being George W. Bush who, rightly in some cases and wrongly in others, had come to symbolize every problem anyone had ever had with America, Americans, and American power in the world. The clichés about Bush personally were a bouquet of American stereotypes, the ones much of the world loved to hate: rich, inarticulate, uninterested in the world, stridently religious, and hasty to act. Obama exploded these stereotypes, but as I wrote the day after his victory over McCain, "The world's multitude of grievances with Bush will quickly be laid on Obama's doorstep if he fails to back up his inspiring rhetoric with decisive action."

Even with front-page issues like the financial crisis, Iraq, Iran, and Afghanistan facing the incoming president, he still had to find the time and the courage to deal with a certain nuclear-armed autocracy that controlled much of the world's oil and gas. In my article I asked the new president to "make it clear he does not consider the people of Russia to be the enemy of the United States." As in most authoritarian states, the Putin regime does not represent the interests of a majority of its citizens. (If it did, it wouldn't have to be authoritarian to stay in power.) Kremlin propaganda works hard to present America as Russia's adversary. With his fresh start, Obama had the opportunity to strike a blow against that image by speaking out against our dictatorial leader in Russia and making common cause with the people Putin was oppressing.

Of course there were complex issues around how Obama dealt with Russia's official president, Dmitry Medvedev, and Russia's real leader, Vladimir Putin. But the central choice was a straightforward one. Obama could treat them like fellow democratic leaders or he could be honest. He could take strength from the fact that he had received nearly 70 million votes while Medvedev had needed only one, that of Putin. Had Obama labeled the Putin dictatorship clearly and openly from the start he might have helped bring hope and change to an entirely different constituency: 140 million Russians.

The first international crisis Obama had to respond to actually came a few months before the election, when Russian and Russian-backed forces in the Georgian breakaway region of South Ossetia finally succeeded in provoking a shooting war with Georgia. Having prepared for this moment for months, Russian ships blockaded Georgian ports and Russian forces sped into Georgia and occupied several cities. It was far beyond the Kremlin's claim that they were involved only in enforcing the peace and it looked like Russian forces might go all the way to the Georgian capital of Tbilisi.

The initial responses to the violence by the 2008 candidates on August 8 could not have demonstrated their differences more clearly. Obama condemned the violence and pleaded, "Now is the time for Georgia and Russia to show restraint." McCain: "Russia should immediately and unconditionally cease its military operations and withdraw all forces from sovereign Georgian territory." After media fallout over Obama's timid remarks and more evidence that Russia was the aggressor, Obama hastily issued another statement to upgrade his language and condemn Russia's "aggressive action."

The differences were dramatic and would only get bigger. As it appeared in *Politico* on August 9, "Obama's statement put him in line with the White House, the European Union, NATO and a series of European powers, while McCain's initial statement . . . put him more closely in line with the moral clarity and

American exceptionalism projected by President Bush's first term."

Just two days later it was clear that McCain's moral clarity had been accurate while Obama's position was embarrassing no matter how "in line" it was with others. Putin issued similar statements calling for both sides to show restraint and cease hostilities while his troops raced into Georgia and provided cover for his South Ossetian allies to wipe out ethnic Georgians from the region. On August 11, both candidates issued longer statements. Obama's was essentially an admission that he had gotten it wrong the first time, although the friendly media didn't portray it that way. And even while he did pin the blame on Putin for the escalation, his conclusion was not about what America's role should be, but Russia's:

"Let me be clear: we seek a future of cooperative engagement with the Russian government, and friendship with the Russian people. We want Russia to play its rightful role as a great nation, but with that role comes the responsibility to act as a force for progress in this new century, not regression to the conflicts of the past. That is why the United States and the international community must speak out strongly against this aggression, and for peace and security."

Incredible. And remember, this was the *tougher* statement he made after being bashed as soft on Russia for two days. Russia's "rightful role as a great nation"? Putin was rolling tanks through a European country as Obama spoke in Hawaii about a KGB dictator acting as a force for progress.

John McCain had long been a staunch supporter of Georgia's shift toward Western-leaning democracy during and after the Rose Revolution in 2003 and the election of US-educated reformer Mikheil Saakashvili to the presidency. The Republican nominee minced no words in his more extensive August 11 statement, embracing the opportunity to flex his foreign policy credentials and to use the conflict to expose Obama's conciliatory approach toward foreign policy as naïveté. McCain did an excellent job putting Georgia into the big picture of why the United States should care about this tiny country in the Caucasus:

"The implications of Russian actions go beyond their threat to the territorial integrity and independence of a democratic Georgia. Russia is using violence against Georgia in part to intimidate other neighbors such as Ukraine for choosing to associate with the West and adhering to Western political and economic values. As such, the fate of Georgia should be of grave concern to Americans and all people who welcome the end of a divided Europe and the independence of former Soviet Republics."

McCain also correctly diagnosed the Russian invasion as a consequence of Western hesitancy: "NATO's decision to withhold a membership action plan for Georgia might have been viewed as a green light by Russia for its attacks on Georgia, and I urge the NATO allies to revisit the decision." McCain finished his statement powerfully: "We must remind Russia''s leaders that the benefits they enjoy from being part of the civilized world require their respect for the values, stability and peace of the world. World history is often made in remote, obscure countries. It is being made in Georgia today. It is the responsibility of the leading nations of the world to ensure that history continues to be a record of humanity's progress toward respecting the values and security of free people."

Can anyone read those statements and not believe that the world would be a safer, more democratic place today had John McCain been elected three months later? Or doubt that Obama's evident timidity encouraged Putin's attack on Ukraine? Of course we have no way of knowing, but I would be willing to bet anything that in the universe where McCain is president, Putin does not invade Ukraine. McCain is often painted as a warmonger in the United States, but calls for friendship don't deter someone like Vladimir Putin, they encourage him. It's a tragedy that thousands of Ukrainians, as well as many Russians, are suffering today because the Obama administration failed to learn that lesson.

197

Obama also failed his first test in the "3:00 A.M. phone call" department as president when the citizens of the Islamic Republic of Iran erupted in protest in June 2009 and the "Green Revolution" participants risked their lives to defend their votes. It was a remarkable moment. Putin and the other members of the "axis of autocrats" were closely watching events in Iran and the Western response. They wanted to know if there would be penalties of any significance for the use of lethal force against nonviolent protestors. Surprisingly, European leaders showed unusual assertiveness in harshly condemning the Iran regime's actions, while the initial response from the other side of the Atlantic was not encouraging.

Only in his second statement, a week into the Iranian uprising, did President Obama realize it was important to speak up for justice and nonviolence, even while he declined to directly express support for the thousands of Iranians who were risking their lives to defend those ideals. I understood Obama's reluctance to provide the Iranian regime with the opportunity to smear the protestors with the brush of American support. But could the leader of the free world find nothing more intimidating than "bearing witness" when it was evident that Ayatollah Khamenei and Mahmoud Ahmadinejad could not care less who was watching?

Senator Richard Lugar and Fareed Zakaria on CNN, among others, defended Obama's extreme caution. Zakaria even compared the situation to how George H. W. Bush responded timidly to the impending collapse of the USSR and its hold on Eastern Europe in 1989. But when has a dictatorship ever used violence as a reprisal to public remarks from a foreign leader? Dictators make their calculations based on force and its likely consequences, not on the genteel bickering of politicians. President Eisenhower said nothing in 1956 and that certainly did not hold back the Soviet tanks that were rolling into Budapest. Little was said in 1968 and the vicious Soviet crackdown in Czechoslovakia still ran its bloody course. Regardless of what Obama or anyone else had said, the Iranian regime would have used all the force at its disposal to keep its grip on power.

On July 7, 2009, Obama gave a speech at the New Economics School in Moscow. It was, of course, a very good speech. Aside from his natural gifts in that department, Obama had several knowledgeable and savvy Russia hands on his team, including future ambassador to Russia Mike McFaul, whom I had known for several years and held in esteem for his support of the color revolutions.

Obama's speech was strong and he gave a consistent message. I said in a press conference after Obama met with me and other opposition leaders that the speech was "less than what we wanted but more than what we expected." He repeatedly emphasized that the important relationship between America and Russia was about the people, not their regimes, which was exactly what I had hoped for. Obama opened direct lines of communication instead of dealing only with official Kremlin channels.

Ideally he would have named names, of course. Obama made some strong statements about the failure of totalitarianism and pointed to the solution of democracy; in fact, he made far stronger statements regarding Putin's Russia than anything we had heard from the two administrations before him. But he avoided criticizing the track records of Putin and Medvedev, the architects and wardens of our dictatorial system. Of course, as their guest in Russia Obama could hardly insult his hosts, but remarking on the anti-democratic trend of the previous nine years would have made the point. Nor did Obama mention Mikhail Khodorkovsky, whose jailing by Putin and continued imprisonment by Medvedev exemplified everything Obama was criticizing about authoritarian states.

But Obama didn't give anything up, either, which impressed me and likely came as a surprise to Putin, who probably expected the young new American president to be eager to make deals to have a big Russian success to report back home. Obama surprised some Republicans in the United States as well. Before he started his trip, several conservative GOP members wrote an open letter to Obama with recommendations: not linking missile defense to nuclear arms reduction, defending the rights of Ukraine and Georgia, and meeting with the opposition. From what I could tell, Obama followed each one.

In my statement to Obama at the meeting, I emphasized that all the conjecture about the power structure of the government in Russia at that time was a terrible waste of time, and that what mattered was that it was anything but a democracy.

My statement went on, "The Russian constitution describes three branches of government. Unfortunately, all three are now contained between the walls of Mr. Putin's office. To all of President Medvedev's talk of liberalization, I can say only that talk is cheap. We have seen no meaningful policy changes in the past year to indicate a new course."

In a reverse mirror image of Reagan's custom with Soviet leaders, I presented the American president with a list of Russian victims of state oppression at the end of the meeting. But I was under no illusion that Obama would ever toss it on Putin's desk.

———

In a sentiment soon to be shared by many Americans, Russians quickly felt let down after a great Obama speech. The strong rhetoric about democracy and shared values faded into a bureaucratic jumble that accompanied Secretary of State Hillary Clinton's gaffe-filled "Reset" meeting with Russian foreign minister Sergei Lavrov earlier in the year.

For just one example, the first meeting of the loftily named US-Russia Bilateral Presidential Commission's Civil Society Working Group took place in Washington, DC, on January 27, 2010. Top Russian administration official Vladislav Surkov was the group's co-chair, despite a letter of protest signed by seventy-one members of the US Congress pointing out that Surkov was "one of the masterminds behind Russia's authoritarian course." The letter also urged President Obama to boycott the meetings until Surkov was replaced, perhaps by someone who hadn't spent his career actively destroying the sort of civil society the working group was intended to promote.

Another potentially awkward part of the DC meeting involved a presentation by the head of Transparency International, the corruption watchdog that on its latest list ranked Russia as number 146 of 180 nations listed, between Kenya and Sierra Leone and by far the lowest of the leading industrialized nations. But Surkov and his Kremlin kin felt no embarrassment. It's even possible they considered that ranking a form of recognition of how far from the path of lawfulness they have succeeded in pulling Russia under Vladimir Putin.

That this ineffectual working group convened at all showed that the Obama administration was placing form over function. Obama's speech in Russia in July raised expectations that his administration would look at the Kremlin's record of brutality at home and transgressions abroad and attempt to ally with the beleaguered Russian people instead of our repressive government. But instead of lines in the sand we got words in the air, with dozens of these commissions established on the American president's initiative, each more wretched and moribund than the last. This one on civil society was simply insulting.

Putin's functionaries were happy to pass the time in the world's capitals being treated as equals instead of being berated for rigging elections and shamed for the growing list of dead Russian opposition figures. But why should the United States provide credentials of legitimacy and good faith by sitting down at the table with such people?

Meanwhile, just a week earlier, an advisory panel set up by Russian president Dmitry Medvedev released a report full of grand liberalization ideas. As positive as this may sound, the institute's chief, Igor Yurgens, then admitted in an interview that in the end "Putin will make any decision he likes" and that "free elections are impossible in Russia today because the Russian population is politically ignorant, passive, and dislikes democracy." His conclusion was that therefore "Mr. Putin and Mr. Medvedev should decide" who was to be president! This was Surkov's design for "sustainable civil society": a Pinochet with a law degree.

These silly commissions only demonstrated that the Obama administration was engaged in a campaign to make people believe problems could and would be solved eventually instead of actually taking the tough steps required to solve them. It was a pattern that would come to dominate his foreign policy. It is true that doing what must be done can be a thankless task and that telling the truth does not always poll well. But promises are for candidates. Fulfilling promises is for leaders.

America may be the world's only superpower, but since we often hear that Russia is Europe's problem, let's check in on how they were doing while Obama was busy retreating on every front. Early in 2011 I was invited to contribute an essay to a European publication on the topic "Russia in Europe: Partners or Challengers?" I almost thought they were joking, but it's a good example of the self-deluded and self-destructive state of mind that gripped Europe at the time when it came to Russia.

In August 2008, Russian tanks crossed an international border in Georgia and a chill ran down the collective spine of all of Europe, especially the former Soviet Bloc nations. Just one month earlier, Russia had threatened a "military-technical response" against Poland and the Czech Republic, including targeting nuclear weapons, when a US missile defense plan was announced. In January 2009, Russia cut off natural gas supplies to hundreds of thousands of people in half the countries of Europe. The bear was back and the bear was hungry.

With just those very recent events in mind, the question proposed by the editors for the title of the essay seemed preposterous.

A partner is usually defined as someone with mutual interests, if not actual friendship or affinity, and who shares in your successes and your hardships. In case after case, for over a decade, the Putin regime that ran the Kremlin—and that does still, as if there were any doubt—took a bluntly adversarial position with Europe and the rest of the Western world. By 2011, however, the Kremlin's most effective weapons were banks, not tanks. The money flow out of Russia was coming close to conquering more of Europe than the twentieth century's most feared strongmen ever did.

For most of the decade, most of Europe's leaders pretended that they could do business with Russia while half-heartedly protesting Putin's demolition of our fragile democratic institutions and the overall crackdown on human rights. Other leaders simply dispensed with the token hypocrisy and embraced the "strong" and "popular" Putin in the hopes of achieving more favorable deals. That Faustian bargain enriched a small circle of elites in both Europe and Russia while Putin steadily turned Russia into a KGB police state.

Then the "Arab Spring" upheaval at the end of 2010 provided Putin with more good news on multiple fronts. To the obvious first: a rise in the price of oil is always the Kremlin's top priority. Years of hoping for an Israeli military strike on Iran that would send oil to $200 a barrel gave way to quietly celebrating the uprisings that Putin hoped would achieve the same price target. Russia's interests in Libya may not have been served by abstaining from the UN Security Council vote on military action, but Russia's ruling junta's cash interests were very well served.

The other bright spot for the Kremlin was the feeble Western reaction when the Saudis sent troops into Bahrain to help quash the rebellion there in March 2011. Unarmed protesters were shot at close range just days after Obama's defense secretary Robert Gates met with the Bahraini monarchy. The United States eventually condemned the violence and Secretary of State Hillary Clinton politely asked the Gulf regimes that the US arms and supports, to "show restraint" in demolishing peaceful protests.

The European Parliament did slightly better, condemning the violent repression of demonstrators, but did so in a nonlegislative resolution with no hint of sanctions or other action. Putin had long wondered how far he could go in repressing domestic opposition without causing a significant backlash. In 2011 he learned there was no limit at all, and that live ammunition against Russian protesters was a viable option.

The Western intervention into the Libyan civil war had lessons for other rogue regimes as well. To Iran it said, "Hurry up!" Gaddafi had publicly given up his nuclear ambitions years ago, to much global acclaim. Meanwhile, Kim Jong-il could kill thousands, do whatever he liked, but was untouchable because the North Koreans had ignored all of the "Unacceptable!" cries from the rest of the world and detonated a few buckets of nuclear slop.

In John le Carré's famous novel *Tinker, Tailor, Soldier, Spy*, spymaster George Smiley cautions an agent on dealing with the KGB: "The only problem arises when it transpires that you've been handing Polyakov the crown jewels and getting Russian chicken-feed in return." The crown jewels of the West are democracy, human rights, and transparency. By cozying up to Putin, Europe betrayed those once sacred contracts for the chicken feed of oil, gas, and everything from automobiles and football teams to actual chickens.

"But wait," I hear the so-called pragmatists say, "oil and gas are hardly trinkets, and anyway, isn't economic engagement the best way to improve the Russian standard of living and, eventually, the state of its politics?" This line of thought has been discredited so many times that by now it is obvious that its proponents use it only as a way to avoid admitting they do not have the courage to stand up to a strongman. But let me discredit it one more time.

First, while the Kremlin has shown a willingness to freeze innocent people to death over a contractual dispute, Russia needs Europe's consumers as much as Europe needs the oil and gas. The pipelines are in place and cannot be redirected. The main alternative client, China, has already driven very favorable long-term deals for cheap Russian energy, so selling there isn't nearly as profitable as selling to Europe. Putin and his cronies know they have a limited window to pocket as much money as they can and they are not going to risk their precious cash flow, not that they have to take any risks when Europe's leaders capitulate preemptively.

As for the second argument, just the phrase "economic engagement" should by now leave a bitter taste in the mouth of anyone with a genuine interest in the advancement of human rights. Russia's elites profited mightily as the price of oil skyrocketed and industries were consolidated into the hands of Putin loyalists. Autocracies share the profits of engagement only as much as necessary to avoid mass societal unrest. When dictators do invest the money they don't steal into the country, it goes into the security forces and propaganda machine, not liberalization of civil society.

The real impact economic engagement had was the reverse of the effect its apologists defend, namely the export of corruption from Russia to its "partners" in the free world. All that oil money has done its job abroad as well, buying respect where it cannot be earned. The Winter Olympics were purchased for Putin's beloved Sochi—the security nightmare and environmental catastrophe of such an event in the small subtropical resort in the Caucasus somehow escaped the International Olympic Committee's eagle-eyed evaluation teams. Then the World Cup was checked off Putin's shopping list, though it's hard to say which side is the less transparent, the Kremlin or FIFA.

I did not use the word "mafia" in a casual way in chapter 8. It is simply a more accurate way of defining the Putin regime than traditional political terms. The boss is the man who can provide protection, who can make deals with the authorities and keep the money flowing in. In this picture, Europe and America are the authorities, the only ones that could stand up to the mafia. But the boss, Putin, has them in his pocket and as long as he keeps the money coming in he will stay right where he is.

It is barely worth mentioning the attempt by some in the West to revive the old sport of Kremlinology by conjecturing on the balance of power between Medvedev and Putin. What matters is that the policies did not change, regardless of the nameplates on the office doors. At no point during Medvedev's presidency was there ever a sign of the cherished liberalization that even some naïve Russians were anticipating.

The final nail in the coffin of the liberalization myth was pounded home by a Moscow judge's gavel at the end of the second trial of Mikhail Khodorkovsky in December 2010. In January 2011, yet more protestors were jailed in Moscow for participating in a rally in defense of free assembly, including former Yeltsin deputy prime minister Boris Nemtsov. The rally was part of Strategy 31, which held sanctioned events every thirty-first day on the calendar to protest the Putin government's unwillingness to grant the rights that are so clear when read in our constitution.

The one European stalwart that seemed to have a bit of backbone was the UK, but the new Tory government was strangely eager to let bygones be bygones. The first case of international nuclear terrorism, the November 2006 murder of British citizen Alexander Litvinenko with the radioactive isotope polonium-210, chilled relations between Britain and a Russian government that quickly gave safe harbor to the prime suspect in the killing. In 2008, the chief executive of the TNK-BP joint venture, a union of flagship UK and Russian companies, fled Russia after a humiliating defeat in a battle for control.

The same man, Robert Dudley, then became CEO of British Petroleum. Just a few weeks after the Khodorkovsky verdict, Dudley, surrounded by representatives of the new Cameron government, proudly announced a stock swap and Arctic exploration deal with Rosneft. Perhaps it was just a cruel accident of timing, but Rosneft is the Russian state company that was the beneficiary of the seizing and looting of Khodorkovsky's company Yukos after he was jailed. It is only a small stretch to suggest that BP was therefore in possession of stolen goods. But cold cash washes away a multitude of sins.

It is hard to say if BP was so eager to cozy up to the Kremlin because the company was having such a rough time on the other side of the Atlantic, where former CEO Tony Hayward was pilloried for the massive Louisiana oil spill. The Americans, at least, looked closely at the BP-Rosneft deal, with US congressman Ed Markey memorably referring to BP as "Bolshoi Petroleum." Meanwhile, Gazprom and Shell announced a joint alliance for exploration. I was only waiting for a proud David Cameron to return from Moscow waving a sheaf of contracts and announcing, "Profit for our time!"

Europe was always quick to criticize Alexander Lukashenko, famous as "the last dictator of Europe," which must get a laugh from the Kremlin. There is little on Lukashenko's résumé of repression that would shame Vladimir Putin, but I suppose huge reserves of oil, gas, and cash can do a lot for one's image. Perhaps if a major oil field were discovered near Minsk, Lukashenko would also be invited to sing karaoke with Hollywood stars and go to parties with Silvio Berlusconi the way Putin was.

It is not impossible to imagine Europe as an equal partner with Russia and not just a necessary evil. While that will never happen with Putin in charge, there are ways Europe's leaders could both stand up to the Kremlin and promote regime change. In a mafia, loyalty matters, but only as long as the boss can guarantee that the money will keep flowing and that he can protect his loyal soldiers. Staying on good terms with Western Europe and America, where Putin's oligarchs also prefer to spend their time and their wealth, is therefore essential. After all, why become a Russian billionaire if you are confined to the shell of a country you looted to become one?

A small circle of oligarchs control Russia and the caste of former and current state security service operatives, known as the *siloviki*, who occupy most of the power centers. Holding that group accountable on a personal level—digging into the legality of their investments, cancelling their precious Schengen visas—would send the message that Putin is no longer so influential, that he can no longer guarantee his allies' fortunes and easy access to the good life abroad. It is a way of targeting Putin and his regime without punishing the Russian people.

I had been promoting such a course of action for many years on both sides of the Atlantic, at least as far back as 2007, when it suddenly began to look like a real possibility in 2011. This was good news, but the reason was rooted in tragedy.

＝＝＝＝＝

Senate 1039, the Sergei Magnitsky Rule of Law Accountability Act of 2011, was designed to go after the visas and financial assets of those responsible for the "detention, abuse, or death" of Sergei Magnitsky, the whistle-blowing young lawyer who died in Russian police custody in 2009 after exposing hundreds of millions of dollars in fraud by Russian officials. The act could also be expanded to cover individuals implicated in similar cases of fraud and human rights abuse. It owed its existence to the astonishing campaign of the indefatigable Bill Browder, Magnitsky's former employer, and "a few good men" in Congress, especially its sponsor, Senator Ben Cardin of Maryland.

The version of what everyone called the "Magnitsky Act" finally came out of Congress as the "Russia and Moldova Jackson-Vanik Repeal and Sergei Magnitsky Rule of Law Accountability Act of 2012." It was the very rare piece of US legislation with overwhelming bipartisan support, so it was curious that the Obama administration seemed bent on thwarting it. (It passed the House on November 16, 2012, with a 365–43 vote and the Senate three weeks later with a 92–4 vote.) After trying to stop it from getting out of Congress for over a year, Obama signed it into law on December 14, 2012.

Apparently the White House was worried about disturbing its cozy relationship with the Putin dictatorship and so had the State

Department create its own list of banned Russian officials from the Magnitsky case, but without releasing the names on it. Of course publicizing the names was the entire point. "Secret deterrent" is an oxymoron.

Or perhaps Obama, who managed to keep it in Congress and off his desk until just after his reelection, was afraid to lend credence to the words of his 2012 opponent, Mitt Romney, who in a March interview on CNN had said of Russia, "Without question our number one geopolitical foe. They fight every cause for the world's worst actors. The idea that he has some more flexibility in mind for Russia is very, very troubling indeed." Obama ridiculed Romney for the remark, even preparing a debate zinger about how the "1980s want their foreign policy back."

You may remember that Romney's shot at Obama's flexibility targeted a "hot mic" moment Obama had had a few days earlier at a summit in South Korea. Obama was overheard telling President Medvedev that "on all these issues, but particularly missile defense, this, this can be solved, but it's important for him to give me space. This is my last election. After my election, I have more flexibility." (The "him" was of course Putin.) Equally revealing was Medvedev's robotic reply: "I understand. I will transmit this information to Vladimir."

Since Putin invaded Ukraine in early 2014, the phrase "Romney was right" has become a motto among those wanting to bash Obama's foreign policy. Romney was right, certainly, and he followed it up with an article in *Foreign Policy* magazine detailing how Obama had dropped the ball on Russia. An excerpt:

> Without extracting meaningful concessions from Russia, [Obama] abandoned our missile defense sites in Poland. He granted Russia new limits on our nuclear arsenal. He capitulated to "Russia's" demand that a United Nations resolution on the Iranian nuclear-weapons program exclude crippling sanctions. Moscow has rewarded these gifts with nothing but obstructionism at the United Nations on a whole raft of issues. It has continued to arm

the regime of Syria's vicious dictator and blocked multilateral efforts to stop the ongoing carnage there. Across the board, it has been a thorn in our side on questions vital to America's national security. For three years, the sum total of President Obama's policy toward Russia has been: "We give, Russia gets."

Bingo. I've added to that fine list here already and so, as with McCain in 2008, you can guess where my US presidential election sympathies lay in 2012. I wasn't aware of it at the time, but in researching for this book I found a passage in Romney's 2010 book, *No Apology: The Case for American Greatness*, that I would like to share because it mirrors some of the thoughts on evil that I wrote in the introduction:

> Evil has been with us from the beginning of time, and it is not going away. Indeed, technology means it is very close. Today, the available means of creating horror are even more deadly than ever before. I submit that it is vital to believe in evil—it is neither confused nor deterred by vacuous introspection. We should study what is said and written by evil men, and take them at their word. Adolf Hitler told the world exactly what his aspirations were in *Mein Kampf* and in his speeches, but at first the world dismissed his claims as political bluster.

This is very true, and I particularly appreciate the part on taking evil men at their word, as it is something I have been saying for years about Putin. Almost since he came into office Putin has spoken forthrightly about his goals. Yes, he also blatantly lies about some things when it's convenient, but on the big issues like centralizing power and his contempt for democracy and civil rights, he speaks plainly and has a good track record of backing up what he says.

This is why it was so frustrating to watch the Obama administration, first through Secretary of State Hillary Clinton and then via her successor, John Kerry, continue to treat Putin as if he would reform his wicked ways if only they treated him kindly enough and offered enough concessions. It turned out Obama would need all of his advertised flexibility in his second term, because he would no longer be able to transmit messages to Vladimir via carrier pigeon Medvedev. He would have to do it in person. Two thousand twelve was an election year in Russia, too.

———

The adjective "Orwellian" has become cheap currency in modern political discourse. Liberals and conservatives alike in democracies like the United Kingdom and the United States enjoy using the term to describe nearly any infringement on civil liberties by the state. Video cameras to deter crime, wiretaps of suspected terrorists, and security checks at airports—all have been deemed worthy reference to Orwell's masterpiece, *1984*. I too sense the importance of protecting personal freedoms, even in a democracy, but those of us who have lived in actual police states would prefer to keep certain words in our lexicon that can describe our far more dire circumstances.

The most powerful theme in Orwell's book is not that of the all-seeing Big Brother, but that of the control and distortion of language, especially in the form of "newspeak." Words take on inverted meanings, words expressing unapproved ideas are eliminated, and human thought itself is curtailed through the reduction and simplification of vocabulary. This attempt to warp reality via information control is not science fiction to anyone brought up reading *Pravda* in the Soviet Union, or anyone living in Putin's Russia today.

And so, the presidential election of March 4, 2012, the most fraudulent in Russian history, was proclaimed "fair and clean" by the state-controlled media. Peaceful civilian protests were dubbed "extremist provocations," and the OMON riot police who brutally suppressed the protestors were "maintaining order." The public outcry and huge protests over fraud in the December 4,

2011, parliamentary elections were answered by even greater corruption and the preordained reinstallation of a KGB lieutenant colonel who clearly aims to be dictator for life.

I would be a poor patriot if I did not point out that *1984* was modeled on the totalitarian state in the dystopian Russian novel *We*, written by Evgenij Zamjatin in 1921 and, of course, banned in the USSR until 1988. There are still elections in Zamjatin's futuristic universe and each year "the Benefactor" is reelected unanimously. Disturbingly familiar.

You might not think that they are banning or burning many books in Putin's "dictatorship-lite," which attempts to mime the functions of an open society and to keep the most clichéd oppression behind the scenes as much as possible. This is partly true, if only because the authorities realize that big piles of burning books look particularly bad on YouTube. Instead, they simply confiscate the books as "extremist materials," as was done in 2012 with 250,000 copies of former deputy prime minister Boris Nemtsov's book detailing Putin's corruption.

The blatant fraud of the December 4 elections was still apparent three months later. In what we call a "carousel" in Russia, herds of voters were moved from polling station to polling station in quantities large enough to clog the center of Moscow with dozens of buses. Fake polling stations appeared just a few days ahead of the election and collected thousands of votes. Threats went out to CEOs, school administrators, and many others directing them to get out the vote for Putin or suffer cuts in funding or worse.

The regime had to adapt to the awareness of the hundreds of thousands of protestors who had taken to the streets in December, much to the surprise of the government and the opposition alike. Webcams were installed in every polling station and tens of thousands of observers arose from the outraged citizenry. This forced Putin's election commission leader Vladimir Churov to rely on tricks that could be performed behind the curtains. Supplementary voter rolls, intended for those who need to vote away from where they were registered, swelled to incredible size.

Unsurprisingly, in the precincts where numbers were available, Putin received a much higher percentage of votes cast from the supplementary rolls than in the regular ones. Absentee ballots were also in high demand all of a sudden, as were the services that allow the infirm to vote from home.

Even all of Churov's wizardry could not get Putin over the 50 percent mark in Moscow, where the official number was just 47 percent even though there were no credible candidates on the ballot. (Our calculations estimated that his real percentage in the capital was closer to 35 percent.) The candidates were all Kremlin approved, from the tired old Communist and Nationalist leaders to the new face of billionaire Mikhail Prokhorov, a Putin creature installed on the ticket to syphon away protest votes. The global media descends only on election day and leaves soon afterward, ignoring the root and branch corruption and repression that is the real story.

As Russians tired of Putin, it remained to be seen if the rest of the world would continue to pretend he was the elected ruler of Russia. President Obama waited a few days but eventually called Putin. The modern dictatorship was taking place behind the scenes, but the performance of a democracy was continuing on stage, and Obama played his part.

This was no surprise, as I had received a preview of the Obama administration's deluded hopes earlier in 2011. Vice President Joe Biden had come to Moscow in March 2011 for talks and he later spoke with me and other opposition members. When Biden arrived he was quite excited after a personal meeting with Putin, saying he'd gone off-script and pressed Putin not to run for the presidency again, saying that it would look terrible and hurt Russia's constitutional integrity. From Biden's proud demeanor and the look on the face of incoming Ambassador McFaul, it was clear this had not been part of the White House's intended message.

I raised my hand to speak and said, "Mr. Biden, you do understand that compared to Putin you and Obama are beggars? You have to go to the Hill for every million while Putin can spend a billion on bribes without signing a piece of paper!" That the Americans still thought Putin cared about what they said or how his actions looked to them or to anyone was, and remains, terribly disappointing.

━━━━━

The Russian protest movement had been transformed at the end of 2011, or so we hoped, after Duma elections that demonstrated a shocking level of fraud even for Russia. Ordinary urban Russians who had done all right under Putin and mostly kept their mouths shut could not accept this latest assault on their dignity. Everyone knew the elections were a joke, and that they had been a charade since 2000. But this time Putin's party, United Russia, had gone too far. The blatant vote rigging pushed hundreds of thousands of Russians into the streets with a unified anti-Putin, anti-United Russia message. It was a beautiful sight to behold.

There were flags from across the political spectrum, which validated my original 2005 protest concept of accepting anyone who would march against Putin, regardless of ideology. The majority, however, had no real political affiliation at all. They were marching against corruption, against impunity, and against Putin. The mask was all the way off, and Putin made it obvious he was no longer interested in pretending to be a democrat. People were simply sick of him.

As the protests continued through December, reaching over one hundred thousand people on December 24, 2011, the protesters were also marching for a relatively new face at the front of opposition marches, Alexei Navalny. He had been arrested at an earlier march and his release was anticipated by huge crowds. In repressive regimes like that of Vladimir Putin there is a constant struggle between the dictatorship and those who oppose it to restrict, or liberate, vital information. Navalny was the vanguard of the "data dissidents." He built a network to reveal the corruption of the Putin regime, relentlessly documenting the kleptocracy case by case, with popular outrage as the result.

Navalny's rise to prominence in the opposition movement was no accident, however. He had worked hard for many years as an organizer and activist. Apart from his persistence and skill, Navalny also possessed the more subtle requirements for leadership in the modern age. His charisma is complemented by a sardonic sense of humor that is ideal for puncturing the propaganda of the gray and humorless Kremlin. His knack for phrasing branded Putin's United Russia as "the Party of Crooks and Thieves" for all time.

Navalny mastered the blogging and social networks that the opposition depends on since we are banned from the mainstream media. As had already been seen in other countries, groups could organize public protests very quickly online. Of course this did not mean you would not be beaten or arrested when you showed up, as many were. I was hardly an expert on flash mobs or even Twitter back then, but I was happy to march with Navalny on several occasions and work together with him and opposition activists old and new.

Navalny and his new breed of followers were largely undeterred for over a year, and we regularly scheduled large sanctioned protests as Putin's formal return to the presidency arrived on May 7, 2012. The refreshed opposition movement was symbolized by white ribbons, noted by Putin with his typical vulgarity: "I thought they were condoms."

The May 6 protests in Bolotnaya Square the night before Putin's inaugural address were the first to be interrupted with serious violence, as the police intentionally shifted the barriers to create bottlenecks and then attacked protesters who were squeezed outside of them. There were over four hundred arrests, including those of organizers Navalny, Nemtsov, and Udaltsov, and over a hundred people with serious injuries.

I was not scheduled to speak that day because the theme of the rally was to provide an opportunity to the activists and speakers who had come from all over the country to be there. And so after reaching the police cordon at around six o'clock in the evening I passed through and headed for my scheduled appearance on Echo of Moscow to discuss the protest and Putin's return. I also had a guest in tow that day, the American political consultant Frank Luntz, who was startled to get an up-close view of Russian democracy in action. He called in to Fox News that evening with his impressions.

"The government we remember of the Soviet Union, of the 80s, appears to be back now," Luntz said. "People are scared. . . . It's frightening to think, but it was almost as though the police wanted to have this confrontation, that they wanted to send this message, 24 hours before Putin comes back into office, that dissention and disagreement is not going to be allowed. They certainly didn't have to do it violently, they certainly did not have to attack. There was no justification whatsoever. . . . I marched in the entire parade and there was a gentleness, there was singing, and chants. These were docile people and they were attacked unfairly."

I watched the entire catastrophe erupt on the live feed from the Echo of Moscow studio. I had been planning to do my spot and return to Bolotnaya to hear the speakers and meet some colleagues, but the entire square had turned into chaos by six thirty. The entire city had been turned into a fortress to prepare for Putin's inaugural the next day and the police were obviously intending to send a message, as Luntz astutely pointed out. The tsar was back and anyone who wanted to march against him had better be prepared to have his skull cracked.

The new crackdown did not end in the streets. The regime targeted the entire Coordination Council of the opposition movement, raiding their homes and even their offices and families' homes. Leaders were called in for interrogation over and over. Even more new anti-protest laws were passed to allow for much higher fines and up to thirty days in prison for a minor civil offense. It was not a headless movement; it required coordination and communications work to bring fifty thousand or more people to the streets. That was still plenty to put the lie to Putin's approval ratings, but it was not enough to topple the regime. There were a few more fairly large rallies up until the May 6, 2013, Bolotnaya anniversary rally that brought tens of thousands of Muscovites out.

On July 18, 2013, Navalny was sentenced to five years in prison on concocted embezzlement charges typical of the kind used to persecute opposition figures. This happened after he had registered the day before as a candidate for the Moscow mayoral race. A bizarre cat-and-mouse sequence then ensued. Navalny was shockingly released, probably for the dual purpose of avoiding making him a martyr and to add some needed quasi-legitimacy to the mayoral election. He was allowed to appear on the ballot and campaign, although of course the Kremlin candidate, incumbent mayor Sergey Sobyanin, had the innumerable advantages of state power and media. Another likely reason why Navalny was released and allowed to run was as a way for the Kremlin to keep the ambitious Sobyanin in his place. Without Navalny on the ballot Sobyanin's result would have surpassed Putin's national 63.6 percent and dwarfed Putin's 47 percent in Moscow. It shows how subtle and dangerous modern dictatorships are that they can employ democratic structures and tools in this way.

Navalny duly finished a distant second and continued his life as a marked man with his convictions and new charges constantly hanging over his head. His last conviction, in December 2014, left Navalny under house arrest and his brother Oleg in jail, a standard hostage-taking maneuver of the KGB old school. They are both prisoners of conscience. Navalny was helping organize a new march on March 1, 2015, when our colleague Boris Nemtsov was murdered on February 27. The march was turned into a memorial parade for our friend.

It is difficult to say what could have gone differently for the public protest movement in that period. If a real revolution was to occur it needed to be early, before the regime formulated a response. Perhaps the huge demonstration on December 24, 2011, on Sakharov Avenue was the best chance if there was one. I was there with nearly every other member of the opposition and there must have been at least thirty other speakers. Navalny came tantalizingly close by saying what many of us had thought for so long:

> I can see that there are enough people here to seize the Kremlin and the White House [federal government building] right now. We are a peaceful force and will not do it now. But if these crooks and thieves try to go on cheating us, if they continue telling lies and stealing from us, we will take what belongs to us with our own hands!

What might have happened had we marched on the Kremlin and the Duma that night? If we had established a camp in Red Square one hundred thousand strong and prepared battlements? Would the people have followed us? Would the thousands of police have opened fire? Would we now be free, or dead?

10

WAR AND
APPEASEMENT

Press conferences are supposed to make headlines, but on June 5, 2013, in Geneva I made a little more news than I had intended. I was there to receive the Morris B. Abram Human Rights Award from the organization UN Watch. It was a great honor to receive an award bearing the name of an American civil rights champion who worked with Martin Luther King Jr. and Robert Kennedy before becoming a global rights figure in co-founding UN Watch in Geneva.

At the press conference a reporter asked a question I have received hundreds of times since I retired from chess: whether or not I feared for my safety and freedom in Putin's Russia. But this time I did not give my usual reply about nothing in life being certain. I answered that if I returned to Russia I had serious doubts I would be able to leave again, since it had become obvious in February that I would be part of the ongoing crackdown against political protestors centered on the Bolotnaya Square case.

"So for the time being," I concluded (if I may quote myself to make the record clear), "I refrain from returning to Russia."

This was not intended to be a grand declaration of leaving my home country, permanently or otherwise. In the context of the question, even the Russia experts among the journalists in attendance failed to pick up anything special about my cautious response. It was only when the *Moscow Times* reported it that the headlines and speculation began to fly.

I was simply expressing the dark reality of the situation in Russia at the time. Nearly half of the members of the opposition's Coordinating Council were under criminal investigation on invented charges ranging from illegal protest to incitement of extremism to embezzlement. This difficult decision was already old news to my family and me; I had not been to my Moscow home since February. Even my fiftieth birthday in April was celebrated in Oslo instead of Moscow, as much as it pained me to make my mother and other close family travel abroad.

My work on the opposition council was generally foreign relations, which entailed lobbying governments and organizations abroad to condemn the human rights record of the Putin regime and to bring sanctions against Putin's government and his cronies. Putin's rage at the passage of the US Magnitsky Act legislation at the end of 2012 convinced me that this was the correct path, and a path that needed to be promoted in Europe as well.

The Moscow prosecutor's office opening an investigation that would limit my ability to travel would have crippled these efforts. It would have kept me from my professional speaking engagements, all of which were abroad since my dissident status had denied me any possibility of earning an income in Russia. A travel ban would also have limited my work with the nonprofit Kasparov Chess Foundation, which had centers in New York City, Brussels, Johannesburg, Singapore, and Mexico City to promote chess in education.

I doubt they would have just locked me up and thrown away the key, although that's what we thought about Mikhail Khodorkovsky and Pussy Riot. It was more the fashion for the prosecutor's office to inflict an endless barrage of charges, trials, and court appearances: death by a thousand paper cuts. It bankrupts the victims financially, physically, and spiritually and keeps them out of the limelight without martyrdom. It causes fear and paranoia in the target as well as in his family and friends. This is the technique they've used against Navalny for years.

When I retired from chess in March 2005 to join the opposition movement, my concept of uniting every anti-Putin element in the country to march together regardless of ideology was harshly criticized. Seeing the 2011–2012 marches with hundreds of flags representing every group from liberals to nationalists all marching together for "Russia Without Putin" was the fulfillment of a dream. But it was a brief dream followed by a rude awakening for the opposition and, sadly, the continued slumber of most of the Russian people.

For his uncontested return to the presidency Putin locked down the capital, turning the center of Moscow into Pyongyang. He has since shown no hesitation in persecuting activists, leaders, lawyers, scientists, or even musicians who dare challenge his power publicly. The phase of attempting to create popular outrage by going through the motions of sham elections was over. Despite the government propaganda, most Russians knew the system was a cruel joke, but this knowledge was not in itself sufficient to get millions of people to risk their safety and freedom against a well-armed police state.

I had also expanded my human rights work in an effort to create an international coalition of dissidents and activists. In 2012 I succeeded one of my heroes, Václav Havel, as the chairman of the Human Rights Foundation (HRF) in New York. Thor Halvorssen, its tireless founder and director, has put together a remarkable series of global events and campaigns with an emphasis on uniting freedom fighters around the world. HRF's annual Oslo Freedom Forum is the epitome of these efforts to bring human rights activists and dissidents together to share information and strategies.

I understood that I could not lead in Russia from outside of Russia and I've had to accept that. I'm still involved in the opposition and in some ways I'm busier than ever working for our cause. To those who have accused me of abandoning Russia, or of giving up, I say that Russia remains my country regardless of where I live or the papers I carry. I will not subject myself to the whims of the thugs and crooks who rule it for the time being. Russia is not Putin. I refuse to be an easy target or to be caged and limited to being little more than a figure of sympathy. It has been painful not to see my eldest son, Vadim, and my mother in Moscow very often, but Klara Kasparova gave me both her name and her fighting spirit, and so I will persist.

———

Two months later, President Obama, too, had personal issues with the Putin regime, canceling a summit meeting with Putin that had been set for August. There were many good reasons for Obama to make this choice, but most of the attention went to Russia's granting asylum to the American fugitive National Security Agency (NSA) leaker Edward Snowden a few days earlier. The coverage reflected the short attention span and limited interest in Russia in the Western press, but it may also be accurate. After all, the list of ways Putin had worked against American and European interests was quite long already, with Syria, Iran, and missile defense on top. But previously Obama had been content to sit down across from Putin and spout the usual blather about cooperation and friendship. If it took a personal jab over the negligible figure of Snowden to at last rouse Obama to stand up to Putin, I suppose that doing the right thing for the wrong reason is better than never doing it at all.

It is human nature to want to put a face on our stories, whether or not it really fits. Like a footballer making or missing a penalty in the final seconds of a game, one individual often gets credit or blame when he is mostly just a diversion from more important stories. One person's central role in a single incident ends up looking more important than the serious issues, which have been building for a long time, that the incident represents. That was the case of Edward Snowden, a traitor and spy to some and a whistleblower and hero to others. I have no special knowledge about his actions or his leaks, but I would surely feel differently about him had he not taken refuge in Russia, where his asylum request tacitly endorsed the dictatorial regime of his gracious host, Vladimir Putin.

My reaction is not only due to Snowden's first statement from Russia, while he was still in legal limbo at Sheremetyevo airport, in which he included Putin's Russia—a police state and patron of despotism worldwide—on his list of nations that "stand against human rights violations carried out by the powerful rather than the powerless." Excuse me? Putin's many political prisoners would disagree quite strongly, as would the many opposition members who have had their emails hacked and their phone calls recorded by the KGB in attempts to discredit them. And Snowden could have been more respectful of the many injured and dead among journalists and his fellow whistleblowers in Russia.

One note on Snowden's NSA revelations, however, speaking as someone who grew up under the all-seeing eye of the KGB and who is fighting its modern rebirth under Vladimir Putin: it is exasperating to hear blithe comparisons between the NSA, and other Western spy or law enforcement organizations, and the vicious internal security regimes of the USSR and East Germany. The NSA is to the Stasi what a bad hotel is to a maximum security prison. It is not what a government does with data that defines it; it is what it does to human beings.

Any encroachment on the personal freedoms and rights of individuals by a government should be protested and debated, absolutely. The mechanisms to protest such abuses must be exercised regularly or they will be lost. But citizens behind the Iron Curtain were not terrified of the intelligence services because of data collection. We lived in fear because we knew what would happen to us if we gave any hint of dissent against the regime. And, as often as not, no data at all was required to persecute, disappear, torture, and murder potential enemies. If a court actually was involved, and evidence desired, it would simply be fabricated. And no, to take on the next argument I often hear, brutal totalitarianism does not begin with surveillance by a liberal democratic state. It begins with terror, it begins with violence, and it begins with the knowledge that your thoughts and words can end your career or your life.

Snowden's acts and his appearance in Moscow had some impact in Russia, but it should not be exaggerated. I've heard claims that Putin learned of Snowden's leaks, then passed his draconian new laws further restricting free speech as a way of "keeping up with the Joneses" at the NSA; it should go without saying that such claims are absurd. Dozens of those laws have been put into effect over Putin's fifteen-year reign, gradually vandalizing the Russian constitution beyond recognition. Putin is always quick to exploit any opportunity to justify his authoritarian ways, but in many cases it is Western leaders and press looking to make excuses for Putin and to avoid calling him a dictator. This is a genetic strength and weakness of the free world, the desire to be "fair and balanced" and to "show both sides of the story" even when it means giving the benefit of the doubt to someone who hasn't deserved it in over a decade. The Western press that never hesitated to refer to Pinochet as a dictator, and with good reason, somehow always finds more polite titles or euphemisms for Putin, the Castros, al-Assad, and even Kim Jong-un.

As for the estimation of Snowden among the Russian opposition, you must realize what his journey looked like in our eyes. The idea that an individual could carry out this espionage mission and then flee to China and take refuge in Russia without any involvement by the KGB is incredibly hard to believe. Combine these logical suspicions with his asylum claim and the aforementioned false equivalency between dictatorships and democracies and Snowden is hardly cut out to be a sympathetic figure among those who respect the universal nature of human rights.

All the attention for Snowden had a parallel in the sudden out-burst of international condemnation of the 2014 Winter Olympic Games that were held in the Russian Black Sea resort of Sochi in February. Numerous protests, both online and in crowds in the United States, Europe, Australia, and elsewhere, were largely in response to the harsh anti-gay law passed in Russia in June 2013, a law with broad and open-ended powers to punish and discrim-inate against gays and anyone who would defend or even talk publicly about homosexuality. Its passage was of a piece with the constant encroachment on free speech and other constitutional rights in Putin's Russia, and also in keeping with the Kremlin's politically convenient, and quite unholy, alliance with the Rus-sian Orthodox Church.

This "homosexual propaganda" law was only the broadest and most recent of many similar ones in a Russia where gays were the routine victims of both official and unofficial discrimination, harassment, and violence. That Russia is a signatory to various European and international conventions that forbid this sort of discrimination had been largely ignored by the European Union and its so-called leadership. So it was welcome to see artists, ac-tivists, and regular citizens stepping into the gap to stand up for Russian human rights, which of course is what gay rights are. Celebrities like Lady Gaga and Stephen Fry made public state-ments, including Fry's eloquent letter to the International Olym-pic Committee and Prime Minister David Cameron to propose moving or boycotting the Sochi Games.

I was pleasantly surprised by this sudden rush of attention to a matter many of us in the opposition had been protesting since Sochi won the bid in 2007. Suddenly my Twitter mentions were full of LGBT-activism accounts sharing my scorn for hosting the Olympic Games in Putin's bigoted autocracy. This was the mer-curial power of social media in action. Serious comments about Russian democracy might be shared a few hundred times, but a photo of a rainbow over Sochi could go viral in ten minutes. As long as it helped raise awareness about the nature of Putin's Russia, both methods were fine with me.

There were already many reasons Sochi should never have been awarded the Olympics. Its character as a subtropical summer resort with weather rarely nearing the freezing point is the most obvious. That Sochi was entirely without the required facilities when the Games were awarded on July 4, 2007, over Salzburg and Pyeongchang, added to the surprise. It was clear from the start that it would be a human and environmental catastrophe for the delicate region. Sochi also borders the North Caucasus, a hotbed of both Islamist terror and Russian military brutality, infamous for terror attacks in Ingushetia, regular bombings in Dagestan, and the horrific Chechen wars.

Many Sochi citizens had their homes and businesses destroyed, and the surrounding area was turned into an ecological disaster zone that only got worse after the area was abandoned a few minutes after the torch was extinguished.

The Putin regime is and always has been about one thing: money. Specifically, about how to move it into the bank accounts of Putin's allies. Hosting the Olympic Games, a first for Russia, as Moscow 1980 was in the USSR, was a perfect way to shift tens of billions of dollars from the treasury and state-owned banks into private hands. Everything from infrastructure to venues and hotels to catering was done by companies hand-picked by the Kremlin, and it was no surprise to find the names of many of Putin's closest pals "going for the gold" a bit early in Sochi. The price tag soared far beyond the promised $12 billion (already a record) to an estimated $50 billion, more costly even than the lavish 2008 Beijing Summer Games. According to the *Economist*, the companies of Putin's old judo buddy Arkady Rotenberg alone received $7.4 billion in contracts. The entire 2010 Vancouver Winter Olympiad cost $6 billion.

Hosting the Games in Sochi was a dubious effort even if the classic old resort town were being turned into Xanadu with Putin as Kubla Khan. But due to epic levels of corruption, most of the money never even made it to Sochi. The construction was shoddy and many of the ambitious projects weren't even scheduled to be built until after the Games. That is, they were never built at all, and they never will be. It is fair to say that Switzerland won the most gold from Sochi regardless of the success of their team.

The International Olympic Committee members must have possessed tremendous faith to entrust the Games to Sochi in the face of such obstacles. Many of my colleagues in the opposition and I protested the bid from the start. When the degree of the chaos and corruption became evident, we petitioned the IOC to move the Games to a different site, even to a less fragile one in Russia. That didn't happen, of course, but the new wave of Sochi protests over the anti-gay law turned a bad situation into an opportunity to turn Putin's showcase into a spotlight that exposed his cruel regime on a global stage.

As a lifelong professional sportsman, first for the Soviet Union and then for Russia, I could not endorse a boycott of Sochi by the Olympic teams. Such maneuvers unfairly punish athletes with no regard for their personal views. I was nearly a victim of "sports politics" myself more than once as a young man. In 1983, I was told I could not travel to Pasadena, California, to play a world championship candidates match against Soviet defector Viktor Korchnoi. The Soviet Sports Committee was already planning to boycott the 1984 Summer Games in nearby Los Angeles in retaliation for the US boycott of the 1980 Games in Moscow. I was initially forfeited for failing to appear and I was fortunate that eventually the match was relocated to London, where I won and continued my ascent to winning the crown in 1985. It is impossible to know what might have happened to my career had the forfeit stood and I had been forced to wait another three years to challenge Karpov.

I believe strongly in the power of sport to break down barriers and to cross borders. The focus should be on sport and the athletes, first and foremost. But sport is part of culture, of life, and there was an opportunity for the athletes and visiting fans and media to have a real impact on human rights in Russia. Everyone remembers the Black Power salutes raised by American sprinters John Carlos and Tommie Smith on the medal podium in Mexico City in 1968. Sochi was ripe for similar gestures, although after a few minor incidents (for example, rainbow-painted fingernails) the teams received stern warnings.

The Sochi boycott that I demanded was a boycott by world leaders, by celebrities and sponsors, by CEOs and fans. It was a revolting spectacle for any head of state to come to Sochi and to sit next to Putin in his stately pleasure dome, pretending it was a world apart from the police state he created. As Stephen Fry's letter pointed out, the world's embrace of the 1936 Berlin Games gave Adolf Hitler a huge boost of confidence. It is politically incorrect to speak of today, but the entire French Olympic team raised their arms in a stiff salute as they passed by the Führer during the 1936 opening ceremony. Debating as some do whether or not it was a Nazi salute or the similar Olympic salute is definitely beside the point. Hitler and the Germans were delighted by the show of deference. (Many teams, including the British and American, refused to salute.) Putin sought similar adulation and validation in Sochi.

By 1936, Hitler's government had already spent years persecuting Germany's Jews. The Nazis also attacked homosexuals, the handicapped, gypsies, and political opponents, a model of oppressing the most vulnerable that Putin is following by going after immigrants, gays, and the opposition. It's a tragedy that the free world always refuses to learn from past mistakes where dictators and would-be dictators are concerned.

The autocrats, in contrast, are eager students of their predecessors. They make careful study of how to gradually remove rights without allowing rebellion, how to crush dissent and hold sham elections while keeping favorable travel and trade status in the West, and how to talk peace while waging war. The motives of dictators vary, it is true—communism, fascism, conquest, larceny—but the drive for total control never changes and their methods are painfully repetitive. In contrast, the idea that free nations have a responsibility to defend innocents from murder and oppression is repeatedly allowed to approach extinction. We only revive it when the latest crisis has already occurred.

Ukraine is the latest victim of this dynamic. Sochi was a Potemkin village and it turned out that the Sochi Games were themselves used as a smokescreen for bigger things. When the EU declined to offer improved terms to enhance Ukraine's integration into Europe in 2013, Putin was quick to step in with his usual mix of threats and bribes, a language his flunky Ukrainian president Viktor Yanukovych spoke fluently. Here is one place where democracy has trouble competing with a wealthy dictatorship. Europe offers committees and vague timelines and in exchange requires transparency and painful reforms. Putin offers hard cash and all he wants is your freedom and your soul.

Unfortunately for Putin and Yanukovych, the Ukrainian people had something to say about this betrayal. When Yanukovych declared that he would suspend preparation to sign Ukraine's EU Association Agreement, Ukrainians came in huge numbers to Maidan Nezalezhnosti, Kyiv's central Independence Square, to protest Yanukovych's attempt to move Ukraine away from Europe and into cold Putin's embrace. "Euromaidan" was born on November 21, 2013, with a few thousand protesters that surged into the tens and even hundreds of thousands over the next few days. The protesters quickly moved from demanding European integration to demanding Yanukovych's resignation. Ukraine was not Russia, they were saying, and they would fight to keep it that way. Tragically, they would have to fight, and die.

In the middle of the night on November 30, Ukrainian special police forces, Berkut, attacked the Kyiv protesters and drove them from the square, injuring dozens. Amazingly, the protest not only regrouped, but was reinforced to greater numbers in response to the attacks. In the first week of December, the protesters organized and set up barricades and a camp in Maidan

Nezalezhnosti. They occupied the Kyiv city council building and demanded that Yanukovych's government resign. Yanukovych went to Sochi on December 6 for an unscheduled meeting with Putin to receive instructions. They did not sign anything to enter Ukraine into Putin's "Soviet Union–lite" customs union trade bloc as feared, but the Ukrainian prime minister announced there would be a major agreement signed on December 17.

December 8 saw the largest protests yet, upward of half a million people in Kyiv according to most media reports. Negotiations by the Yanukovych government went on with visiting EU groups, former Ukrainian presidents, and popular leaders like Vitali Klitschko, the former heavyweight boxing champion and member of parliament. (His younger brother Wladimir is the current champion. They are both enthusiastic chess players.) There were more clashes between the police and protesters on the eleventh but the protesters proved resilient despite the freezing conditions and the government was still wary of using overwhelming force with the world watching. Yanukovych met with Catherine Ashton of the EU and US Assistant Secretary of State Victoria Nuland, whose support for the protests is still used by Russian propaganda to "prove" the entire Euromaidan was a coup plot run by the CIA.

Negotiations continued through December while Maidan became a strange sort of pro-freedom tourist destination, with visiting politicians from all over the world coming to speak to the crowds. Protesters, journalists, and opposition leaders were victimized in raids and attacks by shadowy forces. Incredibly, while it all seemed to be rushing by at the time, with news and surprises coming nearly every day, the standoff continued well into January. Putin kept dangling carrots that Yanukovych was too terrified to reach for. Putin would rather have seen the protesters violently put down than peacefully accommodated, of course. The Kremlin had hoped the Orange Revolution virus had been isolated and contained along Russia's borders and promised Ukraine $15 billion to aid in its quarantine. Yanukovych's panicky turnarounds showed that although he wanted to live like Putin, he did not want to die like Gaddafi.

More violence erupted soon after new anti-protest laws were passed on January 16, including several deaths. Several activists who had gone to the hospital for treatment were abducted and one was later found murdered. Yanukovych attempted to bring the opposition leaders inside his government in an attempt to quell the protests, offering positions to Arseniy Yatsenyuk and Klitschko. The offer was declined.

Throughout Euromaidan, Russian officials made increasingly hysterical accusations about the role of "foreign agents" in the protests. Despite having no evidence, the Kremlin repeatedly accused the Ukrainian citizens of being trained and armed by America and of plotting a violent coup. This line was reminiscent of the way the Soviet Union treated dissidents. If you were against them it could only be because you were a foreign spy, or crazy. The Kremlin could not afford to admit that Ukrainians, the people closest to Russians, were fighting for their freedom. As with Georgia, it was a bad example that could give Russians dangerous ideas.

Despite the resignation of the entire Ukrainian cabinet on January 28, and the Yanukovych government's sudden willingness to make minor concessions to the courageous protestors, tension continued to build in the streets. A Kremlin delegation arrived to discuss things with Yanukovych in private. It was as if the government was waiting for something. The relative calm ended on February 18 as violence erupted over the next several days. Russian-trained snipers from the Ukrainian special forces fired into the crowds. At least eighty people were killed (including a dozen police) and more than a thousand were seriously injured. But again the protesters refused to disappear and this time it was clear they would settle for nothing less than Yanukovych's exit. Euromaidan went from protest to revolution.

Instead of resigning or waiting to be impeached, Yanukovych fled to the safety of his patrons in Russia before he could be brought to justice over the epic scale of his corruption. Photos of his gold-plated palace spread like wildfire on the Internet as the opposition established a new government and scheduled new elections for May.

It is no coincidence that the Ukrainian security forces stormed the Kyiv opposition camps of Maidan during the Sochi Games, which ran February 7–23. Russia invaded Georgia during the Beijing Olympics in 2008, remember. Such spectacles have often provided useful distractions and much of the media that had been in Kyiv had moved to Sochi by the time the worst violence erupted.

Sochi provided a distraction at home for Putin as well. Opposition activist Sergei Udaltsov's trial was delayed until February 18; he faced ten years in prison for "organizing mass riots," which is Kremlin-speak for walking down the street at the front of a protest march—the march that was peaceful until violently crushed by police. The Bolotnaya Square case produced eight guilty verdicts on February 21, again under the welcome distraction of the Olympic Games.

The news showed plenty of photos of a smiling Vladimir Putin posing and raising glasses with deferential politicians, officials, and athletes; exactly the coverage he hoped for while his injustice system created more Russian political prisoners. Putin learned from history that people tire of bad news, tire of hearing sad stories of repression and death. Propaganda works best of all when it is easier to hear lies than to hear the truth, but it cannot change the truth.

As I had feared would happen, Olympics broadcaster NBC and the IOC followed Putin's script and portrayed Sochi as a step toward liberalization in Russia instead of the reverse. Putin used the Games as a distraction from show trials and the most virulent anti-American and anti-Semitic campaigns in decades. How could these stories compete with figure skaters and hockey players? But the Ukrainian people did not play their appointed roles and they fought for their freedom and their lives. Their courage deserves every accolade. The protesters of Euromaidan remind us that no matter how much respect a dictator is paid by foreign leaders during his rule, the story ends the same way: disgrace in the eyes of his own people.

The International Olympic Committee was an eager partner in all of it and of course has a long and dark history of its own. For example, after the triumph of Berlin the next Games were planned for the fascist capitals of Tokyo in 1940 and Rome in 1944. IOC president Thomas Bach's strained protests about how foreign leaders protesting Sochi were "inserting politics into sport" ignored the fact that selling a huge platform for propaganda and corruption to a dictatorship is also "playing politics." By Bach's dubious rationale, the IOC would happily award the Games to North Korea as long as the venues were adequate and the fees were paid promptly.

―――――――――

I knew Putin was not standing by idly while his flunky Yanukovych abandoned Ukraine. I warned in an article in the French paper *Le Monde* on February 24 that "if Putin cannot have all of Ukraine under his fist, he would settle for partition. Already, guided by the Kremlin, Russian-leaning regions of Ukraine like Crimea are talking of 'independence,' which, in the finest Orwellian tradition, would mean exactly the opposite, the loss of freedom as a piece of Putin's neo-USSR."

When Assad and Putin danced a waltz across Obama's red line in Syria in 2013, I warned that dictators and would-be dictators from Caracas to Tehran to Pyongyang were watching closely. Would the West stand up to aggression against a sovereign state to preserve "regional influence"? Did the Obama administration in particular have the courage of its convictions when it came to keeping promises when they were challenged? While there were other factors, I'm convinced that Syria gave Putin added confidence to find out. Putin had returned Russia to a police state and Ukraine, referred to by Putin as "Little Russia," was next on his list. This seemed apparent to me, especially considering the many parallels with the Berlin Games of 1936.

Putin wanted the Sochi Olympiad to be his Peter the Great moment, his beloved Soviet summer resort town turned into an international jewel the way St. Petersburg was built into an imperial capital practically from scratch. Putin also hoped to drum up some patriotic pride with a big circus to serve with thick Russian black bread. This is the sort of delusion that sets in when a despot confuses himself with the state after being too long in power. Absent the feedback mechanisms of a free media and real elections, he begins to believe his glory is the country's glory, that what makes him happy also makes the people happy.

There is a distinction here between Sochi 2014 and the Summer Games in Moscow in 1980 and Beijing in 2008. In those earlier cases, the authoritarian propaganda machine was in the service of promoting the achievements of a country and a system. They were dedicated to the greater glory of Communism, the totalitarian state, the superiority of the system and the athletes it produced. Nobody remembers who presided over the 2008 Games in Beijing and only a few might recall Brezhnev in Moscow. Meanwhile, the chairman of the Russian Olympic Committee never appeared on TV or anywhere else, nor did the director of the Sochi Games. No, the Sochi spectacle was clearly about the ambitions and hubris of one ubiquitous man, something it has in common with the Summer Games held in Berlin in 1936.

I will detour for a moment because this is where I often used to see interviewers and pundits roll their eyes. The phrase "But Putin is no Hitler!" formed on their lips before I'd finished saying the word "Berlin." It is a fascinating and dangerous development in historical ignorance that nearly any mention of Hitler or the Nazis is now ritually scoffed at, from professional journalists to anonymous tweets. It's as if the slow and public evolution of a German populist politician into history's most infamous monster is beyond rational contemplation.

I'm very aware of the dangers of comparing anything bad to the Nazis or Hitler, or everything repressive to fascism, or every act of appeasement to Munich. Overuse leads to trivialization and the loss of meaning, which is also why "genocide" and "Holocaust" must be reserved for very specific things instead of used casually or for shock value. This is the very heart of "Never again" and it must not be forgotten. This is why President Obama's seven-year streak of breaking his 2008 campaign promise to recognize the Armenian genocide matters. How can we fight against the many evils present in our world today if we do not have the courage to face an evil whose ghosts are a century old? So we must be honest and we must be brave enough to call evil by its name, especially the mother of all twentieth-century genocides.

And so it is not at all lightly that I compare a modern one-man dictatorship spreading fascist propaganda to a previous one when it annexes a chunk of a European neighbor on exactly the same pretext of "protecting our blood brothers." It is not out of ignorance or a desire to shock that I compare the cowardice and conciliation displayed today by the leaders of the free world toward Putin with the desperate, futile, and ultimately ruinous appeasement policies of the 1930s toward Hitler. These are coherent and dangerous precedents, not trivial comparisons of two diminutive autocrats each with a penchant for profanity.

Of course the evil of the Nazis defies rational comparison. Of course no one can rival the murderous fiend Hitler became in the 1940s, or the horrors he produced. Of course no one assumes a new world war or an attempt to emulate the Holocaust. But summarily discarding the lessons of Hitler's political rise, how he wielded power, and how he was disregarded and abetted for so long is foolish and dangerous. And as I said in the introduction, back in 1936 even Hitler was no Hitler. He was already viewed with suspicion by many inside and outside Germany, yes, but he stood beaming in that Berlin Olympic stadium and received accolades from world leaders and stiff-armed salutes from the world's athletes. There is no doubt that this triumph on the world stage emboldened the Nazis and strengthened their ambitions.

Intentionally or not, the Putin regime followed the Berlin 1936 playbook quite closely for Sochi. There were the same token concessions in response to international outcries over bigoted laws. A few prominent political prisoners were released right before the journalists arrived. Even the tone of the propaganda had a very familiar ring, as brilliantly illustrated by the writer and journalist Viktor Shenderovich. He quoted a statement by Putin loyalist politician Vladimir Yakunin accusing the Western media of anti-Russian hysteria and hostility and condemning these foreign critics for attempting to disrupt the Olympics. Shenderovich then revealed that half of the statement was actually by Karl Ritter von Halt, the organizer of the Berlin Games, only substituting "Russia" for "Germany" throughout. The transition was seamless.

At the end of February 2014, for the second time in six years, Vladimir Putin ordered Russian troops across an internationally recognized border to occupy territory. This fact must be stated plainly before any discussion of motives or consequences. Russian troops took Ukrainian Crimea by force, and also assisted with the evacuation there of Viktor Yanukovych. This act made Putin a member of an exclusive club, along with Saddam Hussein and Slobodan Milošević, as one of the very few leaders to invade a neighboring nation in the nuclear age. A few weeks later Putin outdid Milošević by formally annexing Crimea, as Hussein did with Kuwait.

Such raw expansionist aggression had been out of fashion since the time of Adolf Hitler, who eventually failed, and Joseph Stalin, who succeeded. Stalin's Red Army had its share of battlefield glory, but his real triumph came at the Yalta Conference in February 1945, three months before the end of the war in Europe. There Stalin bullied a feeble Franklin Roosevelt and a powerless

Winston Churchill, redrawing the Polish borders and promising elections in Poland when he knew that the Communist government the Soviets were installing was there to stay.

Although it is a poignant coincidence, there is more to this look back to World War II than the fact that Yalta is located in Crimea. Putin's tactics are easily, and accurately, compared to those of the Austrian Anschluss and the Nazi occupation and annexation of the Sudetenland in Czechoslovakia in 1938. There was the same rhetoric about protecting a threatened population, the same propaganda filled with lies, justifications, and accusations. Putin also followed the Stalin model on Poland in Yalta: first invade, then negotiate.

Crimea was forced to hold a sham referendum over joining Russia a few weeks later, a vote that took place on the Kremlin's preferred terms, at the point of a gun and with the result never in doubt. That Crimeans had already voted in the past to stay part of Ukraine did not come up.

Putin's move in Crimea came just hours after then–Ukrainian president Yanukovych scrambled up his puppet strings from Kyiv to his master's hand in Russia. He left behind thousands of papers and a few palaces, evidence of the vast scale of his personal and political corruption. His ejection, bought in blood by the courageous people of Ukraine, made Putin look weak. Like any schoolyard bully or crime boss, Putin immediately found a way to look and feel tough again. The historically pivotal Crimean peninsula, with its large Russia-leaning population and geographic vulnerability (and a Russian naval base), was a natural target.

As I have said for years, it is a waste of time to attempt to discern deep strategy in Mr. Putin's actions. There are no complex national interests in his calculations. There are only personal interests, the interests of those close to him who keep him in power, and how best to consolidate that power. Without real elections or a free media, the only way a dictator can communicate with his subjects is through propaganda and the only way he can validate his power is with regular shows of force.

Inside Russia, that force is brought forth against dissidents and civil rights. Abroad, force in the form of military action, trade sanctions, or economic extortion is applied wherever Putin thinks he can get away with it. So far, that has been quite often and so far, Putin has been right.

Despite the predictions of many pundits, politicians, and so-called experts, Putin formally annexed the Ukrainian region of Crimea. Perhaps Putin was not impressed by these critics' sound reasoning and elegant discourse on how his invasion and annexation were against Russian national interests. The main problem with what we can call the "Putin would never" arguments in the West is that they assume Putin and his ruling elite care about Russian national interests. They do not, except in the few areas where they overlap with their own goal of looting as much cash and treasure from the country as possible. It is long past time to stop listening to Harvard professors and think-tank experts lecture us about what Putin would never do and high time to respond to what he is actually doing.

The next obstacle to stopping Putin is the self-imposed paralysis of the leaders of Europe and the G7. The hard truth is that the only sanctions, or actions of any kind, that will affect Putin's conduct are those that directly or indirectly target his hold on power in Russia. It's all Putin cares about because he knows what happens to people like him when they lose that grip. This is why Secretary of State John Kerry's comment to his counterpart Sergei Lavrov after Crimea was so precisely wrong. "We hope President Putin will recognize that none of what we're saying is meant as a threat," Kerry said. "It's not meant in a personal way." With one feeble remark, Kerry took the only things Putin cares about, threats and personal power, off the table.

Obama repeated this mistake two days later when he announced America would not send troops to defend Ukraine. Nobody was asking for troops anyway, and Obama likely thought he was defusing tensions. But where Obama sees a gesture of peaceful intent, Putin simply sees more weakness. Dropping your weapons to calm a hostage situation might work on a scared kid but it doesn't work against someone like Putin. In Putin's eyes, Obama is his only real opponent in the world and his opponent had just voluntarily surrendered one of his greatest advantages: America's overwhelming military strength. On Iran, on Syria, and then again in Ukraine, Obama outsourced his foreign policy to Putin and, by so doing, he crippled the power of the office he holds in ways that will outlast his White House tenure for years.

On March 28, Putin called Obama to discuss Ukraine, although what was said is different from what was heard. Analyzing the discrepancies between the White House and Kremlin press releases of these calls has become a cottage industry and usually you would never guess that the reports are about the same conversation. The White House report mentioned the need for "constitutional reform and democratic elections" in Ukraine and Russia pulling back its troops from Eastern Ukraine. The Kremlin summary referred to the "rampant extremists" in Kyiv and added the separatist Moldovan region of Transnistria to the conversation in a blatant threat to up the ante once again.

I was more interested in a word that wasn't mentioned in either summary: "Crimea." Evidently this chunk of sovereign Ukrainian territory, invaded and annexed by Putin just weeks earlier, had already ceased to be part of the conversation. Just a day earlier, the UN General Assembly had done what the Security Council could not do due to Russia's veto there. The General Assembly resolution in defense of the territorial integrity of Ukraine received a hundred votes and even intense Russian pressure produced only ten allies, a predictable rogue's gallery that included Cuba, Zimbabwe, Sudan, Syria, and North Korea. And yet Obama suddenly appeared ready to let Putin shift the frame of the negotiations to whether or not Russia would conquer *more* of Ukraine.

A month previous, Western pundits had been full of more "Putin would never" predictions, and many warned not to "corner" Putin but to instead offer him a "face-saving retreat" from Crimea. Putin was not interested in any retreat at all and he reversed the tactic against Obama and the West, offering them a face-saving retreat with Eastern Ukraine as the new line in the sand. Over a year later, in the summer of 2015, the fighting there still rages despite several pathetic "cease-fire" agreements that also existed only for Western leaders to save face.

Negotiating with another country's territory as collateral has a long history. The most obvious example is from 1938, when Hitler graciously offered not to take all of Czechoslovakia in exchange for getting the Sudetenland without any complaints from Britain and France. North Korea and Iran also like to have one-on-one talks with the United States, a way of saying nobody else matters. But Ukraine is not USA versus Russia; it's the civilized world versus a dictator, and the United Nations vote supported that assessment ten to one.

The mandate for continued pressure on Putin is clear, if only the West has the courage to maintain it and increase it. Otherwise, just as Czechoslovakia was absent from the "great power" negotiations in 1938, Ukraine's fledgling government will be relegated to the role of a spectator, a patient under local anesthetic watching helplessly as the surgeons slice away. For the United States to participate in talks is well and good, especially as a signatory of the 1994 Budapest Memorandum guaranteeing Ukraine's territory. But Ukrainian representatives should be present at every step and the people of Ukraine must be kept informed throughout before other nations get too far along in deciding what is in Ukraine's best interests.

Putin once again refuted the predictions of his defenders in the West and continued his invasion of Eastern Ukraine. A few months later, as summer approached, thousands of Ukrainians, including many civilians, were dead and hundreds of thousands had been forced to flee. The Ukrainian military was severely overmatched by the "rebel" forces, not that there had ever been a rebel or separatist movement in Eastern Ukraine worth mentioning before Putin discovered a huge and very well-equipped army of them. Europe and the United States refused to provide weapons to Ukraine, limiting themselves to humanitarian assistance and nonlethal aid.

Actions directed at Putin were also shockingly weak despite the clear presence of Russian forces and Russian arms flooding into Ukraine. It's one thing for academics and pundits to calmly sympathize with Putin and his "vital interests" and his "sphere of influence," as if 50 million Ukrainians should have no say in the matter. It's quite another thing for Barack Obama, David Cameron, and Angela Merkel to fret about the "instability" and "high costs" caused by sanctions against Russia, as if that could be worse than the instability caused by the partial annexation of a European country by a nuclear dictatorship, carried out with impunity.

This fecklessness was sad and expected, but I thought it might finally come to an end on July 17 when Malaysia Airlines flight 17 (MH17) was blown out of the sky over Eastern Ukraine by a surface-to-air missile, killing all 298 people aboard. The local separatist leadership immediately boasted about shooting down what they had thought was another Ukrainian military plane, only recanting their statements and deleting their posts when it was revealed to have been a civilian aircraft.

Of course the shock and horror would turn to rage and shame among the leaders of the free world that the war in Ukraine had been allowed to fester. Of course Putin would realize he'd overplayed his hand and attempt to preempt the backlash by withdrawing his forces and his support for Ukrainian separatist terrorists. Of course the fact that two-thirds of the passengers were European (193 of them Dutch) would lead to massive Western protests and stiff penalties against Russia.

Of course none of that happened.

I said at the time that MH17 wouldn't change Putin's calculations in any way, but I hoped it would provoke a Western response that would. Somehow I managed to underestimate the cowardice of the Western world once again. The rhetoric changed a little, and briefly, but little else. An investigation was announced, although it would take a long time to get started since the separatist forces would not allow the wreckage and bodies to be collected until they had looted them. Where was the rage? Nobody believed the separatists' excuses or Russian propaganda about anything other than a Russian missile. Was it because Ukraine was far away, was poor and unimportant, and had been turned into a war zone? Had Putin's forces shot down that same aircraft over Amsterdam or Kuala Lumpur would it have made a difference? I'm not sure I want to know the answer.

So who was to blame? This is not a simple question even if you know the answer. That is, of course the person who pushed the button that launched the missile is to blame; that is the easy part. Shall we just arrest him and try him for murder? Responsibility is a greater concept than that. You have the commander who gave the order to push the button. Then the person who provided the missiles to the separatists. Then there are the officials who opened the border to allow military weaponry to cross into Ukraine and the ministers and generals in Moscow who gave those orders. Then we come to the desk where all power resides in Russia, the desk of the man those ministers and generals obey very carefully: the desk of Vladimir Putin.

Blaming Putin for these 298 deaths is as correct and as pointless as blaming the man who pressed the button that launched the missile. Everyone had known for months that Russia arms and supports the separatists in Ukraine. Everyone had known for years that a mouse does not squeak in the Russian government without first getting Putin's permission. So, yes, Putin is responsible for those 298 deaths, more than anyone else.

But blaming Putin for invading Ukraine—for annexing Crimea, for giving advanced surface-to-air missiles to separatists—is like blaming that proverbial scorpion for stinging the frog. It is expected. It is his nature. Instead of worrying about how to change the scorpion's nature or, even worse, how best to appease it, we must focus on how the civilized world can contain the dangerous creature before more innocents die.

Therefore let us cast our net of responsibility where it may do some good. We turn to the leaders of the free world who did nothing to bolster the Ukrainian border even after Russia annexed Crimea and made its ambitions to destabilize Eastern Ukraine very clear. Is the West to blame? Did they push the button? No. They pretended that Ukraine would not affect them. They hoped that they could safely ignore Ukraine instead of defending the territorial integrity of a European nation under attack. They were paralyzed by fear and internal squabbles. They resisted strong sanctions on Russia because they were worried about the impact on their own economies. They protected jobs but lost lives.

Would this tragedy have happened had tough sanctions against Russia been put into effect the moment Putin moved on Crimea? Would it have happened had NATO made it clear from the start that they would defend the sovereignty of Ukraine with weapons and advisors on the ground? We will never know. Taking action requires courage and there can be high costs in achieving the goal. But as we now see in horror there are also high costs for inaction, and the goal still has not been achieved.

The argument that the only alternative to capitulation to Putin is World War III is for the simple-minded. There were, and always are, a range of responses. Financial and travel restrictions against Putin's cronies and their families and harsh sanctions against key Russian economic sectors may also do some damage to European economies. Until MH17, Europe could argue about how much money their principles were worth. After MH17 they had to argue about how much money 298 lives were worth.

=====

As Russian troops and armored columns advance in Eastern Ukraine the Ukrainian government begs for aid from the free world. That's the same free world Ukrainians hoped would receive them and protect them as one of its own after the protesters of Maidan grasped their victory paid in blood. The leaders of the free world, meanwhile, are still struggling to find the right terminology to free themselves from the moral responsibility to provide that protection. Putin's invasion of a sovereign European nation is an "incursion," much like Crimea—remember Crimea?—was an "uncontested arrival" instead of Anschluss. A civilian airliner was blown out of the sky by Russian-backed and Russian-armed (and likely Russian, period) forces in Eastern Ukraine and, despite the 298 victims, the outrage quickly dissipated into polite discussions about whether it should be investigated as a crime, a war crime, or neither.

This vocabulary of cowardice emanating from Berlin and Washington is as disgraceful as the "black is white" propaganda produced by Putin's regime, and even more dangerous. Moscow's smokescreens are hardly necessary in the face of so much willful blindness. Putin's lies are obvious and expected. European leaders and the White House are even more eager than the Kremlin to pretend this conflict is local and so requires nothing more than vague promises from a very safe distance. As George Orwell wrote in his 1946 essay on language, right before starting work on his novel *1984* (surely not a coincidence), "But if thought corrupts language, language can also corrupt thought." The Western rhetoric of appeasement creates a self-reinforcing loop of mental and moral corruption. Speaking the truth now would mean confessing to many months of lies, just as it took years—and this war—for Western leaders to finally admit Putin didn't belong in the G7.

New Ukrainian president Petro Poroshenko met with President Obama in Washington in September 2014, but Obama's subsequent statement showed no sign he was willing to acknowledge reality. Generic wishes about "mobilizing the international community" were bad enough when it all started. Hearing them repeated as Ukrainian towns fell to Russian troops is a parody. I suggested at the time that Poroshenko should have worn a T-shirt saying "It's a War, Stupid" to the meeting. As Russian tanks and artillery push back the overmatched Ukrainian forces, Obama's repeated insistence that there is no military solution in Ukraine sounds increasingly delusional. There is no time to teach a drowning man to swim.

The United States, Canada, and even Europe have responded to Putin's aggression, it is true, but always a few moves behind, always after the deterrent potential of each action had passed. Strong sanctions and a clear demonstration of support for Ukrainian territorial integrity as I recommended at the time would have had real impact when Putin moved on Crimea in February and March. A sign that there would be real consequences would have split his elites as they pondered the loss of their coveted assets on both sides of the Atlantic.

Then in April and May, the supply of defensive military weaponry would have forestalled the invasion currently under way, or at least raised its price considerably and thereby made the Russian public a factor in the Kremlin's decision-making process much earlier. Those like me who called for such aid at the time were called warmongers, and policy makers again sought dialogue with Putin. And yet war arrived regardless, as it always does in the face of weakness.

As one of the pioneers of the analogy and the ominous parallels, I feel the irony in how it quickly went from scandal to cliché to compare Putin to Hitler in the media, for better and for worse. Certainly Putin's arrogance and language remind us more and more of Hitler, as do the rewards he's reaped from them. For this he can thank the overabundance of Chamberlains in the halls of power today—and there is no Churchill in sight. War comes from weakness, not strength.

As long as it is easy, as long as Putin collects his triumphs without resistance, he gains more support. He took Crimea with barely a shot fired. He flooded Eastern Ukraine with agents and weaponry while Europe dithered. The oligarchs who might have pressured Putin at the start of his Ukrainian adventure are now war financiers with no graceful exit. So many bridges have been burned that the Kremlin's pressure points now are harder to reach.

The humiliating failure of the two peace agreements signed in Minsk proved that leaders of the free world simply refuse to admit that there is no dealing with Putin the way they deal with one another. There is no mutually beneficial business as usual. He exploits and abuses every opening and feels no obligation to operate by the rule of law or human rights inside or outside of Russia. Putin is a lost cause and Russia will also be a lost cause until he is gone. It was an error from the start to treat Putin like any other leader, but now there are no more excuses.

Putin won't back down or be kicked out of Ukraine until credible threats to his power create a split among his elites and advisors. Right now they have no incentive to bet against him. Putin protects them and their assets while the free world they so enjoy living in has made no moves that would finally force them to choose between their riches and Putin. Changing that calculus is the only nonmilitary way to protect Ukraine—and wherever Putin goes next to find new enemies to feed into the propaganda machine that keeps him in power at home.

Obama and Europe's leaders still want to play by the rules even after Putin ripped up the rule book and threw the shreds in their faces. Sanctioning a few of Putin's political hacks is a joke and the Kremlin's elites are right to laugh. To take a phrase from the aptly titled *All the President's Men,* "Follow the money!" Sanction the elites who support Putin, go after all the family members they use to hide their assets abroad, and scrutinize their companies. Putin's oligarchs openly support an administration that directly sponsors terrorists in Ukraine; surely there are ways to go after them and their assets. If existing laws are inadequate to deal with billionaire thugs who enable a dangerous regime, write new ones. And do it quickly.

The Russian military commanders, the ones in the field, are not fools. They are aware that NATO is watching and could blow them to bits in a moment. They rely on Putin's aura of invincibility, which grows every day the West refuses to provide Ukraine with military support. Those commanders must be made to understand that they are facing an overwhelming force, that their lives are in grave danger, that they can and will be captured and prosecuted. To make this a credible threat requires immediate military aid, if not yet the "boots on the ground" everyone but Putin is so keen to avoid. If NATO nations continue to refuse to send lethal aid to Ukraine it will be yet another green light to Putin.

Once again, Putin lies about small things while carrying out his larger threats and goals. He denied there were ever Russian troops in Crimea for a year and then in a Russian documentary aired on March 16, 2015, proudly described deploying thousands of Russian special forces to the Ukrainian peninsula. Of course no one could pretend to be shocked since it had been known practically from the beginning, thanks to satellite photography combined with reporters, bloggers, and locals on social media posting photos of Russian troops and weapons. It should teach us a lesson about what sort of human being he is. If he has a goal, any lies, crimes, or violence needed to achieve that goal are perfectly acceptable and should be expected. After all, he told you what he was going to do. You don't get to complain about how he does it. This is also how Putin has run Russia for fifteen years.

The same circumstances are unfolding with the far larger Russian force in Eastern Ukraine today, which is only growing despite the latest "Minsk II" cease-fire charade. Between "cease-fires" the Russia-backed forces took hundreds of square kilometers more of Ukrainian territory and created hundreds of new casualties. The death toll is now well over six thousand. In a few more months Putin will probably admit to that, too, and perhaps pin medals on the missile crew that shot down MH17. Why not? He enjoys flaunting his lies in the faces of his victims and the leaders of the free world who refuse to protect them. In the same documentary, Putin said he'd been ready to put Russia's nuclear arsenal at the highest level of alert over Crimea. He says things like this because he knows the impact it will have in the West. The people and leaders of the free world that brought down the Soviet empire have forgotten what saber rattling sounds like.

Putin is no master strategist. He's an aggressive poker player facing weak opposition from a Western world that has become so risk averse that it would rather fold than call any bluff, no matter how good its cards are. In the end, Putin is a Russian problem, of course, and Russians must deal with how to remove him. He and his repressive regime, however, are supported directly and indirectly by the free world due to this one-way engagement policy. We must recall the painful memories about the fatal dangers of appeasing a dictator, of disunity in the face of aggression, and of greedily grabbing at an ephemeral peace while guaranteeing a lasting war.

As always when it comes to stopping dictators, with every delay the price goes up. Western leaders have protested over the potential costs of action in Ukraine at every turn only to be faced with the well-established historical fact that the real costs of inaction are always even higher. Now the only options left are risky and difficult, and yet they must be tried. The best reason for acting to stop Putin today is brutally simple: it will only get harder tomorrow.

CONCLUSION

TIMELESS VALUES IN
A SHIFTING WORLD

It is impossible to pinpoint the exact moment at which we stopped looking for leadership from our leaders and started caring only about realpolitik and lesser evils. Before the last rivets of the Iron Curtain hit the ground, as the West patted itself on the back and squandered the peace dividend, voters and parliaments around the world began looking for managers instead of visionaries.

I was reminded of this very keenly on December 11, 2011. Death played a cruel twist when he took the poet, dissident, and human rights champion Václav Havel and the mad over-lord of North Korea Kim Jong-il at nearly the same moment. The media response was predictable, ignoring the leader of the Velvet Revolution and unleashing a flood of conjecture about the twenty-eight-year-old Kim Jong-un becoming the leader of a nuclear-armed prison camp of a nation located right in the mid-dle of Russia, China, and Japan. Concern was understandable, but it was ironic that all that guesswork was taken seriously when no one outside Pyongyang even knew Kim Jong-il was dead for forty-eight hours.

It was worse than ironic that Havel's death, and, more impor-tantly, his amazing life, were swept aside for tales about a luna-tic's love of movies and French cognac. Instead of speculating about an unknown heir in North Korea, what about asking about a successor to the great moral leadership of Václav Havel? Who is there to carry the banner of freedom from oppression in all its forms? The playwright Havel—the artist, the dreamer—lived two-thirds of his life under a Communist regime and knew that liberty had to be fought for with every weapon on every front.

I first met Havel in Prague in 1990, when he was a newly elected president. He was quick to use his new stature to promote the pro-democracy activities of others, especially in what was then still the USSR. I was invited to attend a conference of Soviet dissidents chaired by Vladimir Bukovsky, and Havel insisted that it take place in newly liberated Prague. Incredibly, he was forced to fight elements in his own government that were afraid of offending the Kremlin, and in my recollection Havel was the only senior member of the Czech administration to attend.

At various points during and after his tenure, Havel was criticized for not being an effective executive, for failing to become a politician and a deal maker. But looking at his achievements, especially with an eye on Moscow, such critiques ignore what matters most. Havel presided over the collapse of Czechoslovakia without a drop of blood being spilled at a time when Yugoslavia was in the middle of a horrific civil war. He created the foundations of a democratic establishment free of ties to the Communist and KGB past while Boris Yeltsin failed to root out the entrenched bureaucracy, the *nomenklatura*, and left a KGB successor. Today the Czech Republic and Slovakia are thriving democracies while Russians are fighting the battle for individual liberty all over again. Principles matter, results matter, and Havel succeeded like few others.

Such outspoken courage inevitably serves as a model. Havel served as an ethical tuning fork for Eastern Europeans the way Andrei Sakharov did for the Soviet peoples. His health was already fading when we met for the last time at the Czech embassy in Moscow in 2007, but his eyes saw Vladimir Putin clearly. He was disgusted by those who negotiated with evil instead of calling it what it was.

In a 2004 essay Havel wrote on North Korea, he spelled out the eternal truth about dictators: "Decisiveness, perseverance and negotiations from a position of strength are the only things that Kim Jong-il and those similar to him understand." No talk of appeasement, no treating human rights like just another bargaining chip. If we had more leaders like Václav Havel, we would not have nearly as much to worry about from dictators like Kim Jong-il.

How did we come to such a sad state? When did we go from Soviet dissidents as celebrities and the belief that it was the duty of the free to help the unfree to a world where dictators pose for selfies with snowboarders and the victims of oppression are told to take care of themselves? Believe me when I say I am not harkening back to some never-was golden age of my imagination. I am neither too young to remember those times nor too old to have forgotten them.

═══════

November 9, 1989, was one of the most glorious days in the known history of the world. Hundreds of millions of people were released from totalitarian Communism after generations of darkness.

There is no shortage of scholarship and opinions about why the Wall came down when it did. I am happy to engage in those endless discussions, but we must recognize that looking for a specific cause at a specific moment misses the point. We do know that without the unity of the free world against a common enemy, without a strong stand based on refusing to negotiate over the value of individual freedom, that the Wall would still be standing today and I might still be playing chess for the Soviet Union.

There were alliances and rivalries and stretches of realpolitik for decades. Individuals played a part on both sides, from Ronald Reagan and Margaret Thatcher to Lech Walesa and Pope John Paul II, to Mikhail Gorbachev unleashing forces he could not control. The critical theme was as simple as it was true: the Cold War was about good versus evil, and, just as importantly, this was not just a matter of philosophy, but a real battle worth fighting. Society supported the efforts of those great leaders, and society supported the fight and the principles behind it.

The Wall fell and the world exhaled. The long war of generations was over. The threat of nuclear annihilation that hung over all our heads was ending. Victories, however, even great victories, come at a cost, even if that cost is just letting down one's guard. There were no truth commissions for Communism, no trials or punishments for the epic crimes of these regimes. The KGB changed its name but it did not change its stripes.

And, of course, Western complacency has enabled all its enemies, not just Putin. Today's dictatorships have what the Soviets could scarcely dream of: easy access to global markets to fund repression at home. Not just the petro-states like Russia, Iran, and Venezuela, but the manufacturing states as well. The idea that the free world would use engagement for leverage against dictators on human rights has been countered by the authoritarian states because they are willing to exploit it without hesitation, while there is no similar will in the free world.

Engagement has provided dictatorships with much more than consumers of the oil they extract and the iPhones they assemble. They use Interpol to persecute dissidents abroad; they sponsor or create political parties and NGOs to lobby for their cause; they write op-eds in the *New York Times* full of hypocritical calls for peace and harmony. And all of this while cracking down harder than ever at home. This is engagement as a one-way street. This is engagement as appeasement. This is a failure of leadership on a tragic scale.

Even the greatest ideals and traditions can lose focus after a radical change in the landscape. Symbols help us find that focus, leaving us vulnerable when those symbols disappear. America going to the moon was not so remarkable because there was anything of value there. John F. Kennedy understood that it would

become a symbol of American progress, of challenge, of difficulty, and, of course, of superiority over the USSR.

A generation of new technology was developed thanks to the
space race, technology that would power American industrial
might into the computer age. But not long after this incredible
feat was achieved, the space race fizzled significantly. The symbol was gone and no man has walked on the moon since Eugene
Cernan in December 1972. The symbol of challenge, the symbol
of progress, was confused with the challenge itself. When the
moon was reached, the great quest it represented was quickly
forgotten. As with Hitler and Stalin, a man traveling to the moon
is mostly remembered today as mythology.

The Berlin Wall was more than a symbol, of course. It literally divided a city and represented the divide between the free
and unfree worlds. When it fell, it was easy to forget that those
two worlds, the free and the unfree, still existed even though the
Wall did not. The symbol was gone and so what it represented
was forgotten. Suddenly, evil no longer had a familiar form. As
9/11 taught us, the dangers are real even though the battle lines
are unclear. Allies of convenience have replaced alliances based
on history and values. This is the natural result of over twenty
years of treating everyone like a potential friend, a practice that
emboldens enemies and confuses true allies.

But enemies do exist, whether we admit it or not. They are the
enemies of what America and the rest of the free world stand for.
Whether it is Putin or ISIS, these forces cannot be defeated with
engagement. No, to defeat them will require the unity and the
resolve and the principles that won the Cold War. In chess terms,
our great predecessors left us with a winning position twenty-five
years ago. They gave us the tools to bring down dictators and
showed us how to use them. But we have abandoned these tools
and forgotten the lessons. It is past time to relearn them.

There is a global war under way that most people, even many of its casualties, are unaware is even taking place. I don't have to look back beyond a few months' headlines to count this war's many casualties. A hundred forty-seven murdered at a university in Garissa, Kenya. Sixteen killed in terror attacks in Paris at the magazine *Charlie Hebdo* and at a kosher supermarket. The thousands killed in Eastern Ukraine. The opposition leader gunned down on a bridge on his way home in Moscow. Then there are the countless wounded and imprisoned victims of this global struggle.

Globalization has effectively compressed the world in size, increasing the mobility of goods, capital, and labor. Yet this compression takes place across not only space but time as well, as the twenty-first century's borderless technologies and ideas collide with once sheltered cultures and regimes intent on existing as in centuries past. This is less the famous clash of civilizations than an attempt by these "time travelers" to hold on to their waning authority by stopping the advance of the ideas of an open society.

Radical Islamists set the time machine to the Dark Ages and encourage the murder of all who oppose them. Vladimir Putin wants Russia to exist in the great power era of tsars and monarchs, dominating its neighbors by force and undisturbed by elections and rights complaints. The post-Communist autocracies, led by Putin's closest dictator allies in Belarus and Kazakhstan, exploit ideology only as a means of hanging on to power at any cost. In the East, Kim Jong-un's North Korea attempts to freeze time in a Stalinist prison camp bubble. In the West, Maduro in Venezuela and the Castros in Cuba use socialist propaganda to resist increasing pressure for human rights. Boko Haram warlords employ religion as an excuse to slaughter their rivals. Others, such as the religious monarchies in the Middle East, are guilty by association for creating favorable conditions for violence with their archaic restrictions on free society.

What unites the time travelers is their rejection of modernity, their fear and hatred of what we should simply call "modern values" to replace the obsolete and condescending term "Western values."

Globalization has brought these relics into contact and competition with the modern world that threatens to destroy their environments and authority. This contact also provides them with markets for their natural resources and with the technology they use for murder and repression, so they cannot disengage entirely. The time travelers cannot fight head to head with the ideas and prosperity of the free world, so they use the only weapons they have: ideology, violence, and disregard for the value of human life. They combat the lure of free speech and free markets with irrationality: radical religion and nationalism, cults of personality and dogma, hatred and fear.

Despite the denials of many politicians and pundits it is quite possible to lose a fight you refuse to acknowledge you are in. Even worse, ignoring the reality of the conflict puts more innocent victims on the front lines instead of trained soldiers and law enforcement. There are no easy solutions for homegrown terrorists or nuclear-armed dictators, but we must begin by ending this culture of denial.

———

I've argued elsewhere that history is cyclical; it turned out that the great victory for democracy was not eternal but seasonal. It just took time for the backlash to manifest against our excessive optimism. The mullahs, monarchs, and dictators are pushing back against the threat to their medieval ecosystems. This is the common thread connecting Putin's attack on Ukraine and the murderous Islam-derived ideology that drives al-Qaeda and ISIS, and that drove the Kouachi brothers in Paris and so many others like them. They are pushing back against the modern world, brutally demonstrating the fallacy of "the end of history."

Our goal must be to help those stuck in the past to join the present, and it cannot be done only by force. We must be sincere and make an overwhelmingly attractive case. But this does not mean coddling or tolerating violent extremists or those who create them, at home or abroad. An open society that cannot defend its citizens will not be open for very long. A society that won't fight for freedom will lose it, a truth immortalized by Reagan's statement that freedom "is never more than one generation away from extinction."

Symbols matter in this fight, symbols like *Charlie Hebdo* and the "Bring Back Our Girls" campaigns, and photographs of world leaders marching together for free speech. It is not enough to tell our immigrants, our citizens, and the billions of souls still living in the unfree world that these ideals matter; we must show them. The terrorists and their teachers and the dictators and their enablers are quick to point out every hypocrisy, every double standard. We cannot compromise for, as Victor Hugo wrote in *Les Travailleurs de la Mer*, "Men grow accustomed to poison by degrees."

━━━━━━━

Boris Nemtsov, my longtime friend and colleague in the Russian opposition, was murdered in cold blood in the middle of Moscow on February 27, 2015. Four bullets in the back ended his life in sight of the Kremlin, where he once worked as Boris Yeltsin's deputy prime minister. Photos from the scene showed a cleaning crew scrubbing his blood off the pavement within hours of the murder, so it is not difficult to imagine the quality of the investigation that followed.

Putin actually started, and ended, the inquiry while Boris's body was still warm by calling the murder a "provocation," the term of art for suggesting his enemies are murdering one another in order to bring shame upon his innocent brow. He then brazenly sent a message of condolence to Nemtsov's mother, who often warned her fearless son that his actions could get him killed in Putin's Russia.

Hours after Boris's death, reports said that police were raiding his home and confiscating papers and computers. Putin's enemies are often victims and his victims are always suspects. Boris was a passionate critic of Putin's war in Ukraine and was about to finish a report on the presence of Russian soldiers in Donbass, a matter the Kremlin has spared no effort to cover up. But "Did Putin give the order?" rings as hollow today as it did when journalist Anna Politkovskaya was gunned down in 2006 or when MH17 was shot down over Eastern Ukraine last year.

As long as Putin is in office we'll never know who gave the order, but there is no doubt that he is directly responsible for creating the conditions in which these outrages occur with such terrible frequency. Putin's early themes of restoring the national pride and structure that were lost with the fall of the USSR have slowly run out of steam and been replaced with a toxic mixture of nationalism, belligerence, and hatred. By 2014, the increasingly depleted opposition movement, long treated with contempt and ridicule, had been rebranded in the Kremlin-dominated media as dangerous fifth columnists, or "national traitors" in the vile language they frequently borrowed from the Nazis.

To match the propaganda, Putin shifted more support to the most repressive, reactionary, and bloodthirsty elements in the regime. Among them are Chechen warlord Ramzan Kadyrov and chief prosecutor Alexander Bastrykin, who recently declared that the Russian constitution was "standing in the way of protecting the state's interests." In this environment, blood becomes the coin of the realm, the way to show loyalty to the regime. This is what Putin has wrought in order to keep his grip on power: a culture of death and fear that spans all eleven Russian time zones and is now being exported to Eastern Ukraine.

Boris Nemtsov was a tireless fighter and one of the most skilled critics of the Putin government, a role that was by no means his only possible destiny. A successful mayor in Nizhny Novgorod and a capable cabinet member and parliamentarian, he could have led a comfortable life in the power vertical as a token liberal voice of reform. But Boris was unqualified to work for the Putin regime. He had principles, you see, and could not bear to watch our country descend back into the totalitarian depths.

And so Boris launched his big body, big voice, and big heart into the uphill battle to keep democracy alive in Russia. We worked together after he was kicked out of parliament in 2004 and by 2007 we were close allies in the opposition movement. He was devoted to documenting the crimes and corruption of Putin and his cronies, hoping they would one day face a justice that seemed further away all the time.

Along with a report on Russian soldiers in Ukraine, he had been working hard on the protest march planned for that Sunday in Moscow, a march that became his funeral procession. Boris and I began to quarrel after Putin returned as president in 2012. To me it signaled the end of any realistic hopes that there could be a peaceful political solution to regime change in Russia. But Boris was always hopeful. He would tell me I was too rash, that "you have to live a long time to see change in Russia." Now he will never see it.

We cannot know exactly what horror will come next, only that there will be another and another as long as Putin remains in power. The only way Putin's rule will end is if the Russian people and Putin's elites understand they have no future as long as he is there. Right now, no matter how they really feel about Putin and their lives, they see him as invincible and unmovable. They see him getting his way in Ukraine, taking territory and waging war. They see him talking tough and making deals with Merkel and Hollande. They see his enemies dead in the streets of Moscow.

Statements of condemnation and concern over Boris's murder quickly poured forth from the same Western leaders who have done so much to appease Putin in recent days, weeks, and years. If they truly wish to honor my fearless friend, they should declare in the strongest terms that Russia will be treated like the criminal rogue regime it is for as long as Putin is in power. Call off the sham negotiations. Sell weapons to Ukraine that will put an unbearable political price on Putin's aggression. Tell every Russian oligarch that there is no place their money will be safe in the West as long as they serve Putin.

The response so far is not encouraging, a phrase I tire of writing. Many of the habitual statements of concern and condemnation call for Putin to "administer justice," a plea that could almost could be considered sarcastic. Western media inexplicably continues to give a platform to Putin's cadre of propagandists without challenging their blatant lies.

We may never know who killed Boris Nemtsov, but we do know that the sooner Putin is gone, the better chance there is that the chaos and violence Boris feared can be avoided. It is a chance Russia and the world must take.

━━━━━━

Looking back through history, great changes in the framework between nations have been necessary after a period of great conflict. In 1648, the Peace of Westphalia created the modern age of Europe after the Thirty Years' War. The War of the Spanish Succession was ended by the 1713 Treaty of Utrecht. In 1815, the Congress of Vienna created a new European map after the defeat of Napoleon's France. At the Berlin Conference of 1879 the equilibrium was reestablished after the Russo-Turkish War. At the end of the nineteenth century, the general belief was that this balance would lead to a golden era of peace. Utopian and pacifist literature dreamed of a world without borders right up to the beginning of World War I.

After the First World War we had the Versailles Treaty and the creation of the League of Nations. The League was a failure and the unwillingness to accept this fact led to World War II. On March 5, 1946, in Fulton, Missouri, in his renowned "iron curtain" speech, Winston Churchill spoke about the new dangers to freedom, this time from Communism. It is almost forgotten that he also warned how the newly formed United Nations could fail.

Churchill said of the new organization, "We must make sure that its work is fruitful, that it is a reality and not a sham, that it is a force for action, and not merely a frothing of words, that it is a true temple of peace in which the shields of many nations can someday be hung up, and not merely a cockpit in a Tower of Babel." Unfortunately, Churchill's prophecies have come to pass and today we are stuck with an outdated organization that was developed after WWII to prevent a nuclear clash between superpowers. The old stalemate diplomacy of the Cold War will not help us against suicide attacks and hybrid war. Instead of an entity that exists to freeze conflicts, we need one that can offer real solutions based on modern values.

United military intervention to protect human lives and the greater good must also be kept on the table. The value of human life and the value of human freedom in a new Magna Carta must be defended as if they were borders, for that is what they are. They are borders of time and space, separating those who want to live in the modern world and those for whom modernity is a mortal threat.

I advocate for a return to many of the principles and policies that were dominant in the West during the Cold War. But that does not mean I want to turn back the clock. As the Bible says, "No one pours new wine into old wineskins. Otherwise, the wine will burst the skins, and both the wine and the wineskins will be ruined." We cannot pour the modern wine of globalization and the multipolar world into the old wineskin of obsolete Cold War institutions and regulations. Times change. Circumstances change. Institutions must change. But our values must not.

―――――――

What is to be done? Each situation, each crisis, has its own requirements, of course. The shift of a single pawn changes the entire position. This is why I like to say that I advocate principles, not policies. When you have solid principles and the entire world knows what they are, the policies tend to be much easier to develop and enforce.

It is for leaders, for those who are responsible to their people, to form policies. It is for leaders to consult with experts, to evaluate their options, to consider the consequences, to weigh the short term versus the long term. Making recommendations without the authority to enact them or the responsibility to be held accountable for them is an extravagance. It lends itself to the worst kind of posturing and folly. But I realize that this response, however honest and accurate it may be, is also a form of evasion. No one would be pleased with a doctor who diagnoses you with a deadly illness and then declines to suggest a remedy.

There are many steps that can be taken that require only courage and will. A global Magna Carta is one of them, a document that leads to the creation of a united Democratic nations that upholds and enforces the Universal Declaration of Human Rights. Democracies can take steps now to protect and support those under attack from the dictators, the oppressors, and the time travelers. The free world possesses wealth and power beyond imagining and it must be used to help the unfree to join us or it is power wasted.

Another reason specific policy recommendations are unsatisfactory is that they are inevitably outdated or entirely obsolete. Over the years I have made a long list of things that should be done to respond to Vladimir Putin's dictatorship, for example. Even now, after he has proven my worst fears correct and everyone is telling me how right I was, few of those recommendations have been enacted. Others have been carried, such as sanctions and ejecting Russia from the G7, but too feebly or too slowly to have the deterrent impact I had in mind.

Most of the specific proposals I made nearly a year ago regarding dictatorships, Putin, and Ukraine still stand and I have referenced them throughout the book. Isolate dictatorships that exploit engagement to support oppression. Keep human rights and the value of human life as the backbone of policy, including foreign policy. This does not preclude negotiation or trade within certain parameters, but it must never be doubted that relations will always have strict limits as long as repression exists.

Ukraine should be defended as if it shares a border with every free nation in the world. This means providing arms with which it can defend its borders and financial aid to stabilize the economy Putin is trying so hard to destroy. Take a close look at what America and Europe get from Russia—oil, gas, supply lines—and develop substitutes for them. This is why Putin fears fracking and other technologies that make the West less dependent on his energy exports. And yet this very week, at the end of April 2015, it was reported that the Pentagon has asked Congress for permission to use Russian-made rocket engines. When the leading nations of the free world put their militaries at the mercy of the bad guys, what hope can the victims of the bad guys have?

If appeals to morality and values do not move you, America does indeed have vital interests in Ukraine. As the world's largest economy, military power, and energy consumer, the United States reaps great benefits from global stability. (While big fossil fuel exporters like Russia benefit from instability, which tends to raise the price of oil.) Even if you are a cynical realist or a libertarian isolationist, it is cheaper and more practical to take a stand now over Ukraine than to let it go and then have to worry constantly about even stronger American commitments to the Baltics and Poland, who are NATO members. It is also much safer for Americans, Europeans, and everyone else to maintain a robust global American security umbrella than to encourage rampant military proliferation by closing that umbrella.

It's important to remember that appeasement reflects the overall climate, not just the personal weakness of our elected leaders. From Chamberlain in 1938 to Obama in 2015, the people get what they demand—for a while. Main Street and Wall Street reward politicians who produce attractive short-term results no matter how bad the long-term consequences are. There are few rewards and many penalties for the rare politician who tries to talk about the big picture and the long-term consequences of in-action. Hypothetical questions are dismissed as if it's an unfair "gotcha" to inquire about the future. With no guiding strategy to stick to, democracies lose out to opportunistic dictatorships that can act much more quickly with no checks and balances or people to be accountable to. We cannot wait to act until after the catastrophe is under way. This "wake me up when they take Poland" attitude was foolish in 1938 and it's even more foolish in 2015 because we have the lesson of September 1939—when Poland was invaded—and the six horrific years that followed, to inform us. At least Chamberlain didn't have a history book to tell him what was coming.

I will not say that we are reaching a crisis point or a fork in the road because the tragedy is already unfolding. The decisions made by the leaders of the free world—and by the voters who select them—will decide how tragic it will be. The aggression of Putin and ISIS caught the complacent free world off guard, but that excuse cannot be used any longer and we still have no plan of action. Any politician running for national office should be asked what they will do to make the world safer. Candidates and leaders cannot be allowed to hide behind the flimsy mask of "domestic priorities" in a world of globalized economies and globalized violence.

Whether it is in Ukraine, Syria, Venezuela, Yemen, or Nigeria, the free world should be ready to act to support those who want to live in freedom and to live free from fear. Not just act mili-tarily, after the crisis has already exploded, but act to educate, to build, to help construct societies that appreciate modern val-ues. Even the cynics and isolationists should admit that it is far more moral, economical, and effective to invest in preventing the poverty, fear, and ignorance that often lead to radicalization than punishing that radicalization after it becomes violent. Each billion dollars spent building schools, training teachers, and connecting the isolated to the rest of the world saves $10 billion of war later, after another generation of hungry, angry young men have become vulnerable to the propaganda of anti-modernity because modernity has done nothing for them.

I was honored to participate in the Women in the World Summit in New York City in 2013. I was on a panel with Phiona Mutesi, a teenage chess champion from Uganda, her coach Robert Katende, and Marisa van der Merwe, who co-founded the Moves for Life chess-in-schools program in South Africa. The life experiences of these two remarkable women could not be more different, but they both speak to the importance and power of education, especially in the developing world.

Phiona came from the slums of Katwe in the Ugandan capital of Kampala, growing up in deprivation and fear that few members of our New York audience could imagine. Her discovery of Robert's local chess club became a miracle for Phiona, showing her what she could achieve intellectually. More important than how her chess talent has allowed her to travel the world, she now plans to be a doctor. This is the first and most powerful gift education can provide: a self-confidence that transforms a child's view of his or her potential. Very few kids can truly expect to turn success at football or other physical sports into an education or career. This is also true for chess, but the knowledge that you can compete, succeed, and enjoy yourself on an intellectual level applies to everything you undertake in life.

If there is anything I have learned from my extensive travels all over the world to promote chess in education it is that talent exists everywhere. The question is how to give it the opportunity to express itself and to thrive. This opportunity that education creates is what is lacking in so much of the undeveloped world—and in parts of the developed world as well if we are honest—a shortfall that has wide-ranging and damaging effects. Education is the most effective way to address poverty and violence, even to tackle complex issues of terrorist groups and vicious warlords.

Programs that spend billions on distributing medicine and food to impoverished areas are of course wonderful. Foundations that combat disease and hunger in Africa have saved countless lives. While life may be the most precious gift, it is not enough to play sorcerer only in the morning, to create the sky and not the earth. When you look around the world's trouble spots you see that when kids don't have access to education, many of those who are being saved by Western aid are destined for lives of misery and violence.

Do not misunderstand me. This is of course not an argument against providing life-saving drugs or a denunciation of the brilliant and caring people and programs that provide them. But do not turn away as soon as the babies are born and fed. Do not turn away at all. Look at the young boys enslaved by drug gangs and armies of every stripe, at the unemployed young men who find purpose and profit in victimizing their neighbors, at the girls and women who are inevitably the greatest victims of violence.

The only medicine that can cure these plagues is safe and equal access to a classroom. The best proof of the truth of this may come from the other side, from the brutal groups that burn down schools and shoot schoolgirls in cold blood. It's rare to hear about coordinated attacks on aid that brings medicine and food. These things pose little threat to the Taliban, the regional warlords, or to the corrupt politicians who steal funds that could go to help their people. Religious fanatics, mercenaries, and armies all need healthy recruits, after all.

What these thugs cannot abide is the flourishing of education, with the noteworthy exception of militant religious teaching that often closes minds instead of opening them. They despise the possibility of an educated population, knowing it would mean the end of their kind in a generation. So the Taliban did not just close the schools where fifteen-year-old Malala Yousafzai lived in Swat, Pakistan, they destroyed them. They did not just tell Malala not to go to school, they shot her.

Education in the developing world means far more than keeping at-risk children off the streets. It is the only way to build an economy that can compete in the twenty-first century, as globalization demands. Healthy bodies are not enough as entire populations move from the countryside into cities and as even agriculture becomes a high-tech enterprise. Reading and writing cannot be luxuries at a time when access to the Internet is more prevalent than access to decent plumbing.

Even the most pragmatic know education aid is a good investment. It costs far less to protect and educate children than it does to send in soldiers and cruise missiles to kill them after they have been abandoned and then recruited by thugs into violence and terror. An educated population is less vulnerable to propaganda and more capable of producing the entrepreneurs and leaders who can create economic opportunity.

There are programs that pay opium and cocaine farmers the difference to grow less pernicious crops. It's cheaper and far less violent than fighting a militarized drug war on the borders and in the streets of our cities. Why not invest the same way in kids? How many schools and supplies could be built for the cost of producing and operating one drone? How many teachers, vocational trainers, and guards could be hired for the cost of one special ops deployment?

The Human Rights Foundation works to aid and unite brave people working for individual liberty and justice around the world. Our annual Oslo Freedom Forum brings together hundreds of dissidents, activists, philanthropists, journalists, and policy makers from all over the world. The goal is for every participant to learn and to share and to return home with new strength and new ideas.

In 2014, I presented our Václav Havel Prize for Creative Dissent to Nadezhda Tolokonnikova and Maria Alyokhina of Pussy Riot. It is not often I agree with the Putin regime, but in their case I must make an exception. Their startling performance, their ridicule of Putin, their courage to take a stand with their art, this was not just a cheap prank as their defense lawyer attempted to argue. It was political and it was powerful.

And their trial in Moscow was no trivial persecution. Dictatorships must be feared to survive and so they cannot bear to be mocked. Unlike most observers, Putin, with his dictator's animal instinct, immediately perceived the seriousness of the threat. The result was two years in prison for a performance that lasted fifteen minutes.

And so my last policy recommendation is to listen to the dissidents, even if you do not like what they have to say. They are the ones who reveal to us the dark realities of our societies, the realities that most of us have the luxury to turn away from. Listen to the dissidents because they warn us of the threats that target minorities first and inevitably spread to the majority. Every society has its dissidents, not just dictatorships. They speak for the disenfranchised, the ignored, and the persecuted. Listen to them now, because they speak of what is to come.

"Winter is coming" is a warning, not an inevitable conclusion. The good thing about the seasons of political and social change is that we can affect them if we try hard enough. If we rouse ourselves from our complacency and relearn how to stand up to the dictators and terrorists who threaten the modern world we have built, we can alter our course. Anti-modernity is a dangerous virus, and to remove a virus a reboot or a reset is not enough. We have to build a values-based system that is robust enough to resist the virus at home, smart enough to stop it before it spreads, and bold enough to eradicate it where it grows.

ACKNOWLEDGMENTS

Whenever I'm at risk of sinking into a sea of interesting ideas and intriguing opportunities, my wife Dasha throws me a line and pulls me to the right destination. She knew that this was the right book at the right time.

I very much hope that the book itself recognizes the many individuals who have educated and inspired me during my past ten years as a human rights activist, so I will use this space for those who turned that education and inspiration into a book.

Chris Parris-Lamb, my agent at The Gernert Company, impressed us from the first day we met with his preparation and energy. Chris and our editor at PublicAffairs, Benjamin Adams, were essential in quickly figuring out how to turn a tangle of ideas, history, memoir, analysis, current events, and opinion into a coherent story with a vital message. PublicAffairs founder Peter Osnos has a great nose for news and his enthusiastic support for the book was a tremendous boost.

Special thanks to George R. R. Martin for his marvelous book series, A Song of Ice and Fire, and its derived HBO television series *Game of Thrones,* which inspired this book's title. Putin may be a lot like Tywin Lannister but I'm justifiably afraid to compare myself to any of the characters considering how often they meet gruesome fates!

NOTES

CHAPTER 1: THE END OF THE COLD WAR AND THE FALL OF THE USSR

20 *bring the normal life to my people. The daylight.* A metaphor I adapted from the mirror-smashing scene in a movie that had only just become quite popular in the USSR, Bruce Lee's *Enter the Dragon*!

21 *shaking its political structure to the roots.* George H. W. Bush and Brent Scowcroft, *A World Transformed* (New York: Knopf Doubleday, 1998), Kindle edition, locations 10106–07.

21 *the republics will have their independence.* Fred Waitzkin, *Mortal Games: The Turbulent Genius of Garry Kasparov* (New York: G. P. Putnam's Sons, 1993), Kindle edition, locations 594–95.

22 *trying to save everything he can.* Ibid.

29 *a $2.5 billion aid package that had been delayed.* Curt Tarnoff, *U.S. Assistance to the Former Soviet Union 1991–2001: A History of Administration and Congressional Action*, CRS Report for Congress, updated January 15, 2002.

29 *against its enemies, both internal and external.* Robert O. Paxton, *The Anatomy of Fascism* (New York: Knopf Doubleday, 2004), Kindle edition, locations 4284–85.

CHAPTER 2: THE LOST DECADE

33 *crisis since the end of World War II.* The US and the USSR both agreed on the creation of Israel in 1948 and were the first two countries to recognize it.

35 *consensus for the American role in the world.* Bush and Scowcroft, *A World Transformed*, Kindle edition, locations 11416–20.

37 *much bloodier than we thought.* David Halberstam, *War in a Time of Peace: Bush, Clinton, and the Generals* (New York: Simon and Schuster, 2001), 29.

38 *yesterday America elected the leader of the world.* Garry Kasparov, "Moral Principles Must Underpin U.S. Leadership," *Wall Street Journal*, November 4, 1992, A14.

40   *and advancing the cause of peace.* President Bill Clinton statement to the American people on Kosovo from the White House, March 24, 1999. Full text and video at http://millercenter.org/president/speeches/speech-3932.

CHAPTER 3: THE INVISIBLE WARS

42   *though most are blessedly peaceful today.* The Wikipedia page "Disputed territories in Europe" is fascinating reading and excellent trivia.

49   *what you would have to say to him about that?* President Bill Clinton's news conference with President Boris Yeltsin of Russia in Moscow, May 10, 1995, http://www.presidency.ucsb.edu/ws/?pid=51336.

50   *without even telling Yeltsin. Kommersant* newspaper, May 18, 1995. Referenced in John W. Parker, *Persian Dreams: Moscow and Tehran Since the Fall of the Shah* (Washington, DC: Potomac Books, 2008), 116.

50   *who promoted close political and economic ties with Iran.* Ibid. 117–188.

50   *a more cooperative relationship in the future.* Tarnoff, "U.S. Assistance to the Former Soviet Union 1991–2001: A History of Administration and Congressional Action," CRS report for Congress, updated January 15, 2002.

51   *manage the conflicts they themselves had provoked.* Steven Erlanger, "Five Years Later: Eastern Europe, Post-Communism—A Special Report; East Europe Watches the Bear, Warily," *New York Times*, October 21, 1994.

52   *territorial integrity or political independence of Ukraine.* Budapest Memorandum on Security Assurances, 1994, http://www.cfr.org/nonprolifer ation-arms-control-and-disarmament/budapest-memorandums -security-assurances-1994/p32484.

CHAPTER 4: BORN IN BLOOD

67   *I can stand death—lots of it—but you can't.* Halberstam, *War in a Time of Peace*, 420.

69   *I can't help it. It is my character.* From the film *Confidential Report*, aka *Mr. Arkadin* (1955), written and directed by Orson Welles. Later written as Welles's only novel.

77   *we'll wipe them out in their shithouses.* Prime Minister Vladimir Putin's press conference in Astana, Kazakhstan, September 24, 1999.

79   *Russians believed the security forces were involved in the apartment bombings.* An April 2002 Levada opinion poll revealed that 43 percent of Russians thought this, while 38 percent excluded the possibility; http://www.levada.ru/press/2002041600.html.

81 *liabilities that are too heavy to overcome.* Garry Kasparov, "Russia's Best Election Yet," *Wall Street Journal*, December 21, 1999.

81 *the most destroyed city on Earth.* BBC News, "Scars remain amid Chechen revival," March 3, 2007, http://news.bbc.co.uk/2/hi/programmes/from_our_own_correspondent/6414603.stm.

81 *has fallen in the second Chechen war.* Anna Politkovskaya, *A Small Corner of Hell: Dispatches from Chechnya* (Chicago: University of Chicago Press, 2003), 29.

CHAPTER 5: PRESIDENT FOR LIFE

90 *the empire it served and protected: the USSR.* Masha Gessen, *The Man Without a Face: The Unlikely Rise of Vladimir Putin* (New York: Penguin, 2012), 132.

90 *the ultimate international political performance artist.* Fiona Hill and Clifford Gaddy, *Mr. Putin: Operative in the Kremlin* (Washington, DC: Brookings Institution Press, 2015), Kindle edition, locations 322–27.

91 *resign early and thrust him into the presidency early.* Recounted by Tatyana Yumasheva, Yeltin's daughter and close advisor, on her website; also as reported in the *Telegraph* on January 23, 2010, http://www.telegraph.co.uk/news/worldnews/europe/7063201/Boris-Yeltsins-daughter-attacks-Vladimir-Putin.html.

92 *final historical triumph of the first president of Russia.* Garry Kasparov, "Yeltsin Offers New Hope for the New Year," *Wall Street Journal*, January 3, 2000.

93 *followed the principles of free society.* George Soros, "Bitter Thoughts with Faith in Russia," *Moskovsky Novosti*, February 2000.

94 *very much alive and politically kicking.* Andrei Piontkovsky, "For Whom Putin Tolls?" *Russia Journal*, February 21–27, 2000.

101 *Soviet music was both obvious and shocking.* Critics of American exceptionalism like Putin should keep in mind the new Russian anthem lyrics also include "You are unique in the world, one of a kind"!

CHAPTER 6: THE SEARCH FOR PUTIN'S SOUL

103 *worried him most about Putin in the early days.* Through all of our arguments over the years, Steve's insight and experience make him one of my favorite "sherpas" on how the American foreign policy establishment views Russia, and why. I recommend his articles and books highly, even the ones I disagree with.

104 *how are we ever going to get this right?* Personal email from Steve Sestanovich to author, April 19, 2015.

105   *infamous phrase of British prime minister Tony Blair.* Ian Traynor and Michael White, "Blair courts outrage with Putin visit," *Guardian*, March 11, 2000, http://www.theguardian.com/world/2000/mar/11/russia.ethicalforeignpolicy.

105   *never done anything like that. It's illegal!* Interview with President Bill Clinton on Echo of Moscow radio, June 4, 2000. Cited in Michael Wines, "Clinton in Moscow: The State of Democracy," *New York Times,* June 4, 2000.

106   *beatings, torture and, on occasion, rape.* Malcolm Hawkes, Human Rights Watch statement, March 11, 2000. Cited in the *Guardian*, http://www.theguardian.com/world/2000/mar/11/russia.ethicalforeignpolicy.

111   *the Cold War really is over.* Condoleezza Rice, *No Higher Honor: A Memoir of My Years in Washington* (New York: Crown, 2011), Kindle edition, locations 1450–54.

111   *we will stand together.* George W. Bush, *Decision Points* (New York: Crown, 2010). Kindle edition, locations 3589–91.

115   *developing under conditions of intolerable isolation.* Andrei Sakharov, "A Letter to the Congress of the United States, August 21, 1973," published in *Sakharov Speaks* (New York: Alfred A. Knopf, 1974), 211. Alexei Navalny and I borrowed this technique when we called the Magnitsky Act an "anti-Putin and therefore very pro-Russian piece of American legislation."

115   *it was taken as a rank insult!* Anatoly Dobrynin, *In Confidence* (New York: Times Books, 1995), 163.

116   *without which there can be no mutual trust.* Sakharov, "A Letter to the Congress of the United States, August 21, 1973."

116   *anti-Soviet deed, but a Trotskyist deed.* Christopher Andrew and Vasili Mitrokhin, *The Sword and the Shield: The Mitrokhin Archive and the Secret History of the KGB* (New York: Basic Books, 2000), 317.

116   *the Soviets had to be confronted, not appeased.* Natan Sharansky and Ron Dermer, *The Case for Democracy: The Power of Freedom to Overcome Tyranny and Terror* (New York: PublicAffairs, 2004), 3.

118   *at greater risk than ourselves, who dare to resist.* For some reason this remarkable historical document is difficult to find even in our era of total information. The first Google result for this quote is my own Twitter account! The speech can be found in full for download on the Jackson Foundation's website, http://www.hmjackson.org/publications.

118   *no INTERNAL AFFAIRS left on our crowded Earth!* Out of respect I preserve the capital letters Solzhenitsyn used for "internal affairs" in his Nobel lecture manuscript.

119 *especially if your hands are tied.* Another infamous Rice statement was referring to strongman Alexander Lukashenko's Belarus as "the last remaining true dictatorship in the heart of Europe" in 2005. This has been remembered and repeated endlessly only as Lukashenko being "the last dictator in Europe." Worst of all, she said it while in Moscow! Even if few were ready to call Putin a dictator in 2005, why flatter him so? In 2014, Lukashenko had some revenge by saying that since Putin invaded Ukraine nobody was calling him the last dictator of Europe anymore. He was right.

121 *here with the specific purpose to end the war.* Quotes are from various Russian news reports; several are in English at this BBC report: "Hostage-takers 'ready to die,'" October 25, 2002, http://news.bbc.co.uk/2/hi/europe/2360735.stm.

125 *rise of anti-Semitism last year.* Masha Kondrachuk and Stephen Ennis, "Jews reject Russia claims of Ukraine anti-Semitism," BBC report, November 12, 2014, http://www.bbc.com/news/world-europe-29991777.

128 *a fair trial, by Russian legal standards.* Quoted in a Russian report at Grani.ru in October 2003. Ambassador Vershbow also expressed concern about Russian justice being "applied selectively."

131 *and I wish you courage!* It's available here, also with audio: http://www.rferl.org/content/Text_Of_Closing_Statement_By_Mikhail_Khodorkovsky/2208523.html.

CHAPTER 7: OFF THE BOARD, INTO THE FIRE

137 *to fight for those people and to fight for those things.* Garry Kasparov, "The Great Game," *Wall Street Journal,* March 14, 2005.

139 *orders to arrest you if you try to go.* J. F. O. McAllister; Paul Quinn-Judge; Yuri Zarakhovich, "The Talks that Failed," *Time,* September 13, 2004.

139 *I was going to Beslan to set up talks.* J. F. O. McAllister; "Communication Breakdown," *Time,* September 12, 2004.

140 *broke their silence to denounce it as a cover-up.* "Beslan School Siege Inquiry 'a Cover-up,'" *Herald* (Scotland), February 10, 2007, http://www.heraldscotland.com/beslan-school-siege-inquiry-a-cover-up-1.829305.

141 *hostages who could have been saved were burned alive.* David Satter, *Weekly Standard* 12, no. 9, November 13, 2006.

146 *we will all be to blame!* Gessen, *The Man Without a Face,* 193–94.

157 *Western-style values and universal values.* President George W. Bush, speaking to the pro-democracy organization Freedom House, March 29, 2006.

CHAPTER 8: OPERATION MEDVEDEV

171 *"intelligent" and "of another generation."* USA Today Editorial board interview with Secretary of State Condoleezza Rice, December 11, 2007, http://usatoday30.usatoday.com/news/washington/rice-transcript.pdf.

171 *"troubling" record on human rights.* All quotes are from the set of articles on Putin in the December 19, 2007, *Time* Person of the Year section. These included an interview in which Putin was asked why Russia's elections weren't more open and why I had been jailed. Putin's amazing response: "Why did Mr. Kasparov, when arrested, speak out in English rather than Russian? When a politician works the crowd of other nations rather than the Russian nation, it tells you something." Of course, I was addressing the many foreign reporters in English after already speaking in Russian.

172 *is a potential danger to its own security.* Time, "Adolf Hitler: 1938 TIME man of the year," January 2, 1939.

175 *"gravely concerned" and "strongly condemn."* Quotes from statements of the Extraordinary European Council meetings on the situation in Georgia in August 2008.

184 *caused more damage to the Russian government than her writings.* A remark Putin made to the press in Germany on October 10, 2006, four days after Politkovskaya's murder.

184 *dizzy with the smell of oil and gas!* Václav Havel, quoted widely at the time after the event and cited in the film's press kit.

184 *highest quality in the world.* All quotes are from press coverage of Medvedev's statements at the World Russian Press Congress in Moscow on June 11, 2008.

186 *Russian cities as well as on foreign soil.* The 2009 murder of Kadyrov rival Sulim Yamadayev in Dubai being the most sensational. Dubai police accused Kadyrov's cousin (and state Duma member) of the murder. Yamadayev's brother Ruslan was killed in Moscow in 2008.

187 *if NATO had approved Georgia's MAP [Membership Application Plan] application.* Bush, *Decision Points*, 7945–7947.

CHAPTER 9: THE AUDACITY OF FALSE HOPE

189 *with Marshall and Acheson and Kennan.* Said by Obama during an interview on *Fareed Zakaria GPS*, December 28, 2008. Obama went on to praise the foreign policy of President George H. W. Bush.

191 *in all lands, everywhere.* A version of this appears on a plaque in the stairwell of the pedestal of the Statue of Liberty.

194   *inspiring rhetoric with decisive action.* In my November 5, 2008, op-ed for the Los Angeles Times Syndicate and published widely. Full text available here with no paywall: http://www.theotherrussia.org /2008/11/05/kasparov-on-obama-and-how-russia-sees-america/.

195   *condemn Russia's "aggressive action."* All quotes from campaign press releases, which came out at a furious pace.

196   *American exceptionalism projected by President Bush's first term.* Ben Smith, "'Invasion of Georgia' a '3 A.M. moment,'" *Politico*, August 9, 2008.

197   *the independence of former Soviet Republics.* Senator McCain's entire August 11, 2008, statement on Georgia is worth reading: http://www .realclearpolitics.com/articles/2008/08/mccain_statement_on_ georgia.html.

202   *Mr. Putin and Mr. Medvedev should decide.* Interview with Igor Yurgens at Gazeta.ru, February 2010.

207   *memorably referring to BP as "Bolshoi Petroleum."* Quoted widely in the press, January 14, 2011. Representative Markey was the top Democrat on the House Natural Resources Committee at the time.

210   *policy toward Russia has been: "We give, Russia gets."* Mitt Romney, "Bowing to the Kremlin," *Politico*, March 27, 2012.

210   *dismissed his claims as political bluster.* Mitt Romney, *No Apology: The Case for American Greatness* (New York: St. Martin's Press, 2010), Kindle edition, locations 4916–20.

216   *docile people and they were attacked unfairly.* Transcript of the *Fox News* video clip that's still available online: http://video.foxnews .com/v/1624799524001/anti-putin-rallies-continue-in-russia/?#sp =show-clips.

CHAPTER 10: WAR AND APPEASEMENT

226   *Rotenberg alone received $7.4 billion in contracts.* "Castles in the Sand," *Economist*, July 13, 2013.

233   *Tokyo in 1940 and Rome in 1944.* They were canceled due to the outbreak of World War II. The next Olympic Games were in London in 1948.

233   *a piece of Putin's neo-USSR.* Garry Kasparov, "Les Jeux et la vérité," *Le Monde*, February 24, 2014.

234   *before I'd finished saying the word "Berlin."* My aide Mig Greengard started calling this "the Hitler eye roll" during my many interviews before and during Sochi. He also noted that the eye rolls over these comparisons mostly stopped after Putin annexed Crimea as I'd warned he would.

238   *"It's not meant in a personal way."* John Kerry press conference in London, March 14, 2014.

244   *wishes about "mobilizing the international community."* Obama actually said this ("Remarks by President Obama and President Poroshenko of Ukraine After Bilateral Meeting," September 18, 2014). Many of his remarks look like a parody of diplomatic doubletalk: "And we are going to continue to seek to mobilize the international community to say to Russia that Ukraine desires to have a good relationship with all of its neighbors, both East and West, and that there should be a way in which Ukraine is able to negotiate and trade, and continue the people-to-people links between Ukraine and Russia, but that Russia cannot dictate to them their ability to work effectively with other partners in order to better the situation for the Ukrainian people." Russia had just invaded Ukraine!

CONCLUSION

251   *Kim Jong-il and those similar to him understand.* Václav Havel, "Time to Act on N. Korea," *Washington Post,* June 18, 2004.

256   *calling the murder a "provocation."* Putin's spokesperson, Dmitry Peskov, expressed this just hours after the murder. Putin repeated it the next day.

258   *justice that seemed further away all the time.* The entire 2011 Nemtsov report "Putin.Corruption" is available online in Russian and English at http://www.nemtsov.ru/old.phtml?id=706613. Thousands of printed copies were seized and destroyed as "extremist literature," of course.

260   *not merely a cockpit in a Tower of Babel.* Actually titled "Sinews of Peace," it's simply known as the "Iron Curtain Speech" forevermore. It's worth reading, or hearing, in full if only to marvel at how Churchill, famous for soaring rhetoric, was also keen to discuss an array of details and policy in his speeches. Text and audio here: http://www.winstonchurchill.org/resources/speeches/1946-1963-elder-statesman/the-sinews-of-peace.

260   *the wine and the wineskins will be ruined.* Mark 2:22 (New International Version).

263   *"wake me up when they take Poland."* As actually said to me by Bill Maher on his show *Real Time* on May 1, 2015.

INDEX

ABOUT THE AUTHOR

Photo © Igor Khodzinskiy

Garry Kasparov spent twenty years as the world's number-one-ranked chess player. In 2005, he retired from professional chess to help lead the pro-democracy opposition against Vladimir Putin. In 2012, he was named chairman of the Human Rights Foundation, succeeding Václav Havel. He has been a contributing editor to the *Wall Street Journal* since 1991, and he is a senior visiting fellow at the Oxford-Martin School. His 2007 book, *How Life Imitates Chess,* has been published in twenty-six languages. He lives in self-imposed exile in New York with his wife, Dasha, and their children.

PublicAffairs is a publishing house founded in 1997. It is a tribute to the standards, values, and flair of three persons who have served as mentors to countless reporters, writers, editors, and book people of all kinds, including me.

I. F. STONE, proprietor of *I. F. Stone's Weekly*, combined a commitment to the First Amendment with entrepreneurial zeal and reporting skill and became one of the great independent journalists in American history. At the age of eighty, Izzy published *The Trial of Socrates*, which was a national bestseller. He wrote the book after he taught himself ancient Greek.

BENJAMIN C. BRADLEE was for nearly thirty years the charismatic editorial leader of *The Washington Post*. It was Ben who gave the *Post* the range and courage to pursue such historic issues as Watergate. He supported his reporters with a tenacity that made them fearless and it is no accident that so many became authors of influential, best-selling books.

ROBERT L. BERNSTEIN, the chief executive of Random House for more than a quarter century, guided one of the nation's premier publishing houses. Bob was personally responsible for many books of political dissent and argument that challenged tyranny around the globe. He is also the founder and longtime chair of Human Rights Watch, one of the most respected human rights organizations in the world.

·   ·   ·

For fifty years, the banner of Public Affairs Press was carried by its owner Morris B. Schnapper, who published Gandhi, Nasser, Toynbee, Truman, and about 1,500 other authors. In 1983, Schnapper was described by *The Washington Post* as "a redoubtable gadfly." His legacy will endure in the books to come.

Peter Osnos, *Founder and Editor-at-Large*